Y0-AEA-277

AVARICE DECEIT CONNIVANCE AND REVENGE

AVARICE DECEIT CONNIVANCE AND REVENGE

Two Twisty Crime Screenplays

BY

HERB SCHULTZ

This is a work of fiction. Names, characters, places and incidents either are the product of the author's imagination or are used fictitiously. Any resemblance to actual persons, living or dead, events or locales is entirely coincidental.

Avarice Deceit Connivance and Revenge:
Two Twisty Crime Screenplays

Copyright © 2020 by Herb Schultz
All Rights Reserved
Published in the United States by Major Terata Publications, New York
www.majorterata.com

MAJOR TERATA Publications

This book, or parts thereof, may not be reproduced in any form without permission.

Library of Congress Control Number: 2020915862

Print ISBN: 978-0-9823516-5-9
E-book ISBN: 978-0-9823516-6-6

Designed by: Vince Pannullo
Printed in the United States of America by
One Communications LLC 800-621-2556

CONTENTS

INTRODUCTION

THE WRITERS GUILD OF AMERICA registers about 50,000 screenplays a year. Undoubtedly, tens of thousands of additional unregistered scripts are dumped into the National Strategic Screenplay Stockpile over the same period. Mining this massive pool of cinematic material, Hollywood studios each year release perhaps a couple hundred films. The reality that a tiny fraction of completed scripts gets produced obviously hasn't discouraged pedestrian screenwriters from contributing to an ever-growing inventory of unwanted material. The odds of success are infinitesimally slim, and yet the pursuit of fortune and glory remains robust.

Not that authors of screenwriting instruction books haven't tried to tamp down the enthusiasm. William Akers writes in *Your Screenplay Sucks*, "It is impossible to conceive of the staggering volume of material the system has to contend with. If your script isn't perfect, or as close to perfect as you can get it, then it doesn't stand a chance." Philip Gladwin's *Screenwriting Goldmine* notes that "there are a million other writers out there hacking away at screenplays… so few of their screenplays ever get past the first hurdle of the initial slush pile reader."

That far less than one percent of scripts make it all the way from the grimy, marked-up, three-hole-punched page to the shimmering silver screen should serve as *prima facie* evidence that only the best of the best are plucked for greatness. That with such lush volume from which to choose, Hollywood should consistently deliver high-quality, memorable, and durably entertaining movies.

Sadly, this is far from true.

Having spent hundreds of hours writing and rewriting several scripts over ten years, I can't help but react with a modicum of frustration, bafflement and, ultimately, dismay at the quantity of dreck produced by the American cinema industry. A quick skim of *The New York Times'* TV schedule serves as a proxy for the dim state of affairs. On any given day the TV schedule invariably includes a robust slate of movies airing that evening that *Times* reviewers have tersely panned. Here's an indictment from just one evening's line-up on a random day:

- "Haunted house foolishness" – Dream House
- "Curiously retrograde" – Our Idiot Brother
- "Giant Leap Backward" – Apollo 18
- "Slick facile entertainment" – Valkyrie
- "Wish it were funnier" – Maid in Manhattan
- "Ridiculously derivative" – The Astronaut's Wife
- "Juiceless and nearly bloodless" – Twilight Saga: New Moon
- "Superficial silliness" – Under the Tuscan Sun
- "Not quite coherent" – Drumline

Might this be an aberration? Consider another random day when this lineup was summarily trashed:

- "Like shooting tofu in a barrel" – Wanderlust
- "Less than elementary" – Sherlock Holmes: A Game of Shadows
- "Franchise running on fumes" – Transporter 3
- "Staggeringly bad with genuine spirit of cruelty" – The Butterfly Effect
- "Honey-glazed hokum" – The Help
- "Close-up gore, bloody bore" – Underworld
- "Dumb and sloppy" – Old School
- "Muscle-bound, grunting self-seriousness" – 300
- "Weak cat-and-mouse story" – Heat
- "Will sink your childhood memories" – Battleship
- "Loud, pretentious, flat" – Days of Thunder
- "Funny until you think about it" – The Hangover
- "Self-conscious kitsch" – Clash of the Titans

That's a lot of bad movies for just one evening. Perhaps it's surprising that some big-time actors were attached to these stinkers, including Tom Cruise, Vince Vaughan, Charlize Theron, Daniel Craig, Ralph Fiennes, Naomi Watts, Bradley Cooper and Johnny Depp. How could that happen?

An even better question: how did so many consecutively putrid Adam Sandler movies get the green-light? No one could blame the legion of determined screenwriters who have yet to sell or option a script for feeling demoralized by this spectacle of unjustly rewarded ineptitude - yet we persist. We're routinely scolded that our work contains too much exposition, or that our characters talk on the phone too much, or that act 2 of our script fatally started on page 28 instead of page 25. That last admonition comes from the formula guys who may be most culpable for the broken state of American cinema. The experts will offer a hundred snarky reasons why our scripts are trash, yet remarkably, patently rank material continues to make it on to celluloid. Consider these terrible *Rotten Tomato* scores of the Sandler oeuvre which includes a Netflix-distributed debacle that received a Dean Wormer "zero point zero." (* Sandler gets a writing credit.)

- The Week Of* - 27%
- Sandy Wexler* - 27%
- The Do Over - 9%
- Pixels* - 17%
- Ridiculous 6* - 0%
- Blended - 14%
- The Cobbler - 10%
- Grown Ups 2* - 7%
- That's My Boy - 20%
- Just Go With It* - 19%
- Jack and Jill* - 3%
- Grown Ups* - 10%
- I Now Pronounce You Chuck and Larry - 15%
- The Waterboy* - 35%
- Bulletproof – 8%

How could it be that Hollywood should churn out so much garbage when the industry employs an army of seasoned script readers and supremely talented and well-compensated producers to separate wheat from chaff? Is the quality of the tens of thousands of available scripts so goddamned bad that not even 50 great ones can be identified each year? That seems unlikely. I tend to side with the argument posed in *Screenwriting Tricks for Authors* by Alexandra Sokoloff that the rewrite process in Hollywood is a serious culprit. To make a script fit more in line with a current fad, or sell to a different demographic, new writers are brought in to rewrite. Sometimes many writers, one after the other. Perhaps the assignment is to relocate the action to another place or time, or to exchange the genders of the main characters, or to upend the entire plot. Sometimes producers replace writers simply because their work is poor. Consider the 2013 "winner" of the worst picture, "Movie 43," taglined "The Most Outrageous Comedy Ever Made." Perhaps that's true. It may also be one of the most reviled films of all time, capturing an abysmal 5% rating on *Rotten Tomatoes*. Believe it or not, twenty writers contributed to "Movie 43."

Billy Wilder captured it perfectly when he had his screenwriter character Joe Gillis in "Sunset Boulevard" recap the fate of one of his scripts. "The last one I wrote was about cattle rustlers. Before they were through with it, the whole thing played on a torpedo boat."

SEVERAL YEARS AGO, I began writing novels where the main ingredients were avarice, deceit, connivance and revenge. As I plotted out the stories and developed the characters, I found myself imagining the novels as movies. I drew storyboards with the intention of minimizing exposition in favor of visual language. After completing my fourth book – a collection of short stories called *Sometimes the Sun Does Shine There* – I concluded that a good portion of my work might be suitable for adaptation for the screen. Instead of writing my next novel, I opted to try my hand at screenwriting. Like any rookie, I purchased some "how-to" books and licensed *Final Draft* software to handle the picky formatting rules demanded by the industry. (Doomed is the screenwriter who indents when he should have centered. It screams "amateur.") I noticed how often the advice proffered in some "how-to" books contradicted that in others, yet they all had one thing in common – the treatment of their readers as a bunch of nitwits who have no right to compete to join the professional screenwriting ranks.

One "how-to" author had this wisdom to impart to his naïve readers right up front: "If I can convince you to quit, and only for the price of this book, you should name your next son after me." Nice.

I read dozens of scripts of highly-considered films and found it odd how infrequently they comported with the ironclad commandments put forth in the "how-to" books. That they routinely contained numerous elements that should have caused a reader to reject them after five pages. Perhaps, I thought, the experts selling received wisdom were not completely dialed in. I stopped taking lessons from them and plowed ahead with my first script, an adaptation of a short story about a "stooper" – a man who picks up discarded horse-racing tickets at the track in the hope of finding a winner. Here's the logline for that script: "Left for dead after bungling a petty scam on a sadistic gambler, a lowly racetrack stooper fights back with the help of the gambler's ex-girlfriend to regain his dignity and recover a valuable ticket that rightfully belongs to him." Writing the script seemed to come naturally, and I progressed nicely. Looking for feedback beyond that of some unschooled friends, I sent the screenplay to the now-defunct reviewing service *ScriptShark*. The verdict was pretty harsh. I had made a number of blunders including having too many characters that the audience would not like, and relying on a lazy *deus ex machina* instead of forcing the main character to earn his redemption. Nothing the *ScriptShark* reviewer said was wrong. Still, it disturbed me that I hadn't recognized the flaws myself. It was humbling, but also motivating. I wrote and rewrote the script for more than a year, finally whipping it into what I believe was as good a shape as I could make it. Yet, I harbor no delusion that it will be optioned soon, for the material is rather dark and doesn't align with the kinds of movies making it to the screen, big or small, today.

Most assuredly, my scripts would appeal to a narrow audience. Having watched countless movies screened at the Film Forum, the Angelika, Upstate Films, and the Paris on 58th Street gave me the skewed sense that we're surrounded by millions of committed cinephiles; people who get the inside baseball dialog and appreciate twisty, noir themes. Now I believe sadly that too few of them exist to support production of such stuff. Nonetheless, I moved on from the stooper story to my next screenplay, an adaptation of my novel *Architect's Rendition*. The logline: "Determined to marry his mistress, an architect enlists three associates in a complex scheme to murder his wife… and each other." The "each other" part was inspired by an obscure movie from 1974 starring James Coburn called "The Internecine Project." I remember watching the movie on TV, drawn into the sinister plot in which "a retired agent devises a cunning plan to eliminate those who know too much about his past." Coburn's character, a man with a dicey past who has been nominated for a top government position, must eliminate four acquaintances who know where all the skeletons are buried. His plan: direct each acquaintance to unwittingly kill another of his or her cohort. *Cinema Essentials* says "The Internecine Project" is a peculiar film that plays like a black comedy without any laughs. Coburn's Robert Elliott is a callous murderer, and few of the other characters are sympathetic." Maybe that description could apply to "Architect's Rendition," but I believe there are at least a few laughs among the mayhem.

When I started writing the novel in 2007, I dreamed up numerous methods by which the characters would off one another. I decided the strongest, most believable and least likely to implicate the main character would be those that appear to be random acts. I recalled the infamous case of a pair of cretins who perpetrated several murders in and around America's capital. Dubbed the "D.C. Snipers," in just three weeks in 2002 the two men, hidden inside the trunk of their Chevy sedan, shot and killed ten and wounded three others. After the killers were apprehended, investigators postulated a motive: the mastermind wanted to kill his ex-wife, and believed if she were among several "random" victims, no one would suspect him. Brilliant, whether true or not. I incorporated the idea into *Architect's Rendition.*

I cast the wealthy main character of the novel, Gerald Pfalzgraf, as an architect to make a cinematic homage to the classic, quirky, iconic landscape of Manhattan and its surrounding boroughs. Gerald could have been any professional, but somehow knowing I might eventually adapt the novel for the screen, making him an architect allowed for the inclusion of sweeping shots of New York's finest buildings – as Woody Allen had showcased so well in the opening of "Manhattan."

One day in the future, the movie of *Architect's Rendition* will feature accomplished middle-aged Hollywood actors (looking for that scarce lead character written for someone their age) and fresh talent seeking a challenging role to take the audience on a complex, twisty journey through devious murders that ends in a shocking and tantalizing ambiguous ending. Sequel?

My third novel, *Double Blind Test* tells the story of a successful woman, Tracy Shepard, in the business of alternative dispute resolution – a fancy name for mediation. She's an expert in the art of negotiation who's well-compensated by rich parties locked in disagreement, burning cash on futile litigation, and seeking another way out. During an important business trip, she makes contact with the co-owner of a pharmaceutical lab who cannot agree with his identical twin brother on how to proceed with the development of a breakthrough ophthalmic drug. Tracy is compelled to help the owners resolve their impasse because their drug is designed to cure an insidious eye disease that afflicts thousands, including her father. Ultimately, Tracy invests, and the roller-coaster ride begins.

The concept of using identical twins as a plot device has long intrigued me. Identical twins have often been featured in movies: "The Krays," "Twin Falls Idaho," "Brothers of the Head," "The Social Network," 1977s TV special "The Man in the Iron Mask." But in none of these films do the twins conspire to exploit their unique circumstances to perpetrate a confidence game or some other crime of deception. Yes, crime related to being a twin occurs in the 1952 exploitation flop "Chained for Life," but the scenario is quite mundane. In the movie, starring real-life conjoined twins Daisy and Violet Hilton who also appeared as themselves in "Freaks," one of the twins goes on trial for the capital crime of murdering her sister's boyfriend – raising a plot conundrum most likely drawn from Mark Twain's *Those Extraordinary Twins.* After all, executing the guilty party necessarily results in the death of the innocent twin. Whereas the jury foreman in Twain's short story concludes, "I cannot convict both, for only one is guilty; I cannot acquit both, for only one is innocent; my verdict is that justice has been defeated by the dispensation of God, so you are free to go," the writer of "Chained for Life" lamely leaves it up to the audience to decide the punishment, if any. Without a doubt this flaccid ending violates one and maybe five tenets proscribed in every screenplay "how-to" manual.

A superb example of a film using identical twins as a vehicle for dastardly connivance is "Dead Ringer," starring Bette Davis who plays both twin sisters. One sister (Margaret) has just lost her wealthy husband and now lives in financial security, while the other (Edith) struggles to make ends meet. Circumstances lead to a crime of passion: Edith shoots Margaret dead. In the heady aftermath of the crime, Edith takes over Margaret's identity and embarks on an elaborate but ultimately doomed ruse. (Curiously, Davis played identical twins in an earlier film called "A Stolen Life" in which the sisters inhabit distinct stations in life, empowering the avaricious one to abscond with the identity of the other.) Do you doubt that Bette Davis would have champed at the bit to portray Tracy Shepard?

My vision for the movie "Double Blind Test" was to incorporate an identical-twin-driven device into a cerebral con-game story along the lines of David Mamet's "House_of Games" and "The Spanish Prisoner." Both films feature intriguing characters, sharp dialog, satisfying violence and intelligent twists. These traits guided my effort on "Double Blind Test." Here's the logline: "After a professional mediator is conned by identical twin businessmen who sought her help to resolve a dispute, she meets another woman in a suspiciously similar circumstance, and the two team up to take down the con artists."

CAN SCREENPLAYS LIKE "Architect's Rendition" and "Double Blind Test" compete for producers' attention against scripts written for popular genres like comic book blockbuster, zombie apocalypse gore-fest, low-brow comedy slapsticker, and predictable rom-com? Probably not, but working in my favor are the opportunities for older actors. As more movie stars who gained popularity in their 20s advance into middle age, the availability of good roles for them seems to decline, I think. Screenwriters would develop material catering to a huge cohort of mid- to late-career actors who still retain a sizable fan base – if producers would invest. Just as professional golf invented a "Senior Tour" to profitably showcase still-popular older players who would be forced otherwise to retire into obscurity, Hollywood could step up financing for movies dealing with serious subjects of interest to a mature, financially fit audience, starring seasoned actors boasting centuries of accumulated experience. For certain the profits of such fare would pale against the box office take for a series about a radio-active squid who, by the seventh sequel becomes Speaker of the House, but perhaps if just a fraction of the money wasted on *sui generis* flops could be steered in a different direction, we may just revive the notion of "the *art* of the film."

ARCHITECT'S RENDITION

Determined to marry his mistress, a Machiavellian architect enlists three associates in a complex scheme to murder his wife – and each other.

Architect's Rendition – A Treatment

Act I

IT'S just after the turn of the millennium in New York City, site of some of the world's most iconic architectural gems: Guggenheim Museum, Seagram Building, Lever House, Whitney Museum, TWA terminal, Standard Hotel, New Museum, Hearst Building, IAC Building, Plaza Hotel, Chrysler Building, the United Nations Building. And of course, the wedge-shaped Flatiron Building. A couple blocks from the Flatiron sit the offices of Pfalzgraf Associates, a high-end boutique architecture firm founded by the handsome, well-dressed Gerald Pfalzgraf. Today Gerald sits at his desk – a striking view of the Flatiron Building visible behind him through the floor-to-ceiling windows – reviewing reports generated by a computer program that has captured the internet browsing habits of one of his employees, Oscar Dupree. The content that the program reveals disgusts Gerald – screen captures from Oscar's workstation of graphic, illegal pornography.

As Gerald scrolls through the ugly content, he hears a knock at the door. In pops the head of Oscar. "Sorry to interrupt, Gerald. I'm about to head out. I think the call with Arbogast went well. Anything you need from me?" Gerald, barely masking disgust, shakes his head. After Oscar departs, Gerald stands up, stares pensively out the window at the illuminated Flatiron for a moment, then returns to his desk and shuts down his computer. A copy of "The Prince" by Machiavelli is one among several books on Gerald's desk.

In a contemplative mood, Gerald strolls along a leafy street near Madison Square Park, carrying a stylish briefcase when he passes by a brownstone just in time to hear a man shout obscenities in a foreign language from inside a first-floor apartment. Through the open blinds in the window, Gerald observes an argument between the man, Sinisa and a young woman, Wren. Suddenly, Sinisa clocks Wren hard across the jaw, then storms out of the apartment leaving Wren in a heap. Gerald steps into the shadows and watches Sinisa stride down the block and turn the corner. A moment later, Wren exits the apartment, gingerly rubbing her jaw. A real beauty, she's in her mid-twenties with smooth alabaster skin, willowy arms and shoulder-length golden hair. Wren and Gerald lock eyes for a moment, and just when it seems Gerald might say something, Wren whisks past him. Keeping some distance, Gerald follows Wren along the sidewalk until she ducks into a bar. He turns around and walks away.

Lying in bed the next morning in his plush Fifth Avenue apartment overlooking Central Park, Gerald wakens to the irritating whirring sound of his sweaty wife Morcilla pumping on her step machine. About the same age as Gerald, Morcilla is short and a bit overweight. Without looking at him Morcilla addresses Gerald as he plods past her without acknowledgement. "The decorators are coming at 10. The caterers at 2." The blunt announcement reminds him: socialite Morcilla is to host yet another of her awful parties this evening, attended by dilletantes, snobs, nouveau riche, and all sorts of slithering hangers-on. It's decidedly not his scene.

After the caterers arrive to begin setting up the food spread for the evening's festivities, Gerald concludes the best place for him to be is anywhere out of his house. He heads downtown for a haircut expecting to have his locks trimmed by his usual stylist, but instead he's met by a newcomer filling in. The stylist suggests a cut that would transpose Gerald's part from the left side of his head to the right, on the strength that it suits his face well. Reluctantly, Gerald agrees.

His hairdo newly transformed, Gerald walks the same sidewalk the night he brushed into Wren. He makes it to the entrance of the bar where he last saw her, hesitates a moment, then walks in. Gerald scans the dark, empty bar and spots Wren languidly wiping a glass. He takes a seat at the bar. Wren approaches; a bruise is visible on her jaw. "May I make a cocktail for you?" Gerald orders a Gibson. Wren remarks, "I haven't mixed one of those in quite a while. I hope the onions haven't turned black," to which Gerald replies, "Or black and blue."

After taking a sip of the pungent cocktail, Gerald explains to Wren how the Gibson has come to remind him fondly of the dashing Cary Grant in the Hitchcock film "North by Northwest." This leads to a discussion of the architecture featured in the movie and finally a segue into his own vocation. "I own an architecture firm near the Flatiron Building," She replies, "That might just be my favorite building," adding, "my knowledge of architecture is pretty limited. I'd like to learn more about it, though." Sensing an opening, Gerald remarks, "I'd love to tell you about it." As he says this, Gerald notices Wren rubbing her bruised jaw. "How'd you get that?" Wren replies softly, "You know how." Then, "I like your new haircut. Suits your face well."

Later that evening at Gerald's apartment, Morcilla's society party is in full swing. The place is a beehive of guests all snappily dressed, served by several uniformed caterers delivering hors d'oeuvres. A jazz quartet plays cultured background music on the balcony. A hired photographer mills about documenting the festivities. The Pfalzgraf's butler greets additional guests periodically.

Although this sort of event is the last thing Gerald wants to attend, he holds his nose and plays the role of the dutiful husband to the party's hostess. To a handful of guests, he outlines his firm's pursuit of a contract to design and build a personal art museum for a wealthy client, David Arbogast. Gerald also makes small talk with some artists and gallery owners, as well as a few art collectors. One particularly flamboyant collector, Chappy

Hardwick gushes over the talent of a struggling artist he discovered living and working in a storage unit making sculptures from dried goose droppings. In the middle of the conversation one of the staff call Gerald aside. Excusing himself from the group, Gerald absent-mindedly refers to Chappy as "Chapstick" – a private nickname he invented behind the man's back. Moments later, Morcilla accosts Gerald and excoriates him for insulting her dear friend Chappy. Not in the mood for a confrontation, Gerald pushes back anyway, reminding her of another party where he caught Chappy in their bedroom having sex, and later discovered a bag of cocaine he left behind. A bag of coke that will come in handy later.

Morcilla's party moves along nicely until a guest on the balcony shrieks. Gerald, Morcilla and their guests – including the photographer – rush to the scene to find a very drunken Chappy standing on the edge thirty floors above Fifth Avenue. Chappy utters some barely-coherent accusatory remarks regarding sexual advances toward another guest made by his goose-dropping artist protégé. Gerald talks Chappy off the ledge. Once safely back on the balcony Chappy vomits on Morcilla's Steinway as society swells look on aghast from the sidelines. It's the kind of performance that every hired photographer dreams of capturing at a snooty society soiree.

After the last of the guests have departed, Gerald lies back on a lounge chair in his dimly lit study, a wet rag draped across his eyes. Morcilla walks in, sits on the floor next to Gerald and expresses her appreciation for his help with Chappy's meltdown.

She touches his hand. Gerald removes the rag from his eyes – it's a momentary thaw between the two. Then Morcilla tacks. "Still, I can't understand why you didn't intervene before things got out of hand." Indignant at the accusation of dereliction of duty, and angry at himself for falling for Morcilla's faux entreaty, Gerald retorts, "I didn't invite Chapstick and the rest of those mooches who graze on the expensive food you insist on serving them." The mention of "expensive" lights up Morcilla who rubs it into Gerald that it is her wealth that helped him start the architecture firm and continues to provide financial support. More than anything else, it is Morcilla's insinuation that it is her money that keeps Pfalzgraf Associates that infuriates Gerald most – not because it's false, but because it's true.

A few days later, along with his firm's chief financial officer, Martina, Gerald meets with his banker about securing a loan to expand his office space into the unoccupied floor below his current setup in the building across from the Flatiron Building. As they discuss the details, Gerald notices through the glass walls of the conference room a vaguely familiar face of man speaking with a loan officer in the part of the bank reserved for those with fewer assets and lower credit scores. He wracks his brain to recall how he knows the man.

After the meeting, milling around with Martina on the sidewalk outside the bank, Gerald spots the man again. As the man strides by in a huff, Gerald calls out to him: "Tom Stull?" Tom, who's dressed like a shabby contractor straight from a work site, turns around and looks quizzically back at Gerald. Finally, it clicks. “Gerry Pfalzgraf?” Manhattan Gerald internally cringes at being called “Gerry,” the nickname he had as a lower-middle-class kid living in Western Pennsylvania decades ago. Tom and Gerald had been classmates in elementary school. The two men exchange small talk: Gerald has his architecture firm; Tom runs a construction business he founded after his honorable discharge from the Army as a squad designated marksman. Tom explains that his company has been contracted to make repairs on Interstate 80 in New Jersey, but his cash flow is gummed up, hence the trip to the bank. Tom asks whether Gerald knows of any construction opportunities; Gerald demurs but takes Tom’s business card. The men depart: Gerald into his chauffeur-driven limo, Tom toward the subway.

Gerald is on his way to a lunch appointment with Morcilla in the Meatpacking District where she owns rundown investment property, but first he makes a detour hoping to catch Wren at the bar. Gerald paces the sidewalk outside the bar, deciding whether to enter. After a couple seconds, he does, taking the same barstool he occupied the first time he was there. Wren immediately presents him a Gibson cocktail. “Hello, handsome.” “How did you know?” he asks. She replies, “I saw you wandering around outside. I willed you to come in.” Gerald and Wren finally formally introduce themselves by name. They make some small talk. Wren tells Gerald that she had gone to the Film Forum the previous evening to watch an obscure foreign movie. She lets him know, “Whenever I’m down, I go there to escape.” – a statement that impels Gerald to follow up. “What’s got you down?” Wren quickly clarifies, “I go there when I'm not down too, you know," but it's obvious something bothers her. Gerald takes a long sip of his drink, saying nothing, tempting Wren to elaborate. Eventually she succumbs to the desire to reveal her predicament: Sinisa, the ex-boyfriend who clocked her on the jaw the day Gerald strolled by the apartment, has come back to New York with the intention of rekindling their former relationship. Wren wants nothing to do with him, and suggests to Gerald that Sinisa is a dangerous man. Having shared what she believes to be a sufficient amount of information, Wren pries Gerald for his backstory. He readily admits he's locked in a hell of a marriage, but finding that topic off-putting, he brings up the situation with Oscar and his repulsive downloading proclivities. When Wren asks why Gerald hasn't simply fired the errant employee, he coolly explains, "I might be able to persuade him to do something for me." Wren replies perceptively, "Very Machiavellian."

Gerald finally arrives for his lunch appointment in the Meatpacking District with Morcilla who has been waiting impatiently. As he approaches her table, Morcilla wraps up a difficult phone conversation with the sales manager of an exotic car dealership. She's upset because she feels the sales manager has played a bit of the old "bait'n'switch" with her – a tactic she abhors and refuses to tolerate. After she angrily hangs up, Morcilla digs into Gerald, complaining about his tardiness and pressing him for an update on his meeting with the bankers – all before he even sits down. Inured to such treatment, Gerald ignores his wife and orders a wine flirtatiously from a young waitress. He then reports that the bank has green-lighted the funding for his office expansion, and that he's planning to travel to Pennsylvania to visit David Arbogast about his museum project. Morcilla stuns Gerald with the news that she has decided to renovate her Meatpacking property – a decrepit building Gerald thought would sell. She closes by noting coolly, "I'm going to reconfigure the ground floor into retail space. Going to cost fifty mil, so I won't be funneling any more cash your way."

Wren mixes drinks for a large crowd at the bar when Sinisa shows up looking for her. She's dismayed to see him and reminds him that management has banned him from the premises for past infractions. Sinisa informs Wren that the situation is urgent; she agrees to talk with him briefly. Sinisa explains that he needs money to take care of a $100,000 gambling debt. Wren knows that Sinisa owes the money to organized criminals. Sinisa adds that he'll soon collect $10,000 from a deadbeat in Atlantic City, but his situation remains dire. He proposes a harebrained scheme to rob the bar with her help. Uninterested in abetting a crime, and financially unable to help her abusive ex-boyfriend, Wren summarily blows him off – which enrages Sinisa. In response to Wren's rejection Sinisa gets belligerent: harassing bar patrons, snorting coke in the men's room, knocking over a table. A burly bouncer escorts Sinisa calmly to the door. Everything is fine until Sinisa recoils and assaults the bouncer. Witnessing the pandemonium, Wren confides to a fellow bartender, "I'll probably get fired for this." Enraged, the bouncer heaves Sinisa through the plate glass front door where he lands at the feet of a NYC police officer summoned earlier. "You again? Man, you just don't fucking learn, do you," remarks the office before cuffing Sinisa and hustling him to a waiting black & white.

Following a boring conference call with his bankers, Gerald travels to the bar in the hope of encountering Wren. To his chagrin he learns from a bartender that she's been fired for her association with a miscreant asshole who the night before had been thrown through the front door. The boarded-up door serves as proof of an altercation as described by the bartender. Recalling that Wren once said she likes to watch movies at the Film Forum when she's feeling down, Gerald takes off for the theater on Houston Street where "Rififi" is playing. The movie is almost over when Gerald steps into the mostly empty, darkened theater. He scans the place, and sure enough, she's there. He takes the seat directly behind her. The credits roll, Wren turns to leave and is surprised to see After finishing dinner at Eleven Madison Park, Gerald and Wren walk across the street?"

Sitting together at an urbane lounge near the theater, Wren expresses her feelings of helplessness and doom now that Sinisa has reentered the picture. Gerald inquires as to Wren's plans now that she is newly unemployed, learning that she wants to pursue fine art studies that were interrupted after she moved to Manhattan from Vermont a few years earlier. Gerald suggests architecture which, as he anticipated when he floated the notion, leads Wren to probe about Gerald's profession and his business. She notes that she loves beautiful buildings, but admits she knows little about architecture, adding coyly, "Do you know anyone I could talk to about it?" Gerald plays along, stating that he can introduce her to a guy who owns a top-notch firm, proposing dinner at the highly-rated Eleven Madison Park restaurant not far from the office of Pfalzgraf Associates. He hands Wren his business card. Music to his ears, Wren agrees to the dinner engagement.

Back at the office the following day, Gerald meets with his design team to review the presentation of the museum proposal for the upcoming meeting with David Arbogast. He reminds the team that although his wife Morcilla is a friend of Arbogast's, the relationship will not increase the chances of success. "Arbogast will base his decision on quality of plans. Clarity of vision. Friendships won't mean shit when it comes to this project." Gerald goes on to say that their top competitor – Curtain, Wall, Buckley and Company – also plans to bid for the contract.

Gerald and Wren finish dinner at Eleven Madison Park and now walk across the street through Madison Square Park. Wren's hand sweeps by Gerald's. He lightly takes it without resistance from her. The lighted Flatiron Building is in the near distance, reminiscent of the famous Edward Steichen photograph. Wren reiterates that the Flatiron is her favorite building in New York. Gerald provides some history the building, noting that the wedge-shaped building is like a mighty plow in one of those Depression-Era WPA murals, furrowing Manhattan into Broadway and Fifth Avenue. Wren says she had never thought of it that way. Gerald replies, "It's more apparent from my office." Adding hopefully, "Would you like to take a look?"

Inside the office building, Gerald and Wren exit the elevator onto the unfinished floor that Gerald has acquired. Giving her a brief tour, he notes that the company needs the space to accommodate many new architects he plans to hire to deal with the influx of new business. Gerald then leads her to the staircase leading to the office space one floor up. He produces a security badge but notices that the badge reader securing the door to the stairwell has not yet been installed. Once inside Gerald's office, the couple stand side-by-side at the window taking in the beautifully-lit Flatiron Building. After a moment, Gerald lightly strokes Wren's hair. She says, "I don't like that you're married." "Neither do I," he replies. Wren presses on. "I won't be your mistress. Not for long, anyway." "You won't have to," promises Gerald. He embraces Wren and they exchange a passionate kiss, silhouetted against the floor-to-ceiling windows, skyline shining brilliantly in the background.

The big day has arrived when Gerald and his team – architect Oscar Dupree and engineer Paul Clay – will present their proposal for Arbogast's private art museum. Once inside Arbogast's compound in western Pennsylvania, the meeting attendees on both sides share introductions and pleasantries before Gerald and Arbogast make opening statements. Gerald notes that all the buildings on Arbogast's large compound have been designed by Pfalzgraf Associates, adding that for continuity it would be best to assign the museum project to Gerald's company. He then turns the meeting over to Oscar who delivers the presentation. After he finishes, lunch is brought in and one of Arbogast's men commences with a presentation on the contents of Arbogast's art collection. Suddenly, in the middle of the presentation, Paul let's out a laugh which he quickly stifles. Arbogast is flummoxed and Gerald is mortified. The man continues the presentation, but tension remains high.

Later, during the limo ride back to Manhattan, Gerald erupts in anger. Paul apologizes profusely, blaming the outburst on a joke Oscar whispered to him. Gerald seethes at the possibility that the childish behavior threatens the bid. His ire for Oscar has instantly doubled since he the day he discovered pornography on Oscar's workstation. Livid, Gerald quietly stares out the window in deep thought. The limo drives by a construction site on the Interstate. Gerald spots a truck emblazoned with the name "TS Erection." He thinks for a moment, then removes Tom Stull's business card from his wallet. Perhaps Tom can be of assistance after all.

While Gerald was in western Pennsylvania, Morcilla visited the exotic car dealership to make a stink about the treatment she has received from the sales manager. Accompanying her is Vicki, Morcilla's best friend from high-school. The sales manager greets Morcilla, but she's in no mood for pleasantries. She quickly tears his head off, and makes a demand that throws him off balance. He retreats to his office, promising to work out the details. Alone with Vicki, Morcilla confides that she plans to travel to Barcelona – her family's ancestral city – where she will meet up with David Arbogast. She leaves the not-so-subtle impression that it will be more than a friendly encounter. When the sales manager returns, he announces that he can, after all, deliver the vehicle Morcilla demanded – a brand new, ostentatious convertible exotic car painted bright yellow.

The day after his debacle of a meeting with Arbogast, Gerald awakens once again to the irritating whirring sound of Morcilla pumping her step machine. He takes a shower. When he steps out, the whirring stops and Morcilla intercepts him. "Gerald, what happened at your meeting with David Arbogast?" Confused by the inquiry, Gerald just stares blankly at Morcilla. She continues, "He called me last night to tell me things didn't go so well in your meeting." At first Gerald acknowledges that he has to repair damage, but then recoils at the notion that Arbogast would tell Morcilla about the meeting. He challenges her to explain. She demurs. In no mood to start a fight, Gerald calmly explains that he has the situation under control. Once Morcilla leaves, Gerald angrily yanks a black suit out of his closet, breaking the wooden hanger.

On the sidewalk outside his apartment, Gerald notices a parked flatbed truck bearing Morcilla's new sports car. He approaches the driver. "Hey, I don't suppose that snazzy car is for Mrs. Pfalzgraf." The truck driver confirms it, adding that the woman who bought the car must have some pull because the dealership already had a taken a down payment on it from a famous entertainer. Just more confirmation for Gerald of Morcilla's talent for manipulation.

Gerald is on his way to the office when he receives a call from David Arbogast who informs Gerald that he has invited Curtain, Wall, Buckley and Company to accelerate the presentation of their proposal. Gerald pretends to support the decision to check the competition, expressing confidence that Pfalzgraf Associates will, in the end, offer the better proposal. Inside he's unsettled and furious. As soon as he hangs up, Gerald receives another phone call, this time from a weeping Wren. Holding Gerald's business card, she speaks from inside a restaurant kitchen near her apartment. "I'm sorry. I just didn't know what else to do." Wren explains that Sinisa appeared at her apartment unexpectedly and threatened her. Gerald redirects his limo driver to the restaurant.

The limo arrives and the driver honks the horn. Wren rushes out of the restaurant, jumping into the limo and into Gerald's arms. She makes a move to kiss her savior, but Gerald stops her – not a good idea to reveal his philandering to his driver. Gerald eases Wren away, suddenly noticing her black eye. The limo driver drops the couple off at Madison Square Park where Gerald commits to protecting Wren from the evil Sinisa. He proposes she stay awhile incognito at a room at a boutique hotel that Pfalzgraf Associates holds for visiting clients. Wren responds tentatively: "I don't know what to say. We barely know each other." "Can't you tell I care about you." "Yes, I do. Me too." Gerald fishes for more information about Sinisa, and learns enough to fashion the foundation for a ploy to bring him down. Wren reveals that his full name is Sinisa Ražnatovi, and that he's a coke head, compulsive gambler, and a bone-breaker for organized crime. This last detail disturbs Gerald greatly. Pursuing all angles, Gerald probes into whether Sinisa has any redeeming qualities – or at least a weakness he can exploit. Wren retells the time a drunken Sinisa poured his heart out about how a Catholic priest molested him many times when he served as an altar boy. Gerald feigns sympathy for Sinisa, but he knows these past episodes may be leveraged.

The next day, Gerald takes a cab to a gritty industrial neighborhood outside of Manhattan. He walks to one of the last working pay-phones in New York City that still exists, plucks a card from his wallet and dials the number for TS Erection. Tom answers and Gerald invites him to lunch at a busy chain restaurant in Times Square. The purpose of the meeting is to discuss a business deal. Tom excitedly agrees.

Back home, Gerald calls out for Morcilla. Hearing no response, he enters her bedroom and thumbs through Morcilla's planner. On the current day he notes that his wife is scheduled to attend a fund raiser. He jumps a few weeks ahead and notices an entry about her traveling to Barcelona for several days to oversee a museum exhibition opening. The initials D.A. are penciled in. Gerald grimaces, as he figures D.A. is David Arbogast. He backs up to a couple weeks in the future where he spots an entry about Morcilla going to Vicki's house in New Jersey to plan a high school class reunion. This entry intrigues him.

Act II

Arriving at the office, Gerald walks imperiously past a nervous Oscar without looking at him. The time on a wall clock: 8:45. Fast forward. It's now 6:59 and the place is mostly empty. Oscar stares at the wall clock and when it clicks to 7:00 he shuffles anxiously toward Gerald's office and knocks on the door. Gerald stands next to his computer, hand on the mouse. "Come in," he says. Oscar enters the office with trepidation in his gait. He immediately acknowledges his unacceptable behavior at the Arbogast meeting – presuming this is the reason for the meeting – and apologizes profusely for the transgression. However, this is not why Gerald summoned Oscar. Instead he confronts his employee with the evidence of his download of illicit pornography. Oscar initially denies the accusation, claiming that perhaps someone hacked his computer, but Gerald isn't having it. He continues to shame Oscar with more shocking images until Oscar finally succumbs and admits his guilt. He apologizes once again, but that gesture is far too little for Gerald. Oscar pleads with Gerald, offering to take a pay cut and give up vacation. "Whatever it takes," says Oscar, "I want to stay with the firm. Please, don't fire me. I'll do anything you want." Gerald smiles when Oscar says the words he wants to hear. He accepts Oscar's proposed concessions, but notes that he must perform an additional service to retain his job and avoid being turned over to the authorities. Gerald tells Oscar that the task is somewhat unorthodox, and admonishes him to tell no one about it. Oscar agrees and Gerald lays out the details. After a moment, Oscar reacts strongly. "You're joking, right? I can't do that!" Gerald presses him with threats of prison time if he doesn't comply. Oscar is conflicted. Gerald tries a different angle. "Oscar, this guy is blackmailing the firm. He has damaging information that could keep us from bidding on contracts. We'll lose the museum for sure, and maybe even get hit with some serious litigation. This bastard is a threat to all of us, and we – you – have to make him disappear." Gerald's browbeating has the desired effect, as Oscar reluctantly agrees.

The next day, Gerald has lunch with Tom Stull, the proprietor of TS Erection. They recall humorous and memorable events from elementary school back in Pennsylvania. Among those is Gerald's recollection of the time Tom brought in photos of a bear he shot when he was eight years old. The discussion of the hunt leads to Tom's skill with a rifle, and the fact that he had been a squad designated marksman – a sharpshooter – in the Army. Familiar with Tom's shooting prowess, Gerald mentions he has some work for Tom – but it has nothing to do with TS Erection's construction expertise, as Tom assumes. Rather, Gerald lays out a plot to shoot and kill a person driving a fancy car on Interstate 80 – a location where TS Erection is grading and paving a section of the highway. The idea is to make it appear that a crazed person – like the notorious shooters who randomly killed many innocent people in the Washington, D.C. area – is responsible for the deed. Gerald points out that Tom can quickly take the shot and get back to his job site before law enforcement can arrive. Because of the randomness of the shooting, all the police can do is prepare for another shooting – which won't happen. Of course, Tom is flabbergasted by the request, and becomes agitated in the restaurant. Gerald calms him down and appeals to Tom's cash-strapped situation. The money Gerald is prepared to spend will go a long way toward keeping TS Erection solvent. He adds that he can help influence the bank to ease the terms of Tom's loans. The offers are too rich for Tom to dismiss outright. In the end he agrees to accept a large down payment, with the promise of even more when the task is completed.

In Wren's hotel room at night, Gerald lies in bed next to his young lover, post-coital pleasure on their faces. For the first time, Gerald seriously brings up the notion of leaving Morcilla, while declaring his desire to retain the wealth he requires to maintain and expand his life-style. Gerald expresses his love for Wren, noting that her youth makes him feel young, too. She acknowledges that their age difference is immaterial, and that she feels safe with him. Her mention of safety gives Gerald the opening to pry for more details about Sinisa. He already knows Sinisa had been molested as a child, is a cocaine abuser, and has a propensity for violence. Wren fills in some missing pieces – each serving as a vulnerability that Gerald hopes to exploit. She reveals that he owes $100,000 to organized criminals, and that he plans to go to Atlantic City soon to take back $10,000 owed to him by a gambler. When Gerald asks where in Atlantic City he might go, Wren says she doesn't know for sure, but notes that Sinisa often lit cigarettes using branded matchbooks from the Borgata Hotel – a possible destination. Gerald soaks up all the information, sizing up Sinisa's vulnerabilities.

At home, Gerald watches a documentary on television about the assassination of a Bulgarian dissident by a KGB agent armed with an umbrella tipped with poisonous ricin. Gerald learns ricin is a derivative of beans from the castor plant. Death is assured and pinpointing ricin as the cause is difficult. The story intrigues Gerald. Morcilla steps into the TV room and tells Gerald she's planning to visit Vicki the following morning for a few days to organize their class reunion. She adds, "I'm going to take the new car." Thinking fast, Gerald says that he too has to go out of town. "I need to run down to the job site in Philly for a couple days."

Later, Gerald works at a computer in the public library, taking notes about the effects of ricin poisoning. He clicks, bringing up a foreign patent for manufacturing ricin out of castor beans, taking copious notes on the process. From the library, Gerald travels to an Army surplus store to purchase with cash a used chemical suit, complete with a gas mask. After leaving the surplus store, Gerald drives a rented van along a country road eventually pulling into a tree nursery. He wanders about the potted plants arrayed on the ground, until a worker approaches, asking "How can I help you?" Gerald pulls a paper from his pocket and starts reading from it: "Celosia, gomphrena, portulaca, castor, mercardonia. You got any of those?" The worker takes off looking for the plants Gerald seeks. Soon after, the worker loads a bunch of plants into Gerald's rented van. Gerald pays with cash and drives off down the country lane. Miles later he pulls off the lane and dumps all the plants except the castors into the woods. Wearing rubber gloves, he delicately picks beans from the remaining plants and places them in a Ziploc bag.

Gerald parks outside a trailer at his company's job site Philadelphia. Inside the trailer, Gerald dons the chemical suit and begins to grind up the castor beans. A food dehydrator sits nearby. Later that evening, having completed the transformation of castor beans into highly toxic ricin, Gerald takes off for Atlantic City. On the way, he places a call to the Borgata Hotel to inquire whether a Mr. Sinisa Ražnatovi is a registered guest. The desk clerk on the other end of the line hesitates. "How do you spell... did you say Mr. Ražnatov Sinisic?" Gerald replies, "No," then realizing the flipped nature of the name must be an alias, he quickly pivots. "I mean 'yes'; that's him." Gerald abruptly hangs up and calls Morcilla's cell phone to tell her he must stay in Philadelphia a couple more days. Morcilla, who is lying in bed with Vicki, both naked, blithely acknowledges Gerald.

Gerald passes a sign on the highway that reads "Atlantic City 40 miles." He drives into an isolated, empty rest stop and types a letter on an old manual typewriter. When finished, Gerald walks to a dumpster and tosses the typewriter and a garbage bag containing his chemical suit. He then enters the lavatory to change into a snazzy suit of a unique purplish color and pattern.

Finally arriving at the Borgata, Gerald parks the van, enters the hotel and heads straight to the cage where he purchases $15,000 in chips with which he gambles for a couple hours on blackjack and baccarat. More or less even, Gerald converts his stash into a few high-denomination chips some of which he inserts into a manilla envelope addressed to Ražnatov Sinisic along with the letter he composed at the rest stop. The value of the chips is $10,000 – the precise amount of the debt Sinisa had come to Atlantic City to recover. The letter contains instructions for Sinisa to meet Gerald in the hotel bar. Gerald takes the envelope to the front desk and asks the clerk to deliver it to the addressee.

Fiddling with a cocktail in a booth near the back of the crowded bar, Gerald, checks his watch and looks around, anxiously hoping Sinisa will show. Finally, he does. Sinisa immediately demands angrily to know why he has been offered $10,000 without any explanation. He asks, "How do you know that scumbag Selakovic?" Flummoxed by the question and the strange name, Gerald hesitates. Then quickly presuming "Selakovic" is the debtor Sinisa seeks, Gerald declares he has no connection to the man, but that he is aware of Sinisa's interest in him. Gerald introduces himself as "Paul Geraci," a fixer for a rich businessman who requires the bone-breaking skills that Sinisa possesses. He goes on to explain that the $10,000 payment is meant to clear Selakovic's debt so that Sinisa can concentrate on a new job: a hit on a blackmailer who has been exacting stiff payments from the businessman. "Geraci" offers a payday of $100,000 for the kill. As an aside, "Geraci" notes that the blackmailer is also a pervert who enjoys child pornography. Seeing an opportunity to retire his personal debt to organized criminals, and exact punishment on the kind of person he reviles most – a child molester – Sinisa accepts.

With all the players cast, Gerald places a call to Tom Stull informing him when and where on Interstate 80 his victim will be, adding that "he" will be driving an exotic yellow convertible with the top down. Gerald tells Tom to take a couple pot shots at passing trucks first to establish the ruse that a crazed sniper is responsible for the shooting. Tom expresses concern about doing it as soon as the next day, but Gerald makes it known that the opportunity is too good to pass up. Tom asks how he will be paid for the rest of the money. Before answering, Gerald inquires as to what Tom has done with the large down payment, concerned that he might have squandered it in a conspicuous fashion. Tom assures him that he has stashed the loot in a tool compartment on his pavement grader. Satisfied, Gerald tells Tom to go to a specific subway station at a specific time in the evening after the shooting where an associate dressed as a bag-man will hand over the rest of the money.

Gerald calls Oscar into his office. Oscar looks haggard, fretting that today is the day he'll be sent off to perform the task Gerald laid out previously. Gerald produces a duffle bag containing the costume Oscar is to wear the following evening – that of a grungy bag-man. Having won the bid for the museum, he tells Oscar, "I'm going out to Pennsylvania tonight to see Arbogast. I'll be back tomorrow night. Meet me back here alone precisely at midnight to do a debrief on your mission."

Gerald arrives in the late evening at the Arbogast compound three hundred miles from New York City for a two-day visit – the perfect spot for supporting an alibi. The following morning, he begins a sequence of meetings that keeps him busy throughout the day. That afternoon, Morcilla departs Vicki's house in New Jersey in her brand-new yellow sports car, top down – precisely on the schedule Gerald had learned from his wife's meticulous planner.

Tom and a few workers on his construction crew on Interstate 80 look over papers. Several large pieces of road equipment sit nearby behind cones separating them from rushing traffic on the highway. Tom looks at his watch which reads 3:15. He tells one of his workers, "I'm gonna run ahead to the grading team." Tom hops in his truck and drives off. Arriving at the shooting site, Tom dons camouflage then lies prone in a grassy area amidst trees in a woodsy area near the highway. He peers through a scope on a rifle mounted on a tripod at traffic tooling along the busy interstate. Tom nervously checks his watch which reads 3:50. Unexpectedly, his cell phone rings. He scrambles to turn it off, fearful the call could conceivably establish his location at this moment. Flustered, Tom peers through the scope, spots a long, double-length semi and squeezes off a round that strikes the rear trailer. The truck driver continues on unaware. Tom cocks the bolt-action rifle and takes a shot at a truck hauling new automobiles, hitting one near the rear. He cocks the bolt again, and checks his watch which reads 3:55. He spots a truck bearing the logo of a construction competitor, and with a sinister grin on his face Tom fires a round. This one misses the target and pierces the tire of a mini-van which was behind the truck a second earlier, but lagged back suddenly. The minivan swerves and rolls over. Traffic moving in the opposite direction slows down as the tumbling mini-van sheds parts. Morcilla is among those slowing down. Tom spots the slick yellow car, quickly cocks the bolt and takes the shot that strikes Morcilla in the head, Zapruder style. The car unceremoniously veers onto the grassy median strip and slams to a stop into a grassy knoll. Tom packs his gear and rushes into the dense stand of trees behind him.

Back at the job site, Tom encounters workers milling around, talking among themselves. Traffic is stopped in both directions. Emergency vehicles zoom past, followed by news trucks. A helicopter passes overhead.

At the same time in western Pennsylvania, Gerald and Martina sit at a conference table along with Arbogast and a couple of his aides. An accountant stands at a podium, making a boring presentation. Martina's phone dings with a text message. Gerald eyes her as she silently reads the text. Suddenly, she blurts out, "Oh my god! There was an accident on I80 an hour ago. They think a sniper might've killed a couple drivers." The mention of "a couple drivers" stuns Gerald who was expecting the news of a killing of an individual – his wife Morcilla.

Back in Manhattan, Wren exits the Film Forum where Sinisa waits on the sidewalk holding a tool bag. She is unpleasantly surprised to see him, and demands to know why he's stalking her. On the contrary, he explains that he simply wants to return the watch she surrendered the evening Gerald witnessed Sinisa striking Wren. Given that Sinisa's original purpose in taking back the watch was to help retire his debts, Wren says, "I thought you needed money." Sinisa invites Wren for a drink – just one – to explain his situation. She resists, eventually caving in to Sinisa's persistence. Inside a bar, Sinisa tells Wren that he landed a new high-paying gig that will help solve his financial problems. He explains, "I met some pompous asshole at the Borgata." Sinisa pulls out the business card Gerald gave him and reads aloud the name. "Geraci. Some slick motherfucker in a purple suit. He's got a bigtime client with a problem." Sinisa hoists his tool bag onto the table, and as he fishes around in it, Wren notices with concern that it contains a rope, pliers and an ice-axe. Finally, Sinisa produces the watch and hands it to Wren, imploring her to put it on. Instead she stuffs the watch in her purse, a gesture that angers Sinisa. True to form, he begins to verbally abuse Wren. She makes a move to leave, but Sinisa grabs her by the arm. The commotion attracts the attention of the bartender, and Sinisa relents. Wren bolts for the door. Drinking smugly, Sinisa calls out, "Go ahead and leave. I'll find you again."

Later in the evening in Manhattan, Oscar, dressed in the bag-man costume, shuffles down the stairs into the subway station carrying a garbage bag. The few straphangers on the sparsely populated platform pay no attention to him. Oscar proceeds slowly toward the end of the platform. About 30 feet from the end he spots Tom standing by a support beam with his back to the rails. The two make eye contact. Oscar shuffles in place until he hears the sound of a train approaching the station. Finally, he approaches Tom, coming face to face with him. The train races into the station. Oscar extends the garbage bag toward Tom, announcing, "Here's your payoff, fucker." Tom offers a quizzical look, and as he reaches for the bag, Oscar shoves him into the path of the oncoming train. The brakes screech but it's too late; Tom is crushed under the steel wheels. Oscar rushes up the stairs and out of the station. He ducks around a dark corner and sneaks behind a row of hedges. He quickly sheds the bag-man garments revealing normal street clothes underneath. He stuffs the costume into the garbage bag, steps from behind the hedges unobserved and casually but briskly ambles along the sidewalk. He tosses the garbage bag into a trash can, then hails a cab. He hops in as the sound of blaring sirens builds.

At that moment, in the dark empty floor under construction one flight down from the office of Pfalzgraf Associates, Sinisa rifles a filing cabinet, eventually recovering a brief case. He opens it to reveal bundles of neatly wrapped money bound by ribbons bearing the Borgata Hotel logo – cash that Gerald laundered using casino chips as an intermediary currency. He makes a quick count of the cash, satisfied it's all there. On top of the money rests a package of white powder. A note on the package reads, "A token of our appreciation." Sinisa grins at the gesture. Sitting on the floor by the window, Sinisa the coke-head reliably snorts a fingernail of the powder. By his reaction, it's quality cocaine – the same cocaine Chappy Hardwick left behind at one of Morcilla's parties. Sinisa checks his watch, pulls on gloves and a ski-mask, and ascends the stairs to the office above.

Having completed the task of killing Tom, Oscar sits at his desk to await Gerald's arrival, as requested. Instead it's Sinisa who arrives, forcing Oscar to don a straitjacket. Completely subdued in the jacket, Oscar cries out, "Why are you doing this?" Sinisa barks, "Shut the fuck up, pervert." Called a pervert, Oscar suddenly realizes Gerald has set him up, but it's too late. Sinisa chokes the life out of a writhing Oscar. Sinisa removes the straitjacket, places a noose around Oscar's neck and hoists his dead body onto the desk. He climbs atop the desk, ties the rope to a beam above, lifts up Oscar's body and drops it, simulating suicide. The neck snaps; urine runs onto the carpet. Sinisa stashes the straightjacket into his tool bag and heads to the exit, leaving Oscar to hang limply.

Sinisa stops off at a bar for several celebratory drinks. After a couple hours, fully inebriated, Sinisa arrives at his apartment building and fumbles with his keys at the entrance. Once inside, Sinisa unsuccessfully tries his key at apartment number 4F. Frustrated at his inability to get in, he kicks the door. A large, muscular neighbor opens the door and demands, "What's your fucking problem, pal?" Sinisa is about to engage the man until he realizes he's on the wrong floor at the wrong apartment. The man slams the door in Sinisa's face. Sinisa climbs the stairs, sticks a key in a door marked 5F, and turns the knob. Successfully inside, Sinisa throws a frozen dinner in the oven, sits on the couch and flicks on the TV. He opens the brief case, grabs a stack of money and ogles it lovingly, then takes out the packet of coke, dumps a pile onto a mirror on his coffee table and divides it into three lines. He snorts two in rapid succession. Sinisa changes TV channels rapidly, settling on an old movie. Suddenly, he becomes distressed, puking all over the coffee table. Struggling to breathe, Sinisa staggers about the room, coughing hard. The ricin Gerald has mixed into the cocaine works as designed.

Sinisa stumbles into the hallway, coughing uncontrollably. He presses a button on the elevator, but when it doesn't arrive immediately, he heads for the stairwell. He opens the door to the stairwell, takes an unsteady step and tumbles all the way down, bashing his head against an old-style accordion radiator. Blood seeps from a deep crack in Sinisa's cranium.

Act III

On a hot, sunny morning the following day, Gerald, Martina, Arbogast, and an aide follow the owner of a quarry along a dusty path. Gerald is inappropriately dressed in a dark suit and Italian shoes. He brushes dust off his clothing as the quarry owner leads the gang to a stack of stone slabs to secure approval for their use in the construction of the museum. Just then, Gerald's cell-phone rings, startling him. He steps away from the others. The call is from his secretary at his Manhattan office where lots of action takes place in the background: rubber-necking employees cordoned off from a body bag, cops and EMT's working the scene. Hearing his secretary sobbing, Gerald asks what's going on, as if he didn't know; the others in the quarry party look over at Gerald. His secretary blurts out, "Oscar's dead, Gerald! He hung himself right at his desk. The police want to talk to you." A detective lays out the situation to Gerald and inquires about his plans to return to Manhattan. Gerald replies he'll come back right away.

After he hangs up, the others bombard Gerald with questions. He reports dolefully that Oscar, one of his employees working on the museum project, hung himself above his desk. No one knows why. Almost no one. As the other people express shock and remorse, Gerald receives another call, this time from the New Jersey State Police. It's the news of Morcilla's death by a crazed sniper on Interstate 80. Gerald listens for a moment, then drops the phone and falls to his knees. Martina rushes toward him. "Gerald! What's the matter?"

The following morning, Gerald sits in the back of David Arbogast's private jet, wearing dark sunglasses. He stares out the window at the landscape below. Martina sits a few seats away, reading some papers and occasionally glancing up to check on Gerald. The pilot opens the cockpit door and announces some breaking news. "They just closed Interstate 80 again. A half hour ago that crazed sniper took some more pot shots." Martina responds, "Unbelievable." Gerald peers out the window again. The quizzical look on his face slowly turns into an ever-so-slight smile. He mumbles to himself, "That <u>is</u> unbelievable."

Back home, Gerald drops a piece of luggage on the floor and checks his answering machine. The first message is one of condolence. Gerald shuts off the machine in midsentence. He walks to the couch and flicks on the TV. A news reporter details the arrest of an alleged sniper caught near Interstate 80. For

Gerald, it's a dream come true as the "crazed sniper" theory he imagined will only gain greater credibility – and divert any possible attention away from Tom Stull.

At Sinisa's apartment building, a police officer interviews the neighbor in 4F. He describes Sinisa's rude mistaken intrusion late in the evening, and recalls him stomping around the floor. The officer informs the neighbor that Sinisa fell down a flight of stairs and succumbed to a head injury. The police officer then proceeds to Sinisa's apartment and meets up with the inspector assigned to the case. The officer presumes Sinisa must have been drunk when he fell down the stairs. The inspector agrees. "It certainly looks like an accident. He probably went out for some air and stumbled." The inspector proceeds to examine the briefcase, shocked at the quantity of money inside. The officer speculates the money was a payoff to Sinisa for performing an illegal act; the inspector counters that the money may have been intended as a payment from Sinisa to another criminal who will come looking for it. "We might have ourselves some bait to catch a bad guy," he says hopefully. This theory is in line with Gerald's. He wants the criminals to whom Sinisa owed money to find it, thus removing a reason for them to hunt down Wren.

At Tom Stull's house, a detective interviews Tom's widow, who is unable to provide an explanation as to why her husband would be in the subway at such a late hour. Tom's widow asks whether the police have apprehended the person who pushed Tom onto the tracks. The detective responds that it's just a theory. He explains that no one actually witnessed the event, that no cameras are pointed at that section of the station, and that the motorman simply saw Tom fall into the path of the oncoming train. In the end, the cause of death is determined to be an accident.

Another detective visits Gerald in his office. He offers his condolences for Gerald's loss of his wife, and expresses relief that the sniper who killed her and others was quickly apprehended. The detective then turns his attention to the case of Oscar's suicide. He begins to speculate on a reason when Gerald eagerly volunteers that Oscar had been caught with illegal pornography on his workstation. Gerald goes on to say that perhaps Oscar broke down after receiving a demotion, a pay cut, and removal from a key project. He shows the detective the folder of pornography which prompts the detective to inquire as to why Gerald didn't call in authorities right away. The detective floats the idea that Gerald might have retained the materials as a cudgel. The implication unnerves Gerald, and he mentally scolds himself for being too quick to offer his opinion. He's now worried that the detective could take an outsized interest in what should have been a mundane case.

Gerald arranges to meet Wren for dinner. On his way in the limo he comes across a short article reporting the accidental death of Sinisa. The briefcase full of cash was money well-spent. Inside the restaurant, Gerald sits at a table, drinking a cocktail while he awaits Wren's arrival. She's never late, so her tardiness unnerves Gerald. His paranoia increases after a police car drives slowly past the restaurant. Finally, Wren walks in. The maître d' leads her to Gerald's table where the couple embrace. Wren extends her sympathies for Morcilla's death which she read about in the obituary section of the paper. Gerald explains that he and Morcilla had been working on the financial details of a divorce – which is news to Wren. He says, "I would never wish Morcilla dead, but now that she is, I have to move on. I want to be with you. I love you." Wren responds in kind, adding that she wishes Sinisa would leave her alone and disappear from her life. Gerald says he has a feeling the wish will come true. Later that evening, Gerald and Wren make love in her hotel room, and the following morning have breakfast together in the rooftop restaurant. Gerald gently breaks the news that Oscar committed suicide, and that the odd coincidence of his death and Morcilla's murder on the same day is bound to raise some eyebrows. He recalls the grilling he received from the detective investigating Oscar's suicide. Gerald remarks, "Every husband becomes a prime suspect when his rich wife dies unexpectedly - especially if he immediately takes up with a younger woman. It screams motive." Gerald suggests that to tamp down unwanted scrutiny, Wren take up residence for a while in a cottage he will rent upstate. She's hesitant, but Gerald insists.

On the day before Wren is set to depart for the cottage, she meets up with Gerald by the Hudson River. He wears the same uniquely purplish suit as when he met Sinisa at the Borgata Hotel. The couple express their mutual melancholy at having to be apart for a few months. A chilly wind kicks up. Gerald embraces Wren who thrusts her hands into his jacket pockets to warm them. A moment later she takes out a $500 casino chip branded with the Borgata Hotel logo. "Where'd you get this, Gerald?" Gerald takes the chip and examines it like it's a foreign object. He responds dumbly, "That must be from that time I went to an architect's conference in Atlantic City." Wren takes note of Gerald's outfit, recalling what Sinisa had told her in the bar the night he returned the watch: "I met some pompous asshole at the Borgata. Geraci. Some slick motherfucker in a purple suit." She tentatively asks whether Gerald knows someone named "Geraci." He says "No" flatly, adding, "Who is he?" Wren replies, "I'm not sure. I'm kind of afraid to find out."

The next day, as Wren packs her bags she receives a call from the inspector investigating the origin and purpose of Sinisa's briefcase full of money. He explains that Sinisa possessed her phone number. The inspector goes on to request her presence at the station to answer some questions. Wren assumes Sinisa has been picked up once again for breaking the law, but is aghast to learn that Sinisa is, in fact, dead. At the police station, the inspector explains the details of Sinisa's demise, then proceed to ask her some basic questions. She replies that Sinisa was a drug addict, a loan shark, a gambler indebted to organized criminals. The inspector reveals the existence of the briefcase containing cash wrapped with Borgata Hotel ribbons. The mention of the Borgata momentarily stuns Wren. Noting her reaction, the inspector presses her to reveal more, but she declines, explaining she knows nothing about the money.

Gerald has just instructed an employee to bid on a pavement grader (one that may contain Tom Stull's down payment) at an auction of TS Erection's assets, when his secretary informs him a woman without an appointment has requested to see him. When Gerald spots Wren standing in the lobby, he rushes over and escorts her out of the office. Once out of earshot of his employees and secretary, Gerald asks why Wren isn't at the upstate cottage. Wren reveals she has just come from the police station where she was questioned about Sinisa and his accidental death. Gerald feigns surprise that Sinisa is dead. Before he can ask questions Wren hits him directly: "Do you know someone named Geraci?" Gerald tries to brush it aside having already answered that question in the negative, but Wren persists. She explains how Sinisa was found with a briefcase full of money from the Borgata Hotel, and suggests a connection with the chip she found in the pocket of Gerald's purplish suit. Gerald professes his love for Wren and again reinforces his desire to be together with her. Then, rather than make up more stories, Gerald asks simply, "Would it really matter to you whether or not I knew this guy Geraci?" Wren contemplates the question, then strokes Gerald's face. She's with Gerald, free of the wrath of Sinisa – that's enough for her. She responds, "Not really."

Epilog

Inside Penn Station, Gerald accompanies Wren and her luggage to the track where the train to the upstate cottage awaits departure. Gerald mentions that he's been called to give victim testimony at the trial of the sniper who killed people on the Interstate, noting uncomfortably that the accused has since recanted his involvement in Morcilla's death the first day.

Six months later, Gerald carries Wren across the threshold of the Fifth Avenue penthouse, followed by his butler who schlepps a bunch of luggage. "Welcome to your new abode, Mrs. Pfalzgraf. How about fixing us some drinks?" After Wren finds her way to the kitchen, Gerald paws through a pile of mail, tossing aside the dreck. He stops to open an important looking letter from the district attorney. The DA informs Gerald that the sniper has hired a new lawyer who has filed an appeal based on new evidence discovered since the guilty verdict was rendered three months earlier. New evidence has surfaced consisting of rifle rounds recovered the second day of the shootings that do not match those from the first day. Wren comes out of the kitchen and places a Gibson cocktail on the coffee table. Gerald watches her walk out onto the balcony and admires her beautiful silhouette. He goes back to reading the letter which states that the lawyer intends to assert his client is not guilty of the shooting that killed Morcilla. Gerald blanches. The DA wraps by saying, "Rest assured that the New Jersey State Police will pursue with vigor the identity of a different shooter, should one exist, who was responsible for your wife's murder." Gerald looks at his new young wife soulfully; she blows him a kiss. He sips his Gibson, contemplating impending doom. Might the authorities come looking for him tomorrow, or a decade from tomorrow?

A student of Machiavelli, Gerald mutters to himself, "What a Prince would do now?"

Architect's Rendition

FADE IN.

EXT. MANHATTAN - DAY/NIGHT

Set in Manhattan in the early 2000s, the action opens with a series of shots of some of New York City's finest architectural gems: Guggenheim Museum, Seagram Building, Lever House, Whitney Museum, TWA terminal, Standard Hotel, New Museum, Hearst Building, IAC Building, Plaza Hotel, Chrysler Building, The United Nations Building. The final shot is of the Flatiron Building illuminated at dusk in the manner of Edward Steichen's famous photograph. From there the action moves across Madison Square Park toward an office high-rise a couple blocks away.

INT. GERALD'S OFFICE - NIGHT

Forty-something GERALD, the handsome, well-dressed proprietor of a high-end New York City boutique architecture firm - Pfalzgraf Associates - sits at a sleek desk in his office. A striking view of the Flatiron Building is visible behind him through the floor-to-ceiling windows. Gerald studies a computer program that reports on an employee named OSCAR who has downloaded illegal pornography onto his workstation. Gerald scrolls through the report (which features a head shot of Oscar) and recoils at what must be filthy photos. A KNOCK at the door. In pops Oscar, a lumpy, thirty-ish nerd.

OSCAR

Sorry to interrupt, Gerald. I'm about to head out. I think the call with Arbogast went well. Anything you need from me?

Gerald, barely masking disgust, shakes his head.

OSCAR (CONT'D)

OK, Have a nice weekend.

Oscar steps back out of the office. Gerald stands up, stares contemplatively out the window for a moment, then returns to his desk and shuts down the computer. A copy of "The Prince" by Machiavelli is one among several books on Gerald's desk.

EXT. NYC SIDEWALK - NIGHT

Carrying a briefcase, Gerald walks pensively along the sidewalk in a residential area. He strolls by a brownstone just in time to hear a man SCREAM obscenities in a foreign language from inside a first-floor apartment.

Through the open blinds in the window, Gerald observes an argument between the man, SINISA and a young woman, WREN.

WREN

Here's your fucking watch back.

She tosses the watch onto the coffee table.

WREN (CONT'D)

That's it. I don't have any money to give you. Comprehend?

"Comprehend?" does it. Sinisa clocks Wren hard across the jaw, then storms out of the apartment, heading east. Gerald steps into the shadows and watches Sinisa until he turns the corner. Wren walks out, rubbing her jaw. A real beauty, she's in her mid-twenties with smooth alabaster skin, willowy arms and shoulder-length golden hair. Wren and Gerald lock eyes for a moment, and just when it seems Gerald might say something, Wren whisks by him down the sidewalk to the west.

EXT. NYC SIDEWALK - NIGHT (LATER)

Keeping some distance, Gerald follows Wren until she ducks into a BAR. He turns and walks away.

INT. GERALD'S BEDROOM - DAY

Lying in bed, Gerald wakens to an irritating whirring SOUND. He glances at the clock: 7:30. Gerald reluctantly gets out of bed and walks past the door of an EXERCISE ROOM where his wife MORCILLA works out on a step machine. About the same age as Gerald, Morcilla is short and a bit overweight. She has Mediterranean features. Without looking at him, Morcilla addresses Gerald who plods past without acknowledgement.

MORCILLA

The decorators are coming at 10. The caterers at 2.

INT. GERALD'S LIVING ROOM - DAY

Sitting on a sofa facing a bay window overlooking Central Park, a sweaty Morcilla is on the phone while opening mail.

MORCILLA

I was about to close the deal for the Ferrari when the sales manager tried to charge me an additional 10K for the luggage.

(beat)

Well, it's custom made to fit in the car, but it's not about the money. It's the principle.

(beat)

No, really.

Morcilla looks at a piece of mail, and calls out to Gerald.

MORCILLA (CONT'D)

Gerald! You didn't make a donation to the Whitney, did you? I truly hope you didn't.

INT. GERALD'S BEDROOM - DAY

On the edge of the bed, Gerald rubs his temples.

INT. GERALD'S LIVING ROOM - DAY

Morcilla tosses mail into an expensive-looking trash can as she resumes her phone call.

MORCILLA

Sometimes, Vicki, I wonder where his head is at. Anyway, I'm going to have it out with Signore Enzo, that pompous bidonista.

(beat)

Okay, I'll see you tonight.

Morcilla hangs up the phone and continues to paw through the mail. Gerald walks in with a towel wrapped around his waist. He stares sadly at his wife's chunky silhouette against the big bay window. After a moment, Morcilla looks back at him.

MORCILLA (CONT'D)

What are you staring at Gerald? Don't you have something to do?

Gerald faintly sneers and walks away.

INT./EXT. GERALD'S LIVING ROOM - DAY (LATER)

A RING at the door and the Pfalzgraf's BUTLER opens it. A few uniformed CATERERS with food carts and assorted equipment stand in the lobby outside Gerald's Home.

CATERER

Hello. We're from L'Epicure.

Gerald steps in to take over from the Butler.

GERALD

L'Epicure? Come on in.

(To the Butler)

Show them to the kitchen.

The Butler leads the L'Epicure crew away.

MORCILLA (O.C.)

Is that the caterer?

GERALD

Yeah. L'Eprosy has arrived.

Gerald scoots out the door.

EXT. GERALD'S HOME - DAY

A DOORMAN holds the door for Gerald as he steps onto the sidewalk of his Fifth Avenue building across from Central Park. As he heads to a waiting limo, a TOURIST interrupts, holding a big map flapping in the breeze.

TOURIST

Pardon me sir, but mightcha tell me which way the Guggenheim Museum is?

GERALD

(Pointing up the avenue)

It's about fifteen blocks that-away. It's the building that looks like a gigantic toilet.

INT. HAIR SALON - DAY

As Gerald sits in a barber chair, a fawning, androgynous STYLIST messes with his hair. Finally, he renders judgement.

STYLIST

I think Monsieur would prefer his hair to be parted on the right. Your nose points ever-so-slightly to the right. We can achieve balance with a part on the right.

Gerald appears unconvinced.

STYLIST (CONT'D)

It is not conventional, but can work for a man who is very self-confident.

Gerald looks around and notices a couple other CLIENTS watching him, waiting to hear whether he has self-confidence.

GERALD

Sure. Let's try it.

INT. GERALD'S HOME - DAY

The Caterers stand around beautifully arranged foods, taking bitchy scorn from Morcilla who is thoroughly dissatisfied.

MORCILLA

I was willing to overlook your failure to procure the jamón ibérico de bellota, but smell the snapper ceviche. Just smell it.

A caterer makes a move to sniff, but decides against it.

MORCILLA (CONT'D)

And the frog leg and watercress velouté certainly doesn't look velouté-y enough.

EXT. NYC SIDEWALK - DAY

Sporting his new hairdo, Gerald walks the same sidewalk the night he brushed into Wren. He makes it to the entrance of the Bar, hesitates, then walks in.

INT. BAR - DAY

Gerald scans the dark, empty Bar and spots Wren languidly wiping a glass. He takes a seat at the bar. Wren approaches; a bruise is visible on her jaw.

WREN

May I make a cocktail for you?

GERALD

Gibson, please.

WREN

I haven't mixed one of those in quite a while. I hope the onions haven't turned black.

GERALD

Or black and blue.

Wren touches her sore jaw and departs for the bottle of gin. While she mixes the drink Gerald absentmindedly plays with his hair. Wren returns with the drink; Gerald takes a sip.

GERALD (CONT'D)

Mmmm, perfect. This cocktail always reminds me of Cary Grant. An elegant drink.

WREN

Glad you like it.

GERALD

Did you ever watch "North by Northwest"?

WREN

Once. The plot doesn't make much sense but it's entertaining.

GERALD

I love the buildings. The United Nations, the bad guy's house. The cantilevers, the open plan, the built-in furniture. Sometimes I find the buildings more interesting than the actors.

(Takes a sip)

I'm an architect, in case you couldn't tell. I own a firm near the Flatiron Building.

WREN

The Flatiron, huh? That might just be my favorite building. What do you design?

GERALD

Residences mostly, in the so-called International Style. Steel and glass, flat roofs, pilings, minimal decoration. That sort of thing.

WREN

I'm not too wild about that. Too cold for my taste.

GERALD

Yeah, I get it. It's not for everybody. We're bidding on a contract for a private museum for a big art collector in Pennsylvania. He wants something very Bauhaus.

WREN

My knowledge of architecture is pretty limited. I'd like to learn more about it.

GERALD

I'd love to tell you about it.

Wren rubs her bruised jaw.

GERALD (CONT'D)

How'd you get that?

WREN

You know how.

(beat)

I like your new haircut. Suits your face well.

INT. GERALD'S LIVING ROOM - NIGHT

Morcilla's party is in full swing. The place is crowded with dozens of GUESTS all snappily dressed, along with several L'Epicure Caterers delivering hors d'oeuvres, and a JAZZ QUARTET playing cultured background music on the Balcony. A hired PHOTOGRAPHER mills around documenting the festivities. The Butler greets additional Guests periodically. Gerald speaks with a pair of flamboyant men, CHAPPY and GARTH, when HUMBOLDT, a distinguished German gentleman and his skinny WIFE step into the conversation.

HUMBOLDT

Lovely party Gerald. You look fit. Morcilla tells me you're bidding on a museum for David Arbogast.

GERALD

Yeah. He needs more space to show off his Mapplethorps.

CHAPPY

They must be big. His Mapplethorps.

GERALD

Humboldt, Catharina, may I introduce Chappy Hardwick. A good friend of Morcilla's. And, um, his, uh--

CHAPPY

--This is Garth Barthlemes, my latest discovery. I found dear Garth in a Mini-Storage building along the Westside Highway – actually living inside one of those dreadful units – working like a madman on his absolutely marvelous sculptures of grizzly murder and suicide scenes. Do you know he fashions the crime victims from dried goose droppings? I have more than thirty of Garth's sculptures in my collection.

GERALD

Goose droppings, huh? Canadian? No shortage of that media, I imagine.

GARTH

That's true. And so demanding to work with, what with the smell and all. I'd be honored to have one of my pieces displayed in your office, Mr. Pfalzgraf.

GERALD

Well, uh--

HUMBOLDT

--Morcilla also tells me you're expanding your office space.

GERALD

I'm taking the vacant floor one flight down from the office.

HUMBOLDT

Congratulations, Gerald. Things are obviously going well with the business.

GERALD

Can't complain. I mean I could, but who would listen?

The WINE STEWARD steps in.

WINE STEWARD

I'm terribly sorry to interrupt, Mr. Pfalzgraf. May I have a few minutes of your time to discuss the wine selections?

Gerald scans the room and spots Morcilla talking with a gaggle of guests.

GERALD

I guess so.

(To his guests)

Please excuse me for a moment. Chapst-- uh, Chappy, why don't you tell Humboldt and Catharina how you made a million bucks off of Keith Haring's untimely death?

Gerald and the Wine Steward walk off. In another part of the Living Room some female Guests chit chat.

GUEST #1

I hear Morcilla is thinking about turning her building on Little West Twelfth Street into condos.

GUEST #2

Amazing isn't it? Twenty years ago, men in leather pants with the ass-cheeks cut out had sex in the elevator shaft of that dilapidated building.

GUEST #1

I remember that.

GUEST #2

Then they turn an overgrown train trestle into a park, and voila, "hello gentrification."

GUEST #3

Turning that dump into luxury condos has got to cost 25 mil. Not that she can't afford it, but I bet Gerald wouldn't be too happy.

GUEST #1

Why's that?

GUEST #3

It's no secret that Pfalzgraf Associates stays in business due to Morcilla's, shall we say, largesse.

GUEST #2

In part.

GUEST #3

OK. In part. He'll almost certainly get the Arbogast museum project because Morcilla and David are, shall we say, long time bosom buddies.

The three Guests look across the Living Room past Morcilla who is speaking to Chappy. They spot two new arrivals.

GUEST #2

Oh, look over there? Is that Dodo and Trevor Cholmondeley?

Across the Living Room, Gerald speaks with the Wine Steward who walks off just as the Pfalzgraf's MAID steps up.

MAID

Mr. Pfalzgraf? Mrs. Pfalzgraf ask for you to come to the safe room.

GERALD

Now?

MAID

Si.

INT. GERALD'S HOME/SAFE ROOOM - NIGHT

Gerald and Morcilla face one another in the Safe Room, a secure place where wealthy tenants go during a home invasion.

GERALD

You're out of your mind, Morcilla. I simply stepped away for a second because that asshole wine steward you hired can't make a decision. I never snubbed Chapstick, that sensitive peter-puffer.

MORCILLA

See! You just called him 'Chapstick.' Goddammit, Gerald. That's what he told me. You introduced him to one of your stupid clients as 'Chapstick.' Are you drunk?

Gerald glances at the big drink in his hand.

MORCILLA (CONT'D)

Well?

GERALD

Back off, Morcilla. You remember the last time ole Chappy came to one of your asinine parties. I caught him getting a blowjob in our bedroom.

MORCILLA

And...?

GERALD

I still have the bag of cocaine he tried to hide under the bed. And the dry-cleaning bill. Y'know, getting cum stains out of 400 thread count Egyptian cotton ain't cheap.

MORCILLA

That's disgusting.

(In German)

Stay away from my guests if you're going to behave like a 12-year-old.

Morcilla storms out of the Safe Room. Gerald tosses his drink into a plant and smooths his hair, forgetting at first that it is now parted on the right. He adjusts his tie, sniffs a rose affixed to his lapel, and walks calmly out.

INT. GERALD'S LIVING ROOM – NIGHT

Gerald suffers a stultifying conversation with DODO. He checks his watch a couple times.

DODO

The farmhouse is in Putnam County near the border with Duchess. I kind of wish it was in Duchess. Anyway, the septic system has me nervous. I keep finding what might be, um, toilet paper in the lawn. Is that a bad sign? I want to rent it out next summer. I think the roof has asbestos shingles. That's what the first inspector told me. I was wondering, Gerald, do you know a really good building inspector?

GERALD

Really good? Well, I know a guy who can detect lead paint just by smelling the walls. He's <u>that</u> good.

Trevor joins the conversation.

TREVOR

Dodo, are you trying to squeeze a favor out of our host?

DODO

Well, sort of, but he's not biting.

Garth storms past the threesome in a huff toward the door.

TREVOR

Gerald, did Morcilla tell you I sold an Egon Schiele chalk study last week for an $810,500 profit?

GERALD

How <u>nice</u> for you.

Suddenly a SCREAM from O.C. Gerald, the Cholmondeleys and other Guests in the Living Room rush to the Balcony overlooking Central Park; the balcony where jazz players are assembled and some guests had been dancing.

EXT. GERALD'S HOME/BALCONY - NIGHT

Seriously drunk, Chappy wobbles atop the balcony wall 30 stories above the Fifth Avenue sidewalk. Morcilla and her guests look on in shock while the hired Photographer snaps the lurid action. Chappy points an accusatory finger at a horrified Humboldt.

CHAPPY

If you want him you can have him, but I warn you now, he might be cute but Garth has hemorrhoids. Pretty nasty ones.

GERALD

Get the hell off now before you fall.

CHAPPY

I tell you - I caught Garth in his smelly storage unit attempting anal sex with a Canadian goose.

Humboldt and his wife beat a path to the exit.

CHAPPY (CONT'D)

That's right Herr Humboldt. Take your skinny wench to U-Stor-It and have a ménage à oiseau with Garth the goose-fucker.

GERALD

Will you please get down?

CHAPPY

I don't have to prove that I am creative! All my pictures are confused!

GERALD

OK, I can't argue with that.

(beat)

Look, Chappy, if you fall off the ledge, Garth will just turn your gruesome death into another one of his smelly sculptures. And you'll be forever remembered as a piece of goose shit. Is that what you want?

Chappy looks down at the sidewalk for a moment, then steps gingerly off the ledge back onto the Balcony. As Morcilla approaches, Chappy vomits all over the grand piano as the Photographer captures the affront.

INT. GERALD'S LIBRARY - NIGHT

Gerald sits back in an LC4 lounge chair with a wet rag across his eyes. The lights are dimmed. Morcilla walks in and sits on the floor next to Gerald.

MORCILLA

That was the most awful thing I have ever had to deal with. What a disaster. I'll probably have to get a gag order on the photographer to keep him from selling his pictures to Page 6.

(beat)

I guess it's true: mensch tracht, Gott lacht. Anyway, I appreciate your help with Chappy's meltdown, Gerald.

She touches his hand; he removes the rag from his eyes. A momentary thaw between the two.

MORCILLA (CONT'D)

Still, I can't understand why you didn't intervene before things got out of hand. Didn't you notice Chappy was getting really drunk and that Garth was becoming awfully chummy with your German client? Is he gay?

GERALD

What are you getting at, Morcilla? Those freaks are your friends, not mine. I didn't invite Chapstick, and the rest of those mooches who graze on the expensive food you insist on serving them.

MORCILLA

Expensive? What would you know about that? You're blissfully ignorant when it comes to my money.

GERALD

Go to bed, Morcilla.

MORCILLA

You should have done more to keep things under control, Gerald. You know I'm busy with the guests. You should have kept an eye on Chappy. Especially after you insulted him. You know he can be unpredictable.

GERALD

Maybe I should have just let him take a swan dive off the balcony.

MORCILLA

You're a bastard.

GERALD

And you could have followed along behind him.

Morcilla storms out.

EXT. BANK - DAY

A uniformed DRIVER opens the door to a black limo and out steps Gerald and MARTINA, his dark-haired and pretty power-suited assistant. They walk to the door of a Bank and are greeted by a corporate-looking EXECUTIVE.

INT. BANK/CONFERENCE ROOM - DAY

Gerald, Martina and the Executive sit together at a conference table with papers spread out upon it.

EXECUTIVE

The museum project sounds exciting, Gerald. When do you break ground?

GERALD

We have to win the bid first, but I'm confident Arbogast will choose us over Curtain, Wall, Buckley & Company. I'm going out to Pennsylvania with the team next week to seal the deal.

EXECUTIVE

Well, best of luck. As for the loan to expand your office, we've completed the due diligence and you're pre-approved for the full amount. Congratulations, Gerald.

Gerald nods appreciatively. He looks over at Martina and in the process notices through the glass walls of the Conference Room a middle-aged man (TOM) talking to a LOAN OFFICER. Tom appears agitated, although Gerald cannot hear the conversation.

EXECUTIVE (CONT'D)

Normally we wouldn't do such a large sum, but with Morcilla being such a valued client we couldn't resist.
Gerald expresses mild irritation at the impudent comment.

GERALD

Anything else?

EXECUTIVE

Just a few signatures.

The Executive slides a packet across the table toward Gerald who slides it on to Martina. Gerald stands up, buttons his bespoke suit jacket and shakes hands. He again looks inquisitively at the man engaged with the Loan Officer, as though he knows him but can't recall how.

EXT. BANK - DAY

Gerald and Martina mill about the sidewalk.

GERALD

I'll see you back at the office. I have to meet Morcilla for lunch. You can take the limo. I'm going for a walk.

Tom exits the Bank. He rudely passes between Gerald and Martina. Gerald finally places the face.

GERALD (CONT'D)

Tom? Tom Stull?

Tom turns around and wracks his brain. He's dressed like a contractor straight from a work site. Finally, it clicks.

TOM

Gerry Pfalzgraf?

Tom approaches Gerald.

GERALD

Gerald. Man, it's been, what, 25 years? How've you been, Tom? What are you doing these days?

MARTINA

I'll get all this together for you this afternoon, Gerald.

Martina departs for the waiting Limo. Tom leers at her from behind until Mustapha closes the door.

TOM

Uh, yeah. Long time. I'm doing OK, but not as good as you, I guess. Hot wife, or girlfriend, whatever, you got there.

GERALD

She works for me. I own an architecture firm here in town.

TOM

Nice. I kind of went into the same line of business myself. Construction.

Gerald smirks imperceptibly at the notion that construction is like architecture.

TOM (CONT'D)

After serving four years in the Army.

GERALD

What are you doing in Manhattan?

TOM

I got a contract to do some paving along I80 in Jersey. I'm just here to get my asshole reamed out again by the cocksucking loan officer. A couple a months ago they jacked up my interest rate. Now they want me to put up more collateral which I ain't got. If they repo my stuff, I'm fucked for real.

(beat)

So that's how I'm doing.

GERALD

Damn, that's pretty messed up. Do you have a card?

TOM

I might have one left.

Tom pulls out his wallet and fishes around.

GERALD

Maybe we can have lunch. Catch up on old times.

TOM

Old times?

Tom hands over a wrinkled card with the name of his construction company: TS Erection. Gerald smiles derisively at the company name as he slides the card into his wallet.

GERALD

Y'know, reminisce over the shit we put up with back in Aliquippa.

TOM

Whatever. I'd rather talk about any work you might know of.

GERALD

That too. Listen, I have a lunch appointment coming up.

TOM

OK. Be cool, Gerry.

Gerald is about to correct Tom, but he's already headed toward the subway station, papers bulging from a folder.

EXT. BAR - DAY

Gerald paces the sidewalk outside the Bar, deciding whether to enter. After a couple seconds, he does.

INT. BAR - DAY

Gerald takes the same barstool he occupied the first time he was there. Wren presents him a Gibson cocktail.

WREN

Hello, handsome.

GERALD

How did you know I--

WREN

--I saw you pacing around outside. I willed you to come in. It's so boring here this early in the day.

Gerald smiles and takes a sip.

GERALD

Well here I am. I'm Gerald by the way.

WREN

Nice to meet you. I'm Wren.

GERALD

Like the little bird.

WREN

I have two sisters: Robin and Sparrow, if that tells you anything.

GERALD

I don't suppose your parents raised free range Birkenstocks in the 70s.

WREN

Pretty close.

GERALD

So, my little bird. What's new with you?

WREN

Let's see. I saw "Last Year at Marienbad" at the Film Forum last night after my shift.

GERALD

Great movie. Love the shrubbery. Thank god for the Film Forum.

WREN

Yeah. Whenever I'm down, I go there to escape.

GERALD

What's got you down?

WREN

I go there when I'm <u>not</u> down too, you know.

Gerald takes a long sip of his drink, tempting Wren to elaborate.

WREN (CONT'D)

OK, my tormentor, the guy who hit me that night, has decided to return to the city. He wants to suck me back into his miserable existence. He found out where I live and where I work. It's all bad now.

GERALD

Damn, I'm sorry to hear that.

WREN

I'm sorry to tell it. Makes me seem like a loser.

GERALD

Don't talk like that, Wren. What're you going to--

WREN

--I'm sorry I mentioned it, Gerald. I appreciate your concern, but I don't want to get into it now. Maybe another time.

(beat)

What about you? You strike me as a man who has everything going for himself. What's your cross to bear?

GERALD

Besides being married to a master manipulator for 20 years, not much.

WREN

That's too bad.

GERALD

Yes, it is. But business is great, at least.

(beat)

I am worried though about one of my employees - the one who's handling that museum project I told you about. I discovered he's been downloading some, well, let me just say some very dicey content.

WREN

Yuk. Why don't you fire him?

GERALD

I probably should, but I have to consider all the possibilities. I might be able to persuade him to do something for me.

WREN

Ooo, very Machiavellian.

Gerald lifts his glass in a mock toast.

GERALD

As the Prince once said, "He who seeks to deceive will always find someone who will allow himself to be deceived."

INT. BISTRO - DAY

The Bistro is located in the gentrified Meatpacking District. Gerald walks from the entrance toward a table where Morcilla talks on a cell phone. A glass of wine and a notebook rest on the table in front of her. She glances up at Gerald then without acknowledging him refers to her notebook.

MORCILLA

(In Italian)

If that's how you feel about it, you give me no choice.

Morcilla hangs up the phone and takes a hefty gulp of wine.

MORCILLA (CONT'D)

Gerald, you're late.

GERALD

Nice to see you too, dear.

MORCILLA

Don't be cute. How did your meeting go with the bankers?

GERALD

Fine. I ran into an old--

MORCILLA

--When will they green-light the financing?

Annoyed at the interruption, Gerald flags down a pretty, young WAITRESS and motions her to come over.

GERALD

(Smiling)

Will you bring me a glass of Château de Valflaunès, darling?

WAITRESS

Certainly, sir.

After the Waitress departs, Gerald loses the smile.

GERALD

It's done. The light has been greened. Who were you talking to just now? That Ferrari asshole?

MORCILLA

Signore Enzo, yes. That Ferrari asshole.

GERALD

Why don't you just tell him to go to hell, Morcilla? What do you need the car for anyway? Is there something wrong with the Bentley?

The Waitress returns with Gerald's wine. Morcilla orders.

MORCILLA

(In French)

I'll have the Moules Frites au Pernod.

(MORE)

MORCILLA (CONT'D)

(In English)

What are you having, Gerald?

GERALD

(To the Waitress)

Steak tartare and an endive salad.

MORCILLA

Are you seriously going to eat that?

Gerald hands the menu to the Waitress with an expression that telegraphs "my wife here is a pain in the ass, but it's a cross I must bear." Sympathetic, the Waitress departs.

MORCILLA (CONT'D)

Honestly, Gerald, sometimes I think you do the most disgusting things just to annoy me.

GERALD

As I always say: when in the Meatpacking District, pack meat.

Morcilla shakes her head and sips her drink.

MORCILLA

Oh, and as if it's any of your concern, there's nothing wrong with the Bentley. I happen to like the Ferrari. And I can afford it. Even after propping up your firm.

Gerald stares daggers at Morcilla.

MORCILLA (CONT'D)

I'm sorry, Gerald. I didn't mean that. You're doing a great job. Forgive me. I'm proud of the work you're doing. Really. I just have a lot on my mind, with the charity ball and my building and everything.

She reaches for Gerald's hand but he quickly pulls back and sips his wine.

GERALD

Forget it.

The Waitress arrives with the food. Gerald mashes a raw egg into the beef.

GERALD (CONT'D)

So, what's with the building? You find a buyer for that dilapidated piece of shit?

MORCILLA

It might be dilapidated, Gerald, but it's a hundred yards from the Highline. It would be foolish to sell it now.

Gerald shovels a big load of tartare into his mouth. As he speaks some bloody, yellowish juice oozes down his chin.

GERALD

(With food in his mouth)

Don't tell me you're thinking of renovating it.

Morcilla gags at the sight, and bolts for the restroom. Feeling guilty over his childish behavior, Gerald wolfs down the rest of his meal. He places napkin over the plate just as Morcilla returns and takes her seat.

GERALD (CONT'D)

I'm going out to Pennsylvania next week to meet with Arbogast on the museum project.

MORCILLA

Well, I sincerely hope David gives you the business, Gerald. I've decided to turn my--

(Quotes with fingers)

--"dilapidated piece of shit" into condos. And I'm going to reconfigure the ground floor into retail space. Going to cost fifty mil, so I won't be funneling any more cash your way. Hope you enjoyed your steak tartare.

INT. TAXI (TRAVELING) - DAY

Gerald sits in the back seat in a contemplative mood. Suddenly he feels ill. He calls to his Driver.

GERALD

Pull over. Now!

The Driver complies. Gerald gets out.

EXT. PARK - DAY

Gerald rushes into the Park and vomits. After a moment, he shuffles listlessly back to the Taxi.

INT. BAR - NIGHT

The Bar is packed with drinkers and diners. Wren busily works the bar along with a couple other BARTENDERS. Inebriated, Sinisa steps to the bar, wedging between a MAN and his GIRLFRIEND. Sinisa is a stocky Slav in his 30s. He wears a cheap leather jacket and speaks with an accent. Sinisa calls out to Wren.

SINISA

Wren! Wren, goddammit!

Wren spins around and is shocked to see Sinisa.

SINISA (CONT'D)

Wren! I gotta talk to you.

WREN

You're not supposed to be here.

The Girlfriend hops off the bar-stool and walks off.

SINISA

Just give me a minute.

WREN

What do you want?

SINISA

I need your help. Can we talk, y'know, somewhere in private?

WREN

I'm working. There is no private.

SINISA

Come down to the end of the bar, then. It'll only take a minute.

Wren exhales dramatically. They move to the end of the bar.

WREN

So, what's the big emergency?

SINISA

You know. I need some money.

Wren rubs her jaw.

WREN

Yeah, I vaguely remember something about that.

SINISA

Can't you help me out?

WREN

What about the Piaget watch?

SINISA

That didn't cost you anything.

Wren shrugs.

SINISA (CONT'D)

I'm going to A.C. soon to collect from a deadbeat who owes me 10K. But that's not gonna be enough.

WREN

How much is gonna be enough?

SINISA

More like 100.

WREN

Jesus.

SINISA

Listen, I got an idea. How about you leave the back door unlocked after you leave here tonight? I'll do the rest. Whaddya think?

WREN

What do I think? You're insane.

SINISA

You owe me, cunt!

WREN

Go fuck yourself. Anything else I can do for you?

SINISA

Get me a drink.

WREN

Ask someone else. And you better do it fast before they kick you out again.

Wren leaves to serve another drinker. Sinisa walks back and takes the seat of the absent Girlfriend. He addresses the waiting Man.

SINISA

Are you trying to hit on that blondie bartender, fuckface? That's my wife. You want her to suck your cock you have to get permission from me.

The Man nervously avoids eye contact. His Girlfriend returns and stares angrily at the insolent Sinisa. She turns her ire toward the Man who hasn't immediately jumped to defend her possession of the barstool. Finally, the Man acts.

MAN

Uh, sir, would you please mind--

SINISA

--Fuck you say?

MAN

Um. You're sitting--

SINISA

(Laughing)

--On her face?

(faux serious now)

Oh, I get it. You want me to get up. Right away, sir.

Sinisa gives up the barstool. He extends his hand in reconciliation, and as the Man does likewise, Sinisa knocks the Man's drink all over his pants. The MANAGER of Public Hair witnesses the commotion. As Sinisa walks away, the Manager places a phone call.

INT. BAR/MEN'S ROOM - NIGHT

Sinisa pulls out a packet of cocaine. As he prepares to snort, the Manager and a huge BOUNCER enter.

MANAGER

Sir, you'll have to leave the restaurant. Now. We don't permit drug use on the premises, and we don't tolerate harassment of our patrons.

Sinisa puts his hands behind his head and interlaces his fingers in dramatic fashion.

SINISA

Lead the way, ossifer.

INT. BAR - NIGHT

Closely accompanied by the Bouncer, Sinisa walks toward the exit, then plows drunkenly into a two-top, scattering the food and drink of two PATRONS. With that, the Bouncer grabs Sinisa by the scruff of the neck and hustles him to the door. Sinisa wails. Along with everyone in the Bar, Wren looks on aghast. She addresses a fellow bartender.

WREN

I'll probably get fired for this.

BARTENDER

You know that asshole?

Just as Sinisa and the Bouncer get to the exit, Sinisa escapes from the Bouncer's grip and bites him on the hand.

BOUNCER

You fucking animal!

The Bouncer shoves Sinisa violently through the glass door, shattering it. Sinisa falls at the feet of a POLICE OFFICER. The Police Officer hoists Sinisa to his feet, flips him around and cuffs him.

POLICE OFFICER

You again? Man, you just don't fucking learn, do you?

The Police Officer cuffs Sinisa and hustles him to a waiting black & white.

INT. GERALD'S OFFICE - DAY

Gerald sits at his desk listening to the bank Executive over a speakerphone. He peruses his computer.

EXECUTIVE

(Over speakerphone)

That's basically it, Gerald. You have the funding to expand your office, and if - ha ha - I mean when you get the museum contract, we're ready to extend the construction loan for your spec houses to twenty-five--

GERALD

--Thirty, John.

EXECUTIVE

(Over speakerphone)

Oh yeah, sorry. Thirty million.

GERALD

Just for that, I want thirty-five.

EXECUTIVE

(Over speakerphone)

Funny, Gerald.

GERALD

I'm serious. Bump it to thirty-five. I'll put in a good word with your board. Or I suppose I could persuade Morcilla to--

EXECUTIVE

(Over speakerphone)

--Be cool, Gerald. Thirty-five is doable.

GERALD

Shit, I should have pushed for fifty. Talk to you later.

EXECUTIVE

(Over speakerphone)

Thank you so--

Gerald hangs up.

EXT. BAR - NIGHT

Gerald approaches the bar and takes stock of the boarded door where glass once was. He cautiously steps in. A Bartender approaches.

BARTENDER

What're you drinking?

GERALD

Is Wren here?

BARTENDER

Wren doesn't work here anymore.

GERALD

Uh, um, what happ-- Any reason--

BARTENDER

--You saw the door, right? I guess her ex-boyfriend came looking for her and made a bit of a mess.

GERALD

Jesus. I don't suppose--

BARTENDER

--No idea.

GERALD

What happened to the ex?

BARTENDER

Cops took him away. He was busted here before. I think that's why Wren got the boot. Apparently, they blamed her for his presence.

GERALD

Jesus, what bullshit.

EXT. FILM FORUM - NIGHT

The marquee indicates "Rififi" is playing.

INT. FILM FORUM - NIGHT

Gerald steps into the darkened theater where the movie is underway. He scans the room, locates Wren and sits behind her. The credits roll, Wren turns and spots Gerald.

GERALD

Can I buy you a cocktail?

INT. LOUNGE - NIGHT

The Lounge is urbane and lightly attended by other well-dressed couples. Gerald and Wren sit at a quiet table, each with a cocktail.

GERALD

How'd you like the movie?

WREN

Probably better than you did. How much of it did you catch? The last five minutes?

GERALD

I've seen it before. Great noir story.

WREN

Kinda like my life.

GERALD

That guy - quite the bad penny.

WREN

Well, given he's Serbian, I'd say he's quite the bad dinar.

GERALD

I gather you're in the market for a new job, thanks to, um--

WREN

--Sinisa.

GERALD

You have anything lined up?

WREN

I'm thinking about going back to school. Finish my art degree, maybe.

GERALD

What about architecture? That's an art form that can pay the bills.

WREN

I love beautiful buildings, but I don't know the first thing about becoming an architect. Do you know anyone I could talk to about it?

GERALD

Let me think. Yeah, I know a guy who owns a top-notch firm right here in Manhattan. They're designing a museum as we speak.

WREN

Sounds intriguing. Can you put me in touch with him?

GERALD

He's going to meet the client later this week, but I'm sure he can make time to explain the business to you over dinner. Say, Thursday evening, 8:00, Eleven Madison Park?

WREN

This Thursday? I'm not sure I can make 8:00.

GERALD

8:05?

WREN

That's better. Would you please inform your colleague I'll be there at 8:05 this Thursday?

GERALD

Done. I mean, I certainly will.

Gerald hands Wren a business card.

GERALD (CONT'D)

Here's his number in case you want to confirm.

INT. GERALD'S OFFICE - DAY

Seated at his desk, Gerald presses a button on his intercom.

GERALD

(Into intercom)

Janet, can you send in Oscar and his team?

Oscar and his team of architects, including engineer PAUL, walk into the office and take seats.

GERALD (CONT'D)

OK, men. We're going to meet with David Arbogast and amaze him with our proposal. We have funding, so no excuses. The presentation for the museum has to be orgasmic. You know what I mean, right Oscar.

Oscar appears flummoxed.

GERALD (CONT'D)

I want Arbogast to blow a load when he sees our proposal.

OSCAR

Uh, yeah, Gerald. Sure. We'll bring him to climax if that's what it takes.

GERALD

Good. Now you might be lulled into complacency because my wife has a long-time friendship with David. That whole Jeff Koons-Barcelona exhibition thing. But believe me - Arbogast will base his decision on quality of plans. Clarity of vision. Friendships won't mean shit when it comes to this project.

PAUL

There's nothing to worry about, Mr. Pfalzgraf. We'll kick ass out there.

GERALD

I appreciate your optimism, Paul. Oscar, I trust you've explained to Paul just how formidable a competitor Curtain, Wall, Buckley and Company can be.

OSCAR

Yeah, Paul, I'll tell you offline.

GERALD

You do that, Oscar. For the rest of you - make no mistake, Curtain, Wall is ten times bigger than we are, and that old fuck Richard Curtain - bless his 90-year-old ass - studied under Frank Lloyd Wright.

OSCAR

I think Arbogast, with his property so close to Falling Water, won't want to hire a firm that will propose a Wright-like building.

GERALD

I tend to agree. I just don't want to take any chances. OK, take me through the pitch, Oscar.

Oscar flips on a projector, and a schematic image of a sleek, modern building appears on the screen.

EXT. ELEVEN MADISON PARK - NIGHT

Wren and Gerald walk together away from the restaurant, waiting to cross the street toward Madison Square Park.

WREN

That was spectacular. I've never devoted that much time to eating a meal in my whole life.

GERALD

Glad you enjoyed it, Wren. I don't think I've ever devoted that much time to a conversation in my life. You're fascinating.

The WALK sign illuminates. Wren's hand sweeps by Gerald's. He lightly takes it without resistance from her.

EXT. MADISON SQUARE PARK - NIGHT

The lighted Flatiron Building is in the near distance looking like the famous Steichen photograph.

WREN

Mmmm. My favorite building.

EXT. FLATIRON BUILDING - NIGHT

Gerald and Wren look up at the building.

WREN

I just love the detail.

GERALD

Yeah. Daniel Burnham went a little overboard on the dentils and pilasters and those things at the top that look like cartouche. Pretty much the opposite of what my firm designs. Still, it's a marvelous structure.

(beat)

It's like a mighty plow in one of those Depression-Era WPA murals, furrowing Manhattan into Broadway and Fifth Avenue.

WREN

I never thought of it that way.

GERALD

It's more apparent from my office. Would you like to take a look?

WREN

Love to.

INT. PFALZGRAF OFFICES - NIGHT

Gerald and Wren wait outside the elevator.

GERALD

First, I'll take you to the floor I just leased. I hope to have it built out in a few months. We really need the space.

The elevator doors open and the couple step out.

INT. PFALZGRAF OFFICES/UNFINISHED FLOOR - NIGHT

Gerald escorts Wren around the vacant space.

GERALD

I'm planning to hire 15 new people before the end of the year. Maybe more if we get the subcontract for a high-rise on 57th.

(beat)

Let's take the stairs up to my office.

Gerald produces a security badge. Close-up of the badge reader in a box on the floor, not yet installed. He stuffs the badge back into his pocket. Gerald opens the door and he and Wren walk up the stairs.

INT. GERALD'S OFFICE - NIGHT

Standing side by side, Gerald and Wren take in the beautifully lit Flatiron Building. After a moment, Gerald strokes Wren's hair.

WREN

I don't like that you're married.

GERALD

Neither do I.

WREN

I won't be your mistress.

(beat)

Not for long, anyway.

GERALD

I promise you won't have to.

The couple embraces. Gerald and Wren kiss - silhouetted against the floor-to-ceiling windows, skyline shining brilliantly in the background.

INT. LIMO (TRAVELING) - DAY

Gerald, Oscar and Paul ride in the limo along Interstate 80.

OSCAR

I hope we didn't go overboard on the square footage. Still seems awful big to me.

GERALD

Arbogast's collection is awful big. He owns Basquiat, Keith Haring, Chuck Close, Mapplethorpe, Jeff Koons. All top notch stuff. Shit, the Koons collection will need 10,000 square feet by itself. Those huge balloon figures take up a ton of space.

OSCAR

Well, I can't wait to get started.

GERALD

Listen, Oscar. Just because we've done four other buildings for him doesn't guarantee we'll get the commission. It's a freaky business.

PAUL

Isn't your wife--

GERALD

--Yes. My wife is a good friend of Arbogast's. Honestly, I'm not sure if that helps or hurts.

OSCAR

Well, our proposal is rock solid. I'm not worried.

GERALD

And that worries me.

EXT. ARBOGAST'S PLACE - DAY

The limo advances through a stately gate up a long, treelined driveway, passing stylish, modern buildings. The limo passes a vacant area with some idled construction vehicles, and large dumpsters.

INT. LIMO (TRAVELING) – DAY

The Limo passes the vacant area on Arbogast's Place.

GERALD

There it is boys. Site of the future Arbogast Museum.

OSCAR

And hookah lounge.

Paul chuckles.

EXT. ARBOGAST'S PLACE - DAY

The limo pulls to the front entrance of a large, thoroughly modern house. A well-dressed, elderly MAN-SERVANT awaits.

INT. ARBOGAST'S PLACE - DAY

The Man-Servant leads Gerald and team into a Conference Room where ARBOGAST greets them, accompanied by a few AIDES. Arbogast is about 60 and modestly overweight. He's dressed in a well-made double-breasted suit, and wears his thinning, grey hair slicked back.

ARBOGAST

Gerald, so good to see you. How's Morcilla?

GERALD

David… Lovely to be here. Morcilla sends her regards. It's too bad you couldn't make her party.

ARBOGAST

I saw some pictures. Sorry I missed the festivities.

Gerald is momentarily thrown off balance at the notion there are pictures from the party.

GERALD

Uh, let me introduce you to a couple of my people.
Oscar Dupree, team leader on the project.

Oscar steps forward and shakes hands.

OSCAR

Pleased to meet you, Mr. Arbogast.

GERALD

And Paul Clay, one of my engineers.

Paul shakes Arbogast's hand.

PAUL

How do you do.

ARBOGAST

(Points to his employees)
That's Harold McCullough, my curator, and Bob Wolfe, my accountant.

The two men wave from across the long conference table.

ARBOGAST (CONT'D)

I have lunch coming soon. Let's get started, shall we, Gerald?

Everyone sits down except Gerald who stands at the head of the table, and Oscar who sets up a laptop projector.

GERALD

David, Pfalzgraf Associates has designed every building on your property. We are in the best position to ensure the look of your new museum will provide the esthetic continuity you must have. That your compound deserves.

(beat)

I'm confident what you'll see today is a handsome building that establishes a bold presence yet integrates cleanly with the overall site parameters. Now I'd like Oscar to take you through the details. Oscar?

Gerald takes a seat. Oscar projects an image of a modern-looking structure on the screen.

OSCAR

As Mies Van Der Rohe once said, "Architecture starts when you carefully put two bricks together."

INT. FERRARI SHOWROOM - DAY

Morcilla and her long-time friend VICKI wander about the Ferrari Showroom, admiring the various exotic automobiles on the floor. Morcilla runs her hand along the fender of one.

MORCILLA

You like this one, Vicki? Feel the curves.

Vicki runs her hand along the sensuous fender and smiles.

MORCILLA (CONT'D)

This is the car I've been trying to buy from these people for the past month. The Modena in Rossa Corso red. Now after all this time, I'm beginning to fancy that convertible Spider over there.

(Gestures to the car)

Giallo Fly Yellow. Gorgeous.

VICKI

It certainly is, M.

Disturbed that Morcilla has made an unannounced appearance, ENZO the sales manager hustles from his office.

ENZO

Signora Pfalzgraf! Why you not tell me you come in today? How can I help you?

MORCILLA

Save it, Enzo. Are you going to sell me the Modena with the luggage included or not? Yes or no - right now.

ENZO

Well, I uh, we, uh. Yes, of course. I throw in the lug--

MORCILLA

--Throw in? You mean like floor mats?

ENZO

I meant--

MORCILLA

--Forget it, Enzo. I've changed my mind. I'll take that yellow Spider instead.

ENZO

Um, that one already has a deposit on it.

MORCILLA

So? Do you really think I care about your little business details?

(beat)

Have the car delivered to my garage. I'll have my accountant settle the bill next week.

ENZO

Signora Pfalzgraf--

MORCILLA

--You <u>are</u> aware that I can take my business to that very nice dealer in Greenwich, right, Signore Enzo?

ENZO

Yes, but the Spider is, shall we say--

(In Italian)

--somewhat more expensive.

MORCILLA

(In Italian)

No more expensive than my time wasted haggling with you.

(In English)

Are we settled? Or shall I spend a day in Connecticut meeting with your charming competitor?

ENZO

Excuse me for a moment, Signora Pfalzgraf.

Enzo departs for his office.

VICKI

He seems all hot and bothered.

MORCILLA

He should. My calendar is jammed. The building renovation, the charity ball, the zoo annex. And somewhere in there I have to wedge in Barcelona for a week.

VICKI

Barcelona. Nice. Will you be meeting David there?

Enzo returns.

ENZO

Signora Pfalzgraf. Will it be satisfactory if we ship the Spider to your garage next week?

MORCILLA

Of course.

(To Vicki)

Of course.

INT. ARBOGAST'S PLACE - DAY

Oscar finishes his presentation. The projector casts an image of large sculptures set about a courtyard outside the museum. A KNOCK at the door and a WAITER pokes his head in.

ARBOGAST

Lunch has arrived. Harold, you don't mind showing Gerald the collection while we eat, do you?

The Waiter sets up the food while Harold steps to the head of the table. He starts his presentation with an image of a large balloon-shaped animal. Gerald unwraps a piece of expensive-looking chocolate and pops it in his mouth.

HAROLD

Acquired by Mr. Arbogast in 1994, this piece is 22 feet tall and weighs 7 tons. There are several more like it in the collection.

As Harold speaks, Oscar leans over and whispers to Paul.

HAROLD (CONT'D)

I point this out because we must accommodate adequate entrance and egress for--

Harold is interrupted by a stifled guffaw from Paul. Everyone at the table stares at Paul incredulously. Gerald in particular is appalled.

PAUL

--I'm sorry--

Gerald is livid, but doesn't show it.

GERALD

--Harold, please continue.

Arbogast looks on quizzically as if he's thinking "what the fuck?" Gerald stares at Paul like he wants to kill him.

HAROLD

Um, as I was trying to say, you have to consider the immense size of these sculptures.

EXT. LIMO (TRAVELING) - NIGHT

The limo pulls out of Arbogast's place.

INT. LIMO (TRAVELING) - NIGHT

The limo is tooling along Interstate 80. Uncomfortable silence until Gerald finally blows his stack.

GERALD

What the fuck was so funny back there? Are you two insane? Jesus Christ, Arbogast is our top client and you two assholes are goofing around like second graders.

PAUL

I'm sorry Mr. Pfalzgraf. Oscar made a joke and I couldn't help myself.

GERALD

Oh, he did, did he?

OSCAR

Paul lost his cool, Gerald. I just asked him why my piece of chocolate had corn in it.

GERALD

That's hilarious, Oscar. I know you can tell by the way I'm laughing my fucking ass off.
(beat)
So help me god, if we lose the museum...

OSCAR

Gerald--

GERALD

--Shut up. Both of you. Don't talk. I have to think.

Gerald turns away and looks out the window at the passing landscape. The limo drives by a construction site. Gerald spots a truck emblazoned with the name "TS Erection." He takes out Tom's business card from his wallet and studies it.

INT. GERALD'S BEDROOM - DAY

Gerald wakes up to the whirring SOUND emanating from Morcilla's step machine. He glances at the clock: 6:30. Gerald gets out of bed and heads to the shower. The whirring stops and Morcilla intercepts him.

MORCILLA

Gerald, what happened at your meeting with David Arbogast?

GERALD

Huh? What do you mean?

MORCILLA

I, uh, he called me last night to tell me things didn't go so well in your meeting.

GERALD

David Arbogast called you? About a meeting with me? What's going on, Morcilla? Why would he do that?

MORCILLA

He wants to give you the contract for the museum, but he's worried about some of your employees, Gerald. He's concerned your team might not be up to the task. Have you spoken with him?

GERALD

It's the first thing I plan to do this morning. But I asked you: why would he call you?

MORCILLA

(Childlike)

I don't know. I'm just relaying to you that he likes your proposal.

GERALD

I don't--

MORCILLA

(Forcefully now)

--Look, Gerald, you have to straighten out your operations. You can't bring half-wits to meetings with important leaders in the art community like David... Arbogast.

After an odd pause, Gerald responds coolly.

GERALD

You're right, dear. I really should fire Oscar. He's becoming more of a liability as time passes. If Mr. Arbogast calls you again, please remind him we will work two hundred percent to make his museum a masterpiece of design and functionality.

Morcilla shrugs and leaves. Gerald angrily yanks a black suit out of his closet, breaking the wooden hanger.

EXT. GERALD'S HOME - DAY

Gerald walks toward his waiting limo but when he notices a truck parked behind it bearing Morcilla's new yellow Ferrari Spider, he approaches the TRUCK DRIVER instead.

GERALD

Hey. I don't suppose that snazzy car is for Mrs. Pfalzgraf.

TRUCK DRIVER

Yeah. I was supposed to load a different car for her but my boss told me she decided on this one instead.

GERALD

I see.

TRUCK DRIVER

She must have some pull, cuz my boss told me this one already had a deposit on it. Some rock star dude.

GERALD

That Mrs. Pfalzgraf sure must be a persuasive woman.

TRUCK DRIVER

Apparently.

Gerald walks to the limo.

GERALD

(Sotto voce)

Fucking manipulative is more like it.

INT. LIMO (TRAVELING) - DAY

Gerald talks to Arbogast on the phone.

GERALD

David? Gerald.

INTERCUT WITH ARBOGAST'S OFFICE

ARBOGAST

Hello, Gerald. Nice of you to call. Listen, my staff and I really enjoyed your presentation yesterday. The design concepts look to be very integral to the compound.

GERALD

Thank--

ARBOGAST

--I wanted you to know however that I've asked Richard Curtain to come by personally to size up my requirements. Perhaps you've come to believe I would give you the contract without competitive bid, but I must say I am a trifle concerned with the professionalism of your team.

Gerald mouths the word "fuck."

GERALD

David, you have every right to consult whomever you choose. In fact, I think that's being very smart. But I'm confident you'll decide on us after you have evaluated all the factors. David, we've designed all the buildings on your property. Whatever Curtain, Wall, Buckley comes up with won't work. It may be a subtle design element, but it won't work.

ARBOGAST

Have a great day, Gerald.

As soon as Arbogast hangs up, Gerald's phone rings. He answers. In the background he hears the CLANG of pots and pans.

INT. VIETNAMESE RESTAURANT KITCHEN - DAY

Sporting a shiner, Wren is on the phone in the kitchen of a Vietnamese Restaurant where cooks and dishwashers work. She holds Gerald's business card.

WREN

(Sniffling)

Gerald? Can you hear me?

INTERCUT WITH THE LIMO

GERALD

Wren? What's wrong? Are you crying?

WREN

I'm sorry, Ger. I just didn't know what else to do.

GERALD

What's going on? What's all that noise?

WREN

I'm in the kitchen of the Vietnamese restaurant down the block. Sinisa came to my apartment this morning. He threatened me.

GERALD

Where is he now?

WREN

I don't know. I'm afraid to go home. What should I do?

GERALD

Give me the address of the restaurant. I'll come get you.

EXT. VIETNAMESE RESTAURANT - DAY

A HONK from the limo draws Wren out. She runs to the opened back door and dives in.

INT. LIMO (TRAVELING) - DAY

Wren embraces Gerald and makes a move to kiss him.

GERALD

Not here. Let's go to the park and talk.

Gerald eases Wren away, suddenly noticing the black eye.

GERALD (CONT'D)

Jesus, Wren. You didn't tell me he hit you.

He lovingly caresses her eye.

EXT. MADISON SQUARE PARK - DAY

Standing on the sidewalk next to Wren, Gerald signals to his Driver to leave. The couple walk into Madison Square Park and take a secluded bench.

GERALD

Don't worry, Wren. I'll protect you from that scumbag bastard. My firm holds a room at the Gansevoort Hotel for out-of-town clients. You can stay there while I figure something out.

WREN

I don't know what to say. We barely know each--

GERALD

--Can't you tell I care about you.

WREN

Yes, I do. Me too.

GERALD

I need to know more about this creep. Sinisa, right?

WREN

Yeah, Sinisa Ražnatovi. Coke head, compulsive gambler, breaker of bones for the Serbian mob.

GERALD

Mob? What? He's into organized crime, too? Jesus, Wren, what were you thinking?

WREN

He's very jealous, Ger. Watched me like a hawk. The only time I'd ever get a break was when he went to Atlantic City to collect on debts.

GERALD

Damn. How did you get away?

WREN

He disappeared. Simple as that. Never even left a note. I assumed he found a better gig. Didn't matter. I was free.

GERALD

Then the cat came back. I know this guy's an asshole, but you were with him for a while. Does he have even one redeeming quality?

WREN

I guess like all tough-guys, Sinisa is deep down a child, suffering with childhood issues. He told me about a time he was an altar boy and a priest molested him. Pretty bad stuff. Sinisa actually cried like a baby when he told me that story. It was the only time I truly felt sorry for him.

GERALD

Wren, I want you to check into the Gansevoort Hotel under the name Dominique Francon. Tell them you're with Fountainhead Productions in town to meet with Pfalzgraf Associates.

(Writes on a paper)

Give them my passcode - LC4. Say you'll be staying for a few weeks.

Gerald hands the paper to Wren.

WREN

Why do I have to use a phony name?

GERALD

It's for your protection. And mine, too, I suppose.

Gerald pulls out his wallet and hands some money to Wren.

GERALD (CONT'D)

Buy yourself some clothes and whatever else you need, Wren.

WREN

Thank you so much.

GERALD

We'll figure things out, Wren, I promise.

Wren snuggles up to Gerald.

WREN

I know we will.

She gives Gerald the passionate kiss she wanted to give him back in the limo.

GERALD

I'd love to spend the rest of my day right here with you, but I gotta get to the office. Why don't you grab a cab to the hotel and freshen up? Take care of that eye.

Wren gives Gerald another juicy one, then walks off to hail a cab. Once Wren departs, Gerald hails a cab too.

EXT. INDUSTRIAL NEIGHBORHOOD - DAY

The cab drops off Gerald in a gritty industrial neighborhood. He walks to one of the last working pay-phones in New York that still exists, plucks a card from his wallet and dials.

INTERCUT WITH TOM STULL'S HOME

TOM

TS Erection, Tom here.

GERALD

Tom, Gerald Pfalzgraf. How's the erection business?

TOM

Um, OK. What can I do for you?

GERALD

I was wondering if you'd like to have lunch with me in the city this week. I have some job prospects.

TOM

Shit, yeah. I've got another appointment at that fucking bank on Thursday morning. Should be available after that.

GERALD

Perfect. Meet me at Bubba Gump Shrimp – it's in Times Square. 12:30, OK?

TOM

I know that place - great seafood. I'll see you at 12:30.

Gerald hangs up.

GERALD

(Laughing)

TS Erection. Jesus H. Christ.

INT. GERALD'S HOME - NIGHT

Gerald walks in.

GERALD

Morcilla. You here?

Hearing no response, he walks into the Bedroom and proceeds to look through Morcilla's notebook at her busy schedule. On the current day he notes that his wife is to attend a fund raiser. He jumps a few weeks ahead and notices an entry about her traveling to Barcelona for several days to oversee a museum exhibition opening. The initials D.A. are penciled in. Gerald grimaces. He backs up to a couple weeks in the future where he spots an entry about Morcilla going to Vicki's house in New Jersey to plan a high school class reunion.

INT. PFALZGRAF OFFICES - DAY

Gerald walks imperiously past Oscar without looking at him. Oscar is tense. The time on a wall clock: 8:45.

INT. PFALZGRAF OFFICES - NIGHT

It's now 6:59 and the place is empty. Oscar stares at the wall clock and when it clicks to 7:00 he walks nervously toward Gerald's Office, and KNOCKS on the door.

INT. GERALD'S OFFICE - NIGHT

Gerald stands next to his computer, a hand on the mouse.

GERALD

Come in.

Oscar enters, trepidation in his gait.

OSCAR

Gerald, I got your email. I've been shitting bricks all day. Let me say right off how sorry I am for my behavior in front of Arbogast. Completely inappropriate.

GERALD

I want to talk to you about something very serious. I installed software a few weeks ago to track what employees are doing on their workstations. Here's what it reported on you.

Gerald pivots his computer screen so Oscar can see a decidedly onerous pornographic image.

GERALD (CONT'D)

There's a lot of this kind of material in your folder. I assume you know this not only violates your condition of employment, but is also illegal.

OSCAR

I, uh, don't know, uh, why you think I would download such stuff. I mean, anyone could have--

GERALD

--Spare me, OK? I can call in the software people as witnesses to testify on the infallibility of their program. Do you really want--

OSCAR

--OK, OK.

Oscar rubs the back of his neck for a moment. Then he faces Gerald.

OSCAR

I got carried away. It's really nothing. But it will never happen again, I swear.

Gerald clicks to bring up another ghastly image. Oscar winces.

OSCAR (CONT'D)

You're right, Gerald. I was stupid. I admit it. I could've gotten the firm in trouble. I'm really sorry.

GERALD

Not good enough.

OSCAR

I'll take a pay cut, give up my vacation. Whatever it takes. I want to stay with the firm. Please, don't fire me. I'll do anything you want.

Gerald smiles when Oscar says what he wants to hear.

GERALD

Good. Here's the story. I am going to dock your pay, but I also have a task you must perform. Something a bit unusual.

OSCAR

Well, sure Gerald, if it means avoiding dismissal. Or prison.

GERALD

Let me make it clear that what I'm about to describe to you must be kept in complete confidence. You cannot discuss it with anyone else. Understand?

Oscar nods.

GERALD (CONT'D)

Any word out of you and I'll turn you in. Now, sit down.

Oscar takes a chair.

INT. PFALZGRAF OFFICES - NIGHT

Gerald and Oscar can be seen talking but not heard through the glass wall of Gerald's Office.

Gerald lays out his task to Oscar. After a moment, Oscar reacts strongly.

INT. GERALD'S OFFICE - NIGHT

OSCAR

You're joking, right? I can't do that!

GERALD

Yes, you can, and you will. Unless you'd rather spend the next 20 years getting your asshole reamed out twice a day. That's a lot of reaming: 20 times 365 times 2.

Oscar is conflicted.

GERALD (CONT'D)

That's 14,600 asshole reamings - not counting leap years.

OSCAR

I trust your math, Gerald, but--

GERALD

--Oscar, this guy is blackmailing the firm. He has damaging information that could keep us from bidding on contracts. We'll lose the museum for sure, and maybe even get hit with some serious litigation.

(beat)

Shit, Oscar, this bastard is a threat to all of us, and we – you – have to make him disappear.

OSCAR

Well, he does sound like trouble.

GERALD

He is.

OSCAR

And I certainly don't want to go to prison.

GERALD

I know you don't.

OSCAR

But what if I get caught?

GERALD

No one will find out. People will think it was a random act of senseless violence. Happens all the time in the Big Apple.

OSCAR

Can I think about it overnight?

GERALD

No. I need your answer now.

Oscar walks to the window and gazes out.

OSCAR

The Flatiron Building... tonight, it looks just like that old Steichen photo in the lobby.

Oscar turns toward Gerald, resigned.

OSCAR (CONT'D)

I don't want the firm to get in trouble, Gerald. And I can't go to prison, that's for sure. Just let me know when you need this thing done.

GERALD

OK, Oscar. Hey, it might not even be necessary. Although the more I get to know your predilections, I suspect you might enjoy it. Who knows? Get your things and go home.

INT. BUBBA GUMP - DAY

Gerald and Tom sit together at a corner booth in the tourist-infested BUBBA GUMP restaurant. Gerald picks at a salad while Tom digs into a huge pile of deep-fried gorp.

TOM

(with mouth full)

This shit is awesome. You wanna try a piece?

GERALD

Uh, no thanks, Tom.

(beat)

Man, I can't believe how many years it's been since we went to that lame-ass school. Remember that dunce, Sheila something? Kept the whole class back. Couldn't even turn a fraction into a decimal.

TOM

Yeah, she was stupid but she knew how to give a killer blowjob.

Gerald is suddenly deflated by the prospect that Tom may be a more accomplished cocksman than himself.

GERALD

Really? In fourth grade?

TOM

Yup.

Tom plows on with his greasy food while Gerald takes a moment of reflection. Finally, Gerald resumes the conversation.

GERALD

Hey, do you remember that show-and-tell when you brought in a picture of a bear you shot.

TOM

Sure. I bagged him with a 300 Savage right below the ear.

GERALD

Somebody told me at a class reunion that you joined the army and became a sniper.

TOM

Kinda. I was an SDM, not a sniper.

(beat)

SDM – squad designated marksman. Y'know, a sharpshooter.

Gerald nods as though he understands the distinction.

TOM (CONT'D)

So, what is it you wanted to meet about? Need some paving done?

GERALD

I do need some work done, but it's not paving. Or anything construction related, in fact. Before I describe it, I want you to know I'm ready to make it very worth your while. Nice payday. I'll also use my influence with the bank to get your credit line increased. And I'll throw some of my firm's business your way.

TOM

I don't get--

GERALD

--I'll even try to shut down the investigation into your wife's credit card fraud problem.

TOM

How do you know about Tori?

GERALD

I know a lot of things, Tom. For instance, I know if you turn down my offer, you'll never fill another pothole again. Unless you take a dump in it.

TOM

How's that?

Gerald casually pops a tiny tomato into his mouth.

TOM (CONT'D)

(Angrily)

What's with the threats? You want my boot up your fucking ass?

GERALD

Relax, Tom. You haven't even heard what the job is about. Just listen to me, OK?

TOM

Fuck.

GERALD

You're familiar with the section of Interstate 80 that runs through east Jersey, right?

TOM

Sure. I'm working on it right now.

GERALD

And I know you're a great shot.

TOM

Huh? So fucking what?

GERALD

I know this sounds strange, but I want you to take a few random potshots at some vehicles driving on I80.

Incredulous, Tom stops chewing, holding food in his cheek.

GERALD (CONT'D)

I'll give you the exact time and location later. You'll shoot a few semi-trailers, maybe a dump truck. Hit them someplace where the driver won't notice. At the exact time you're taking these shots, someone will be driving an unmistakable car on the highway. The top will be down. You can't miss it. Make that one a head shot.

TOM

Are you crazy? Jesus Christ!

GERALD

I'm not crazy. I'm dead serious. I need this to happen.

TOM

Forget it.

GERALD

Big payday. You need that to happen, don't you, Tom?

Tom calms down a bit, and chews and swallows the rest of his food.

TOM

Why am I even talking to you?
(beat)
What if I get caught? I could get life. Maybe even the fucking chair. Go to hell, motherfucker.

Some DINERS turn toward the agitated Tom. Gerald notices the sudden curiosity.

GERALD

Tom, calm down. You're not going to get caught because the whole thing will go down in a few minutes. By the time the cops get to the scene you'll be back at your job site. They'll figure they have some deranged killer on their hands, like that DC sniper. They'll focus their energy on catching him when he strikes again. But you're never going to strike again. The shootings will remain an unsolved mystery.

(beat)

Also, Jersey doesn't have a death penalty. I'm not sure any state uses the electric chair anymore, now that I think about it. Not sure.

TOM

You're out of your fucking mind. Pure psycho.

Tom eats aggressively, then abruptly puts his fork down.

TOM (CONT'D)

If I do this, you'll bail out me and Tori? Why? Who's gonna be driving the car?

GERALD

That's none of your concern. The less you know the better. Suffice it to say you'll be helping my company by eliminating a greedy, cocksucking blackmailer.

TOM

You know if I get caught, you're going down with me, Fuckzgraf.

GERALD

Tom, you're not going to get caught. I have confidence in you. I also have fifty K in tens and twenties set aside – my fifty percent down-payment. The rest of the money and the other favors will come after the deed is done.

TOM

No good. It'll cost you way more than that. A quarter mil. You're talking murder here my friend.

Tom starts to stand up.

GERALD

Tom, sit. Please. I meant to say 'my twenty percent down payment.' OK? I agree - a quarter mil is appropriate for what I'm asking you to do.

Tom slowly retakes his seat.

TOM

Shit. I had you pegged all wrong when I saw you in the bank the other day. You're a scumbag.

GERALD

What's it gonna be, Tom?

After a delay, Tom responds.

TOM

When would I get the money?

GERALD

I'll get you the 50K tomorrow. Don't spend it right away - stash it for a while. When the job is done, I'll arrange payment of the rest. You just sit tight and wait for my call with the details on when and where.

TOM

I don't know, man.

GERALD

Yes, you do. I'll call you with the details when I have them. How was your scampi?

INT. HOTEL - NIGHT

Gerald lies in bed next to Wren, post-coital pleasure on their faces.

WREN

That was special.

GERALD

You're beautiful, Wren. Being with you makes me feel 20 years younger.

WREN

I can tell.

GERALD

Not just when we make love, but all the time. Does it bother you that I'm that much older than you? I mean--

WREN

--Age doesn't matter to me. You're wonderful, Ger. You make me feel safe. I like that, especially now.

GERALD

Has that bastard contacted you?

WREN

No. But I'm still--

GERALD

--He has to go once and for all. You can't go on like this, knowing he could show up at any moment.

WREN

Yeah, well…

Gerald sits up, ready to get serious.

GERALD

Besides him being a sexually molested drug addict, what other problems does Sinisa have?

WREN

He owes a ton of money - a hundred thousand he told me - to the mob.

GERALD

Well, that's another useful vulnerability.

WREN

That night he punched me out… you remember. Sinisa came begging for help. I gave him back an expensive watch, but that wasn't good enough. I guess he thought I was hiding a fortune from him.

GERALD

What's he planning to do next?

WREN

Who knows? He told me he's going to Atlantic City soon to collect on a debt. It's only ten thousand, but some poor slob will probably lose the use of a limb in the process.

Gerald ponders the situation for a moment.

GERALD

Where in Atlantic City?

WREN

I don't know for sure. He used to come home with matches from the Borgata Hotel sometimes. I assume he stayed there.

GERALD

Borgata, huh?

WREN

What happens next, Gerald? I can't stay in a hotel forever.

GERALD

Not forever, but a little longer would be safer.

WREN

And I have to start looking for a new job.

GERALD

I'm not sure that's such a good idea, Wren.

WREN

I don't have a choice. I need the money.

GERALD

I can help with that.

WREN

I'm sure you can, but I'm not too keen on that idea. You're married, and like I already told you, I can't be on the payroll as your mistress.

GERALD

What if I wasn't, y'know, married?

WREN

I don't want to be the reason you--

GERALD

--You wouldn't be. I've wanted to get out for some years now.

WREN

Really?

GERALD

Morcilla is tough to be with. Plus, I think she might be screwing one of my clients. She's probably plotting right now to cut me loose. I have to get ahead of it. I have to make a plan.

WREN

Like what?

GERALD

I don't know yet. I just want to get out with my fair share.

(Chuckles)

Y'know, all of it.

(beat)

Wren, I want you to be with me in my life. Live with me in my house. It has a fantastic view of Central Park. You'd love it.

WREN

I'm sure I would.

(beat)

Will.

INT. GERALD'S LIVING ROOM - DAY

Intrigued, Gerald watches a true story on TV about the assassination of a Bulgarian dissident by a KGB agent armed with an umbrella with a tip poisoned with ricin. Morcilla enters.

MORCILLA

I'm going to Vicki's house tomorrow to plan the class reunion. I think I'll take the Ferrari. Is it supposed to rain?

GERALD

Only if you put the top down.

MORCILLA

Mr. Optimism.

Morcilla steps out. The TV announcer notes that ricin is a derivative of beans from the castor plant. Death is assured and pinpointing ricin as the cause is difficult unless someone suspects it. Gerald calls out to Morcilla O.C.

GERALD

Morcilla, I have to run down to that job site in Philly for the next couple days. Fucking builders always think they know better than the architect.

MORCILLA (O.C.)

I wonder why that is.

(beat)

By the way, David Arbogast called. He said he has some good news to tell you.

GERALD

I still don't understand why he calls you about my business.

INT. PUBLIC LIBRARY - DAY

Gerald works at a computer in the Public Library, taking notes about the effects of ricin poisoning. He clicks, bringing up a foreign patent for making ricin out of castor beans.

INT. ARMY SURPLUS STORE

Gerald buys a used chemical suit, complete with a gas mask. He pays with cash.

EXT. COUNTRY ROAD - DAY

Gerald drives a rental van along a country road before pulling into a TREE NURSERY.

INT. TREE NURSERY - DAY

Gerald exits the rental van and wanders about the potted plants arrayed on the ground. A WORKER steps up.

WORKER

Can I help you?

GERALD

I'm looking for some ornamentals. That's what my wife asked me to get, anyway. Ornamentals.

Gerald pulls a paper from his pocket and starts reading.

GERALD (CONT'D)

Celosia, gomphrena, portulaca, castor, mercardonia. You got any of those?

WORKER

Give me the list. Let me check.

EXT. TREE NURSERY - DAY

The Worker loads a bunch of plants into Gerald's rental van. Gerald pays with cash and drives off down the country lane.

EXT. COUNTRY ROAD - DAY

Gerald pulls off the country road and dumps most of the plants into the woods. Wearing rubber gloves, he delicately picks beans from the castor plants and places them in a Ziploc bag.

EXT. JOB SITE TRAILER - DAY

Gerald parks in the van in front of the Trailer, and heads for the door carrying a duffle bag.

INT. JOB SITE TRAILER - DAY

Wearing the chemical suit, Gerald grinds up castor beans on a workbench. A food dehydrator sits nearby.

INT. VICKI'S HOUSE - DAY

Vicki's House is a nicely appointed colonial. Vicki and Morcilla sit at a table covered with papers and photographs.

VICKI

It seems like we just had our 10th reunion. And, poof, here we are planning the 25th.

As Vicki reaches for a pair of scissors, Morcilla briefly caresses her hand.

MORCILLA

You look the same as you did on graduation day, V.

INT. RENTAL VAN (TRAVELING) - NIGHT

Gerald calls the Borgata Hotel. A DESK CLERK answers.

DESK CLERK (O.C.)

Borgata Hotel. How may I direct your call?

GERALD

Can you connect me to a guest? Sinisa Ražnatovi?

DESK CLERK (O.C.)

How do you spell-- Did you say Mr. Ražnatov Sinisic?

GERALD

No. I mean, yes. Yes. That's him.

DESK CLERK (O.C.)

Thank you. Please hold while I connect--

Gerald hangs up. Then he places another call.

GERALD

Morcilla? Listen, I'm going to be stuck here for a couple more days. I'll be back on the weekend.

INT - VICKI'S HOUSE - NIGHT

In bed, naked, Morcilla hangs up the phone. Pull back to reveal she's in bed with Vicki.

VICKI

Who was that?

MORCILLA

Nobody.

EXT. HIGHWAY - NIGHT

Gerald's van passes a sign: "Atlantic City 40 miles." He drives into an isolated, empty Highway Rest Stop.

INT. RENTAL VAN - NIGHT

Parked in a Highway Rest Stop, Gerald types a letter on an old manual typewriter.

EXT. HIGHWAY REST STOP - NIGHT

Gerald walks to a dumpster and stashes a garbage bag and the typewriter. He walks into the lavatory. A moment later he walks out wearing a snazzy suit of a unique purplish color and pattern.

EXT. BORGATA HOTEL - NIGHT

Gerald parks the van and walks into the Borgata Hotel.

INT. BORGATA HOTEL/CAGE - NIGHT

Standing at the Cage, Gerald hands over $15,000 and receives the equivalent in chips from the CAGE WORKER.

INT. BORGATA HOTEL/CASINO - NIGHT

Gerald plays cards at a blackjack table. As he plays, a minor disturbance erupts at a different blackjack table across the room where an agitated Sinisa can be seen taking issue with another player's perceived incompetence.

INT. BORGATA HOTEL/CASINO - NIGHT (LATER)

Accompanied by a few ASIAN PLAYERS and a CROUPIER Gerald wins a big hand at baccarat.

GERALD

That about gets me back to even. I'm gonna cash out. Give me a couple 5K chips, OK?

The Croupier settles up and hands over two $5,000 chips along with additional chips.

INT. BORGATA HOTEL/LOBBY - NIGHT

Gerald inserts the previously typewritten letter and the two $5,000 chips in an envelope, seals it and walks to the Front Desk where the Desk Clerk awaits.

DESK CLERK

Good evening, sir. Checking in?

GERALD

No. I have a letter for a colleague. Ražnatov Sinisic. Can you see that he gets it? It's for his meeting.

Gerald hands the letter to the Clerk.

DESK CLERK

Of course, sir.

INT. BORGATA HOTEL/ROOM - NIGHT

Sinisa stumbles into the Room and crashes onto the bed. He notices a FLASHING light on the phone and dials the front desk. After another moment, he lashes out at the Desk Clerk on the other end.

SINISA

Well, fucking bring it up to me.

INT. BORGATA HOTEL/BAR - NIGHT

Gerald sits alone in a booth in the back of the Bar, sipping a Gibson. He checks his watch, fiddles with the drink, and scans the bustling bar. Finally, Sinisa walks up and sits across from Gerald.

GERALD

Thank you for--

Sinisa produces the two $5,000 chips.

SINISA

--What the fuck is this? How do you know that scumbag Selakovic?

Gerald hesitates for a split second, parsing the introduction of an unknown person "Selakovic."

GERALD

Uh, what does it matter, Sinisa?

SINISA

That's another thing. How do you know my name?

GERALD

Look. I specialize in solving problems. That means I'm good at getting information.

SINISA

Did Selakovic hire you, Mr. What-the-Fuck?

GERALD

Geraci. Paul Geraci.

Gerald hands Sinisa a fake business card. He takes a chance.

GERALD (CONT'D)

Selakovic. He owes you 10 grand, right?

SINISA

Yeah.

GERALD

No, he didn't hire me.

SINISA

Then why--

GERALD

--I have no interest in him other than to move him out of the way. I need your complete attention. I have a very important client who seeks someone with certain special skills that I believe you possess. We're willing to pay off Selakovic's debt so you can concentrate on a job for my client. One worth 100,000 dollars.

Sinisa lights a cigarette. A COCKTAIL WAITRESS in a skimpy outfit appears.

SINISA (CONT'D)

Captain and coke, babe.

GERALD

Another Gibson, please.

As the Cocktail Waitress leaves, Sinisa stares at her ass for a moment, then returns his attention.

SINISA

Go on.

GERALD

An employee in my client's company possesses damaging information; enough to cause insolvency for the company and incarceration for my client. You do know what insolvency means, yes?

Sinisa nods unconvincingly.

GERALD (CONT'D)

This asshole has blackmailed my client for a year. Now he's demanding double. You have to understand - it's a problem that can't be solved by firing him. He's gotta go. With prejudice.

SINISA

Tell me about the money.

GERALD

Fifty when you show up at the job site. The other fifty when it's all over. All cash deal, small bills. I'll explain the details.

The Cocktail Waitress returns with the drinks. Gerald hands her a $100 chip.

COCKTAIL WAITRESS

Thank you so much, sir.

The Cocktail Waitress departs.

GERALD

Another thing, this employee is a disgusting pervert. He likes little boys. Let me show you something we found on his computer.

Gerald produces one of Oscar's illicit photos. Sinisa takes the photo and looks on with a combination of pain and fury. He slugs down his drink.

GERALD (CONT'D)

I can't understand these pedophiles. Can you?

Sinisa angrily crumples the photo.

SINISA

I'd kill this fucker for nothing. What does your boss want me to do?

EXT. RENTAL CAR COMPANY - DAY

Gerald drives the rental van into the lot of a Rental Car Company situated in an industrial area in an outer borough.

EXT. INDUSTRIAL NEIGHBORHOOD - DAY

Gerald enters a pay-phone booth. He sprays the mouthpiece with Lysol, then makes a call.

GERALD

Can you talk?

INTERCUT WITH TOM STULL'S OFFICE

TOM

Yeah, I can talk. What do you want?

GERALD

I think you know. Are you familiar with the Route 604 area of Allamuchy? There's large stand of trees on a bluff overlooking I80.

TOM

Yeah, sure. We're doing work down the road a piece.

GERALD

Good. Tomorrow, on or about--

TOM

--Tomorrow? Are you fucking nuts?

GERALD

On or about 4 in the afternoon, a bright yellow Ferrari convertible driven by my nemesis - your target - will pass over the rise from the west. There's no way you can miss seeing it. Very flashy vehicle.

TOM

I asked you: are you fucking nuts? I can't get it together in one day.

GERALD

Yes, you can and you will. You took my 50 grand. That's a commitment in my book. Besides, I've got another 200 burning a hole in my pocket that I'm sure you can use.

(beat)

Listen, Tom, this is an opportunity I can't pass up. It's the first reliable info I've gotten on the bastard's exact movements. I may never get such solid intel again. We have to nail him tomorrow. No choice.

A long silence.

GERALD (CONT'D)

You still there?

TOM

Shit. Alright. I just want to get this over with. What about the rest of the money?

GERALD

What did you do with the 50 grand I already gave you? I sincerely hope you didn't spend it all.

TOM

I stashed it like you said. It's in a tool compartment in my grader. Nobody knows about it, okay? Now, how do I get the rest of my money?

GERALD

At 11 in the evening, after the deed is done, go to the Seventh Avenue 14th Street subway station. The 1 train. Wait at the far south end of the platform. A guy dressed like a bagman will deliver the rest of your payoff. A month later, one of my subcontractors will hire you to pave the parking lot of a mall we're constructing in Ohio. And I'll have a talk with an old fraternity buddy in law enforcement about your wife's credit card problems. After that, we never speak again.

TOM

Very neat.

GERALD

Do you want the fucking money or not?

TOM

Of course. Be cool, man. Shit. I'll get it done tomorrow.

GERALD

Remember: no cell phones. Don't leave any cartridges or other shit laying around. Just take the shot and leave. And don't forget to pick your ass.

TOM

What?

GERALD

I told you. My guy - the bag-man - will scratch his balls as a signal to you. You reciprocate by picking your ass. Simple enough?

TOM

Yeah.

GERALD

Are you sure you got it all?

TOM

Yeah, yeah.

GERALD

Good. Now tell it all back to me in detail.

INT. PFALZGRAF OFFICES/LOBBY - DAY

Gerald steps off the elevator into the lobby. His receptionist JANET sits behind a desk.

GERALD

Good morning, Janet.

JANET

Welcome back, Gerald.

GERALD

Tell Oscar to come my office.

INT. GERALD'S OFFICE - DAY

Gerald stares out the window at the Flatiron Building. A KNOCK on the door.

GERALD

Come in.

Looking haggard, Oscar shuffles in holding a balled-up handkerchief. His face is reddish and pimply.

GERALD (CONT'D)

Are you alright Oscar? You look like shit. Sit down. We have important work to do tomorrow night.

OSCAR

(Coughs)

Oh. I was hoping you were going to tell me the problem went away somehow.

GERALD

No, the problem didn't go away somehow, Oscar. The son-of-a-bitch is all too alive and well. Just yesterday I had to pay him not to contact Arbogast and scotch the museum deal. Cost me fifty K. This can't go on, understand?

OSCAR

Well, of course, Gerald.

GERALD

Don't go soft on me. The job is a cinch to pull off, and when it's done, you'll be on the road to recovery. You'll get your old pay back... and a new client. You're a good architect, Oscar. Don't blow it.

OSCAR

A new client? Really? Jeez, Gerald, that would be outstanding. And all that crap with the internet: that goes away, too, forever. Right?

Gerald nods. Oscar pushes his crusty hair out of his eyes and rubs some pimples on his forehead.

OSCAR (CONT'D)

I'm sorry I look so bad, Gerald. I've been in a real funk lately.

GERALD

On the contrary, you look perfect for your role tomorrow. Really shitty. Mr. Dupree, you're ready for your close-up.

Oscar smiles wanly.

OSCAR

OK, Gerald. And the day after - I start my life over.

GERALD

That's what I like to hear, Oscar. Confidence. Listen, I'm going to Pennsylvania tonight to see Arbogast. I'll be back tomorrow night. Meet me back here alone precisely at midnight to do a debrief on your mission.

Gerald produces a duffle bag from behind his desk and hands it to Oscar.

GERALD (CONT'D) Your costume. Wear it well. And don't forget to scratch your balls.

Oscar takes the duffle bag and opens the door just as Martina KNOCKS on the door. She pokes her head in.

MARTINA

Gerald, the limo's waiting. Are you ready to go?

INT. LIMO (TRAVELING) - NIGHT

Gerald and Martina sit in the back of the Limo. She pores over some papers.

GERALD

What's the schedule?

MARTINA

Dinner tonight with Mr. Arbogast and his team. Presentations all day tomorrow. Financial stuff, mostly. We'll show our latest designs. Then another dinner tomorrow, this time with some artists and society types.

GERALD

Good lord.

MARTINA

Day after tomorrow, Mr. Arbogast wants you to visit a quarry nearby his compound.

GERALD

What the hell for?

MARTINA

According to his guy, Arbogast wants your opinion on the color of the stone for the balustrades.

GERALD

Jesus. I suppose I'll have to tour a paint factory to decide whether to use satin or semi-gloss.

INT. TOM'S BASEMENT - NIGHT

Standing by a work table, Tom checks out his rifle. He stows it and ammunition into a case. As he inspects the scope, the SOUND of a door opening. His wife TORI calls down to him.

TORI (O.C.)

Tom, what are you doing down there?

Tom quickly scuttles the scope into the case and shoves everything under the work table.

TOM

Uh, just getting some things together for work tomorrow. I gotta scope, uh, check out that new job site I was telling you about.

Dressed in pajamas and a robe, Tori sidles next to Tom.

TORI

That one in Ohio? You don't have to go there tomorrow, do you?

TOM

Yes, Tori. I told you. It's a big job. Decent money.

TORI

But it's so far away.

TOM

It's not that far. I'll drive out there in the morning, check it out, make some measurements and shit, and come back. Probably midnight.

TORI

I got a letter this afternoon. I had to sign for it.

TOM

You signed for it? Why did you do that? Who's it from?

TORI

I think the district attorney. I'm afraid to open it.

TOM

You're afraid to open it, but you signed for it?

TORI

What was I supposed to do?

TOM

Fuck. Look, the guy with the Ohio job knows people who can help get you out of this. I don't know the details, but--

TORI

--You told him about me? How come?

TOM

Do you want to go to jail? Listen, you fucked up with your stupid eBay scam. I'm trying to help you.

TORI

Who is he?

Tom shakes his head at revealing too much.

TOM

Leave me alone, Tori. I gotta get my shit together for tomorrow. Go back upstairs and pack me a lunch for the road.

EXT. VICKI'S HOUSE - DAY

Sun shines on Morcilla's yellow Ferrari in the driveway.

INT. VICKI'S HOUSE - DAY

Morcilla and Vicki are in bed together, naked. It's 2:30 according to the clock on the dresser.

VICKI

C'mon, M., get up. If Sherwood catches us like this--

MORCILLA

--OK, Babe. I need a minute. I haven't had sex like that in God knows how long.

VICKI

You and Gerald? No?

Vicki picks up her bra from the floor and starts dressing.

MORCILLA

I suppose after 20 years, the friction intensifies, and not in a good way. Sometimes I wonder if Gerald is out screwing someone younger. Maybe even some young guy.

Morcilla likewise gets dressed.

VICKI

Really? That's shocking. Are you thinking about splitting up?

MORCILLA

Who doesn't after 20 years? But, right now, no.

VICKI

What about David?

MORCILLA

I'll see him in Barcelona next month. It'll be fun, then I'll come home. That's all.

VICKI

Do you think Gerald will pop home one of these days and ask for a divorce?

Morcilla laughs derisively.

MORCILLA

And jump off the gravy train? My wealth is well-protected from Mr. Pfalzgraf. He'd be stupid to divorce me. I'd have to die before him – and that's not happening. He thinks drinking is an aerobic exercise.

A door SLAMS O.C. It's Vicki's HUSBAND

HUSBAND (O.C.)

Afternoon, honey! Is that Morcilla's sexy yellow Ferrari I see in the driveway?

VICKI

Shit.

Morcilla and Vicki quicken the pace.

EXT. JOB SITE - DAY

Tom and a few WORKERS on his construction crew look over papers. Several large pieces of road equipment sit nearby behind cones separating them from rushing traffic on the interstate highway.

TOM

You got it? A hundred yards before the bridge, not fifty like these fucked up plans say.

CREWMEMBER #1

Yeah, yeah. I got it.

Tom looks at his watch which reads 3:00.

TOM

OK. I'm gonna run ahead to the grading team.

Tom hops in his truck and drives off.

EXT. - VICKI'S HOUSE - DAY

Vicki speaks to Morcilla who's in the Ferrari with the top down.

VICKI

It's a pity we didn't make more progress on the class reunion.

MORCILLA
I guess that means I'll just have to come back out here again next week. Bye, Babe.

Vicki strokes Morcilla's hand. Morcilla backs out of the driveway and speeds down the suburban lane.

EXT. WOODSY AREA - DAY

Tom dons camouflage then lies prone in a grassy area amidst trees in a Woodsy Area near the Interstate Highway. His rifle is mounted on a tripod and he peers through the scope at traffic tooling along the busy interstate. Tom nervously checks his watch which reads 3:50. Unexpectedly, his cell phone rings. He scrambles to turn it off. Tom gets serious now. He presses his eye against the scope, spots a long, double-length semi and squeezes off a round that strikes the rear trailer. The unaware truck driver continues on. Tom cocks the bolt-action rifle and takes a shot at a truck hauling new automobiles, hitting one near the rear. He cocks the bolt again, and checks his watch which reads 3:55. He spots a truck bearing the logo of a construction competitor, and with a sinister grin on his face Tom fires a round. This one mistakenly pierces the tire of a mini-van which was behind the truck a second earlier, but lagged back suddenly. The minivan swerves and rolls over.

TOM

Fucking shit!

Traffic moving in the opposite direction slows down as the tumbling mini-van sheds parts. Morcilla is among those slowing down. Tom spots the yellow Ferrari, quickly cocks the bolt and takes the shot that strikes Morcilla in the head, Zapruder style. The Ferrari abruptly veers onto the grassy median strip and slams into a knoll. Tom packs his gear and rushes into the dense stand of trees behind him.

EXT. JOB SITE - DAY

Workers mill around, talking among themselves. Traffic on the opposite side is stopped, whereas the interstate adjacent to the Job Site is eerily vacant. Emergency vehicles zoom past the Job Site, followed by news trucks. Tom, now in his regular clothes, steps into the conversation.

TOM

What the hell is going on?

WORKER #1

Obviously, a wreck back there, Tom.

TOM

Yeah, I figured that. Any idea what happened?

A helicopter passes overhead.

WORKER #2

Maybe it was a fuckin' sniper.

Tom blanches.

WORKER #1

Oh, c'mon.

TOM

You hear a gunshot or something?

WORKER #2

No. I'm just sayin'. Maybe it was some fucker like that nigger in DC.

TOM

Jesus Christ. Would you please not use the N-word. What's the matter with you?

WORKER #1

The DC guy was a nigger?

TOM

Listen, there's no sniper. Some guy probably ran off the road, texting or something.

INT. ARBOGAST'S PLACE - DAY

Gerald and Martina sit at a conference table along with Arbogast and a couple of AIDES. A pencil-neck ACCOUNTANT stands at a podium, making a boring presentation. Gerald struggles mightily to pay attention.

ACCOUNTANT

David, the FASB gives a nonprofit collecting organization the option of capitalizing its collection. But if you don't, you'll have to certify that you're preserving the collection for public exhibition or research or something educational.

ARBOGAST

That makes sense.

ACCOUNTANT

Yes. If you sell pieces from your collection, you'd have to use the proceeds to acquire other works.

ARBOGAST

Well, I could always use another Koons. I hope your team factored in enough floor space, Gerald, for new acquisitions.

GERALD

Huh? Yes, David, we considered--

MARTINA

--May I say, Mr. Arbogast: exhibiting the Koons balloon figures juxtaposed with your Mapplethorpe photos of large penises is pure genius.

Gerald grins nervously, looking at Arbogast in anticipation of a spicy retort as when Paul Clay embarrassed the team.

ARBOGAST

Very perceptive, Martina. Do you have curatorial training?

MARTINA

I took a course. Nothing formal, but I have a passion for art.

ARBOGAST

Good for you.

(beat)

By the way, Gerald, why didn't you bring your man, uh, Oliver--

GERALD

--Oscar? He's bent over his desk busily working on the project right now.

INT. OSCAR'S APARTMENT/BATHROOM - DAY

Oscar is bent over the toilet retching.

INT. OSCAR'S APARTMENT - DAY

Oscar shuffles out of his Bathroom and glumly studies a pile of ragged, dirty clothing on his bed. The bag Gerald handed him back at the office sits nearby, opened and empty. Oscar looks at himself in the mirror with disgust.

INT. ARBOGAST'S PLACE - DAY

BACK TO SCENE.

ARBOGAST

Glad to hear it. OK, let's continue. Accounting rules fascinate me. I wanted to be an accountant when I was a kid.

Gerald sighs. Martina's phone DINGS with a text message. Gerald eyes Martina as she silently reads the text.

MARTINA

Oh my god! There was an accident on I80 an hour ago. They think a sniper might've killed a couple drivers.

GERALD

A couple? What?

ARBOGAST

Insanity.

GERALD

More than one!? I mean--

AIDE

--Didn't you take 180 to get here, Mr. Pfalzgraf.

MARTINA

Yes, we did.

ARBOGAST

Pure insanity. Gerald, maybe you should take a different route back to New York tomorrow.

GERALD

Why?

MARTINA

Does the limo have bullet-proof glass, Gerald?

GERALD

What?

ACCOUNTANT

These crazy snipers will keep shooting until they're caught. They think they're still in Vietnam and Charlie is lurking all around. The shooter is probably military.

GERALD

Well, I wouldn't--

MARTINA

--Who's Charlie?

ARBOGAST

Please be careful, Gerald.

(To the Accountant)

Jacob, I have a few questions about that FASB rule.

The Accountant flips to the next chart.

EXT. FILM FORUM - NIGHT

Wren exits the Film Forum where Sinisa is waiting on the sidewalk holding a tool bag. She is startled to see him.

SINISA

I've been looking all over for you Wren. You're not at the bar.

WREN

Thanks to you. Why are you stalking me?

SINISA

I'm not stalking you. I just wanted to give you back the watch.

WREN

I thought you needed money.

SINISA

I did. Now I don't. Listen, have a drink with me.

WREN

I can't.

SINISA

C'mon, Wren. One drink.

INT. DIVE BAR - NIGHT

Sinisa and Wren sit in a booth opposite one another. The tool bag is on the seat next to Sinisa.

SINISA

Wouldn't you like something besides water?

WREN

I'm fine. What do you want?

SINISA

You, of course.

WREN

I knew it. I'm leaving.

SINISA

Wait. Please. I'm getting my shit together. I got a new job. The pay is good, and it's gonna keep on paying.

WREN

Good for you.

SINISA

Yeah, I met some pompous asshole at the Borgata named Garcia... No, that's not it.

Sinisa pulls out the business card and looks it over.

SINISA (CONT'D)

Uh, Ger--

Wren's eyes widen. Sounds like her nickname for Gerald.

SINISA (CONT'D)

--Geraci. Some slick motherfucker in a purple suit. He's got a bigtime client with a problem. I'm gonna help him out of it and it's worth a hundred grand to me.

WREN

Um, congratulations, I guess.

SINISA

So now you see. I'm doing good.

Sinisa hoists the tool bag onto the table, and as he fishes around in it, Wren notices with concern that it contains a rope, pliers and an ice-axe. Finally, Sinisa produces a box and hands it to Wren.

SINISA (CONT'D)

Here's the watch. I'm sorry I asked you for it back. Put it on.

Wren takes the box and stuffs it in her purse.

WREN

Anything else?

SINISA

Why are you such a bitch?

Wren makes a move to leave but Sinisa grabs her by the arm.

SINISA (CONT'D)

I love you. I'll take care of you. After tonight, I'm gonna be debt free. Then I can squeeze this Geraci fuck for more. It's gonna be good. Come back to me, Wren.

WREN

Let go. You're hurting me.

Sinisa makes eye contact with the BARTENDER who has taken an interest in the looming altercation. He lets go of Wren and she bolts for the door. He calmly takes a drink.

SINISA

(Calling out)

Go ahead and leave. I'll find you again.

Sinisa reorganizes the contents of his tool bag.

INT. SUBWAY STATION - NIGHT

Oscar, dressed in the bag-man costume, complete with phony grungy teeth, shuffles down the stairs into the Subway Station carrying a garbage bag.

The platform is sparsely populated with just a few straphangers who don't pay attention to Oscar. He proceeds slowly toward the end of the platform. When he's about 30 feet from the end he spots Tom standing by a support beam with his back to the rails. When the two make eye contact, Oscar scratches his balls. In response, Tom picks his ass. Oscar shuffles in place until he hears the faint SOUND of a train approaching the station, then he walks to Tom.

Oscar and Tom are now face to face. The train races into the station. Oscar extends the garbage bag toward Tom.

OSCAR

Here's your payoff, fucker.

Tom offers a quizzical look, then reaches for the bag. As Tom does so, Oscar shoves him into the path of the oncoming train. The brakes SCREECH but it's too late; Tom is crushed under the train. Oscar rushes up the stairs.

EXT. SUBWAY STATION - NIGHT

Oscar hustles out of the Subway Station, bolts around a dark corner and sneaks behind a row of hedges. He quickly sheds the bag-man garments revealing normal street clothes underneath. He pops out the grungy teeth and stuffs everything into the garbage bag. Oscar steps from behind the hedges unobserved and casually ambles along the sidewalk. He tosses the garbage bag into a trash can then hails a cab. As he hops in the blaring SOUND of sirens builds.

EXT. MADISON SQUARE PARK - NIGHT

The cab deposits Oscar at Madison Square Park. Oscar strolls ebulliently toward the offices of Pfalzgraf Associates. He looks up at the illuminated Flatiron Building and smiles. Gerald was right; Oscar liked it.

INT. PFALZGRAF OFFICES/EMPTY FLOOR - NIGHT

In the dark Empty Floor under construction one flight below the Offices, Sinisa rifles a filing cabinet, eventually recovering a brief case. He opens it to reveal bundles of neatly wrapped money bound by ribbons bearing the Borgata Hotel logo. He makes a quick count of the cash, satisfied that it's all there. He finds a package of white powder included with the money. A note on the package reads "A token of our appreciation." Sinisa grins at the gesture.

Sitting on the floor by the window, Sinisa snorts a fingernail of the powder. By his reaction, it's quality cocaine.

SINISA

Goddamn! Gle kurtsa ti u slamnatome sheshiru!

He snorts some more.

SINISA (CONT'D)

That's gonna make things easier.

He checks his watch, pulls on gloves and a ski-mask, and takes a last-minute admiring look at the Flatiron Building. He walks to the stairway past the box sitting on the floor containing the badge reader.

INT. PFALZGRAF OFFICES - NIGHT

Oscar sits at his cubicle, fidgeting nervously. Suddenly, from the adjoining cubicle the masked Sinisa appears.

SINISA

Stand up motherfucker and turn around! Don't look at me!

Stunned, Oscar stammers.

OSCAR

Who-- What do--

SINISA

--Shut up asshole. I told you to stand up and turn around right fucking now!

Oscar complies. Sinisa takes a straitjacket from his tool bag and tosses it on Oscar's desk.

SINISA (CONT'D)

Put this on.

Oscar starts to put it on like a regular jacket.

SINISA (CONT'D)

Not like that, fool. Turn it around.

Oscar fumbles with the straitjacket, dropping it on the floor before getting it right. Sinisa buckles him tight.

SINISA (CONT'D)

Now get down on the floor and face the wall.

Whimpering, Oscar drops to his knees and falls on his face.

OSCAR

Why are you doing this?

SINISA

Shut the fuck up, pervert.

OSCAR

Pervert? What? Is this about Gerald--

Sinisa kicks Oscar in the gut, shutting him up. He takes a rope fashioned with a noose from the tool bag, slips it over Oscar's head and pulls the knot tight. Oscar thrashes about, but Sinisa straddles his body and pulls even tighter until Oscar ceases to move. When he's certain Oscar is dead, Sinisa hoists the corpse onto the desk and removes the straitjacket. Then he loops the rope over an exposed beam above the desk and ties it tightly. Sinisa climbs atop the desk, lifts up Oscar's body and drops it. The neck SNAPS and urine runs onto the carpet. Sinisa stashes the straitjacket and tarp into the tool bag and heads to the exit.

INT. DIVE BAR - NIGHT

A well-oiled Sinisa puts down a shot, chased by a beer. He barks as order to the Bartender.

SINISA

One more time, bud.

The Bartender sets him up, and takes some money from a few moist bills on the bar.

EXT. SINISA'S APARTMENT BUILDING - NIGHT

Inebriated, Sinisa fumbles with his keys at the entrance to the Apartment Building.

INT. SINISA'S APARTMENT BUILDING - NIGHT

Sinisa unsuccessfully tries his key at apartment number 4F. Frustrated at his inability to get in, he kicks the door. A large, muscular NEIGHBOR opens the door.

NEIGHBOR

What's your fucking problem, pal?

SINISA

My problem? What's your fuck--

Sinisa spots the apartment number - not his.

SINISA (CONT'D)

--Oh, sorry, man.

NEIGHBOR

You should be, you drunken asshole.

The Neighbor slams the door in Sinisa's face.

EXT. SINISA'S APARTMENT - NIGHT

Sinisa sticks a key in a door marked 5F, and turns the knob.

INT. SINISA'S APARTMENT - NIGHT

Sinisa throws a frozen dinner in the oven, sits on the couch and flicks on the TV. He opens the brief case, takes out a stack of money and ogles it lovingly. He takes out the packet of coke, dumps a pile onto a mirror on his coffee table and divides it into three lines. He snorts two in rapid succession. Sinisa changes TV channels rapidly, settling on an old movie. Suddenly, he becomes distressed, puking all over the coffee table. Struggling to breathe, Sinisa staggers about the room, coughing hard.

INT. NEIGHBOR'S APARTMENT - NIGHT

The Neighbor intruded upon by Sinisa earlier glares angrily at his ceiling. The STOMPING of feet is heard O.C.

EXT. SINISA'S APARTMENT - NIGHT

Sinisa stumbles into the hallway, coughing uncontrollably. He presses a button on the elevator, and when it doesn't arrive immediately, he heads for the stairwell. He opens the door to the stairwell, takes a step and tumbles all the way down, bashing his head against an old-style accordion radiator. Blood seeps from a deep crack in Sinisa's cranium.

INT. HOTEL - NIGHT

Wren makes a call and gets a recorded greeting from Gerald.

WREN

Ger, I miss you terribly. I hope your meeting is going well. I suppose you heard there was a shooting on the interstate. Please be careful on your way back.

Wren is about to hang up, then she continues speaking.

WREN (CONT'D)

I, uh, Sinisa tracked me down. He's got me scared. I'm sorry to bother you with my shit. I just can't wait for you to come back, that's all. I love you.

EXT. QUARRY - DAY

On a hot, sunny morning, Gerald, Martina, Arbogast, an Aide and the QUARRY MASTER trudge along a dusty path into the Quarry. Gerald is inappropriately dressed in a dark suit and Italian shoes. He brushes dust off his clothing as the Quarry Master leads the gang past a stack of stone slabs.

QUARRY MASTER

We can cut the balusters and balustrades you want from the same vein as the lintels.

Gerald's cell-phone RINGS, startling him. He steps away from the others.

INT. PFALZGRAF OFFICES - DAY

Lots of action takes place in the background: rubber-necking employees cordoned off from a body bag, Cops and EMT's working the scene. Janet is on the phone. A Detective DUNN is by her side.

JANET

Gerald? Gerald? Oh, Gerald. The police are here.

INTERCUT WITH QUARRY

GERALD

(loudly)

What's going on?

The others in the Quarry party look over at Gerald.

JANET

(sobbing)

I was the first one to come into the office this morning, and I found... I saw... Oscar's dead, Gerald! He hung himself right at his desk. I found him hanging from the ceiling. It was awful. The police are here now. They want to talk to you. Janet hands the phone to Dunn.

DUNN

Mr. Pfalzgraf, I'm Detective Dunn with the NYPD. How are you this morning, sir?

GERALD

How am I? My secretary is sobbing, for Christ sake.

(beat)

I'm sorry, Detective. What's going on there?

DUNN

I regret to inform you that one of your employees, uh...

(beat)

...Oscar Dupree committed suicide last night, probably around midnight. That's just a bit after the time he badged in. Hung himself right next to his desk. We didn't find a note or any other kind of communication. So far, we've had trouble identifying a next of kin.

GERALD

I, uh, I'm shocked. I don't know what to say. Next of kin? I don't know who that would be. I'd have to check his personnel file. He wasn't married and had no children as far as I know.

DUNN

Do you know of a reason why he mighta done this? Did he seem depressed or desperate or anything?

GERALD

Well... I... Oscar was having some problems at work, which I'd rather not discuss over the phone.

DUNN

When will you be back in town, sir?

GERALD

As soon as I can. Probably late afternoon.

DUNN

Your secretary told me you're in Western PA. Please be advised that traffic through New Jersey on I80 and adjacent highways will probably be slow as the State boys there hunt for that sniper. You heard about that I assume.

GERALD

Yes, terrible. Thank you, Detective.

Gerald hangs up.

MARTINA

What's the matter Gerald? Is something wrong?

GERALD

Oscar. He... The Detective. Oscar killed himself last night. Right by his desk.

ARBOGAST

What?

MARTINA

Oh my god!

GERALD

Last night, I guess. Damn.

Lots of chatter among the others as Gerald paces about aimlessly. Then, Gerald's phone rings once more. He tightens up and answers the call he hopes for yet dreads.

OFFICER (O.C.)

Mr. Pfalzgraf? Mr. Gerald L. Pfalzgraf, Fifth Avenue, New York City?

GERALD

Yes?

OFFICER (O.C.)

My name is Lieutenant Colonel Maria Esposito of the New Jersey State Police. Are you the husband of Morcilla Calatrava Pfalzgraf, also of Fifth Avenue in New York?

Gerald listens for a moment, then drops the phone and falls to his knees. Martina rushes toward him.

MARTINA

Gerald! What's the matter?

FADE TO BLACK.

INT. JET (FLYING) - DAY

Gerald sits in the back row of David Arbogast's private jet, wearing dark sunglasses. He stares out the window at the ground below. Martina sits a few seats away, reading some papers and occasionally glancing up to check on Gerald.

The PILOT opens the door to the cockpit and announces some news to the two passengers.

PILOT

It's a good thing you two are up here instead of down there. They just closed interstate 80 again. A half hour ago that crazed sniper took some more pot shots. Fired on a charter bus full of seniors heading to Atlantic City.

MARTINA

Unbelievable.

Gerald peers out the window again. The quizzical look on his face slowly turns into an ever-so-slight smile.

GERALD

(Sotto voce)

That is unbelievable.

INT. GERALD'S HOME - NIGHT

Gerald walks into his home, drops a piece of luggage on the floor and checks his answering machine. The first message is one of condolence. Gerald shuts off the machine in midsentence. He walks to the couch and flicks on the TV. A NEWS REPORTER details the arrest of an alleged sniper caught near Interstate 80.

NEWS REPORTER

(On TV)

The suspect, Silas Crowder, was apprehended about a half-hour after reports of a shooting this afternoon along Interstate 80 in the town of Allamuchy.

(beat)

According to a law enforcement official, Mr. Crowder took credit for yesterday's shootings in the same area that took the lives of two drivers and wreaked havoc for hours on the busy thoroughfare.

INT. SINISA'S APARTMENT BUILDING - DAY

A POLICE OFFICER interviews the Neighbor one floor below Sinisa's apartment.

NEIGHBOR

He was drunk as a skunk. Didn't even know what floor he was on. I heard him stumbling around upstairs.

POLICE OFFICER

He fell down a flight of stairs.

NEIGHBOR

What a surprise.

POLICE OFFICER

Bashed his head on a radiator. Did you notice if he was carrying anything? A tool bag, maybe? Or a brief case?

NEIGHBOR

Nah. I was too pissed off. Where is he now?

POLICE OFFICER

The morgue.

NEIGHBOR

Jesus.

INT. SINISA'S APARTMENT - DAY

The Police Officer enters Sinisa's Apartment and addresses INSPECTOR REINKING who checks out the scene. The air is smoky.

POLICE OFFICER

God, what's that smell?

INSPECTOR REINKING

Burned TV dinner. I think it was Salisbury steak once upon a time.

POLICE OFFICER

The downstairs neighbor says the victim was visibly drunk before he fell down the stairs.

INSPECTOR REINKING

Yeah, it certainly looks like an accident. There's a line of coke and a puddle of barf on the coffee table. He probably went out for some air and stumbled.

Reinking examines the brief case.

POLICE OFFICER

He was a real problem child. Last time I saw him a bouncer hurled him through a glass door. I picked him up a couple other times for smalltime drug shit.

INSPECTOR REINKING

Does this appear small-time to you?

Reinking shows the brief case revealing bundles of hundred-dollar bills tied with Borgata logo'd ribbons.

POLICE OFFICER

Holy shit. There must be--

INSPECTOR REINKING

--Fifty grand at least.

POLICE OFFICER

Looks like our boy just got paid for doing something naughty.

INSPECTOR REINKING

Or maybe he was getting ready to pay somebody who will soon come looking for it. We might have ourselves some bait to catch a bad guy.

INT. CORONER'S OFFICE - DAY

C.U. of the Coroner's report for Sinisa Ražnatovi on a computer screen; "Accidental" is typed into the space marked "Cause of Death."

INT. TOM'S HOUSE - DAY

A DETECTIVE sits with a teary Tori and her yipping lap-dog.

DETECTIVE

Why do you think your husband was in the subway at that hour of the evening, Mrs. Stull?

TORI

I don't know. He told me he was going to Ohio. Maybe he changed his mind. Or came back early.

DETECTIVE

He worked in Jersey. I wonder why he was in Manhattan late at night.

TORI

I have no idea, detective. Honest.

DETECTIVE

That's too bad. You should try harder to remember. Who was Mr. Stull supposed to meet in Ohio?

TORI

Just a guy with a paving job. He wouldn't tell me who.

DETECTIVE

Why not?

TORI

Tom hated to talk about his work. I asked but he wouldn't say.

(beat)

Did you catch the person who pushed him onto the tracks?

DETECTIVE

Well, that's just a theory. No one saw what happened. The security cameras don't point to where your husband fell. But some people we interviewed said they saw a disheveled homeless guy wandering near there around that time.

(beat)

It's really impossible at the moment, Mrs. Stull, to be sure what happened. He could have fallen.

TORI

(Bawling)

What am I gonna do now?

INT. CORONER'S OFFICE - DAY

C.U. of the Coroner's report for Tom Stull on a computer screen; "Accidental" is typed into the space marked "Cause of Death."

INT. PFALZGRAF OFFICES/LOBBY - DAY

Gerald shuffles somberly into the Office and receives a hug of condolence from Janet.

JANET

Gerald, we're all so sorry for your loss. I can't believe what happened. How are you doing?

GERALD

Not so good, Janet. It's all so mind-boggling.

JANET

A Detective Dunn is in the guest office.

GERALD

He's here now?

INT. GERALD'S OFFICE/GUEST OFFICE - DAY

Gerald walks into the Guest Office where Dunn is pacing around. Gerald extends his hand.

GERALD

Detective Dunn. Gerald Pfalzgraf.

The two shake hands.

DUNN

Mr. Pfalzgraf, let me first express my condolences for the unfortunate death of your wife. So tragic and unnecessary.

GERALD

Thank you, Detective.

DUNN

I'm just so glad they captured that hillbilly Crowder before he could inflict any more mayhem.

GERALD

Thank god. How can I help you?

DUNN

I want to finish up my investigation of the suicide of your employee. I spoke to some of your employees. One of them - Paul Clay - told me about an embarrassing incident with one of your clients--

GERALD

--Detective, I think I know the reason Oscar committed suicide. Nothing to do with a client. I discovered he had downloaded child pornography on his workstation--

Gerald turns on his computer and types a command.

GERALD (CONT'D)

--And I slammed him pretty hard. I threatened to turn him over to the authorities if he didn't straighten out. I demoted him, cut his pay, took him off a key project.

DUNN

Interesting.

GERALD

I suppose the pressure got to him. Here's what the tracking program captured from Oscar's screen.

Gerald turns the monitor so Dunn can see.

DUNN

(Disgusted)

Jesus! Why didn't you notify the authorities right away? You must know this is kinda stuff is illegal.

GERALD

I thought if I was strict with him, and I got rid of the stuff, y'know, replace his workstation with a new one, he'd toe the line going forward.

DUNN

But you didn't get rid of the stuff. You kept a copy.

Gerald fights the urge to swallow.

DUNN (CONT'D)

Why did you monitor Mr. Dupree's computer? Did you suspect him of something?

GERALD

Not particularly. I monitored all the employees.

DUNN

I see. Did you hold this over his head - as a threat maybe?

GERALD

Detective Dunn, please understand. I had the software installed to protect my company's intellectual property. I had no idea Oscar was downloading this material until I looked at the files. I didn't want to ruin the man's life by turning him in. I focused my attention on executing, um, meting out a combination of punishment and reward. A carrot-and-stick approach, if you will.

DUNN

Carrot-and-stick. I see. So, again, why did you keep these files?

GERALD

In my business, it's common for architects who get fired to file lawsuits later, claiming bias or discrimination. I wouldn't put it past Oscar, so I kept the files in case I needed to show his termination was based on a legitimate reason.

Dunn jots something onto his note pad.

DUNN

Well you really should have called in the authorities. Transmission and possession of child pornography is a serious felony. I'll be calling in the department's IT specialists to go through your company's computers to ensure nothing else illegal has been archived. With your permission, naturally.

Gerald nods.

DUNN (CONT'D)

It must be very hard to deal with the death of your wife and the suicide of your employee, y'know, both happening at the same time. Bizarre, really.

(beat)

I appreciate your cooperation, Mr. Pfalzgraf.

GERALD

Thank you, Detective Dunn.

DUNN

You know, to lose an employee, Mr. Pfalzgraf, may be regarded as a misfortune; to lose both an employee and a wife looks like carelessness.

GERALD

How's that?

DUNN

Oscar Wilde. The Importance of Being Earnest? Oh, never mind, I thought you might recognize it. Have a nice day.

Dunn exits the Guest Office, leaving Gerald with a nervous, quizzical look on his face.

EXT. HOTEL/ROOFTOP POOL - DAY

Wren lies on a chaise lounge by the Hotel's Rooftop Pool, eating a sandwich and reading the newspaper. She spots a small headline in the obituary section that reads "Morcilla Pfalzgraf, Art Patron, Socialite, Victim of 'I80 Sniper'". She nearly chokes on her sandwich.

INT. CHURCH - DAY

Morcilla's funeral mass has just broken up. In attendance are David Arbogast, Gerald's Mother, Chappy Hardwick and his new boyfriend, some of Gerald's employees, members of Morcilla's family, Vicki and Sherwood. Gerald mills around by the front pew with other mourners offering condolences. Vicki approaches Gerald.

VICKI

I'm so sorry, Gerald. And so sad. What a tragedy.

(beat)

Y'know, Gerald, Morcilla told me she thought you might be having an affair.

GERALD

What?

VICKI

With another man. I hope that's not true, Gerald.

GERALD

Oh, for god's sake, Vicki.

Gerald turns and walks away. Vicki call out to him.

VICKI

Why did you change your hairstyle, Gerald?

Gerald keeps on walking.

INT. CORONER'S OFFICE - DAY

C.U. of the Coroner's report for Morcilla Pfalzgraf on a computer screen; "Homicide" is typed into the space marked "Cause of Death."

INT. LIMO (TRAVELING) - NIGHT

Gerald reads the NY Post in the back seat. He scans page after page stopping when he sees a brief article of interest. The headline: "Man dies in fall." C.U. of the article reporting "The man, identified as Sinisa Ražnatovi was found dead of head injuries at the bottom of a stairwell." Gerald mutters to himself.

GERALD

Best 50 grand I've ever spent.

The Limo pull up to a trendy-looking Restaurant. Gerald addresses his Driver.

GERALD (CONT'D)

I'll find my own way home later, Mustapha. Take the night off.

INT. RESTAURANT - NIGHT

Dressed in an expensive suit and tie, Gerald sits alone at a table near the back in a dark Restaurant, sipping a cocktail. He checks his watch and eyes the entrance. Gerald tenses up when a police car drives slowly past the window of the Restaurant, its lights flashing. After a moment Wren walks in, dressed runway-stylish. A MAITRE D' leads Wren to Gerald's table. Gerald stands and the two lovers embrace and kiss.

GERALD

Wren, you look lovely.

He holds the chair for Wren, then takes a seat.

WREN

Ger, I don't know what to say. It's such a shock. What a senseless crime. I'm really sorry. How are you holding up?

GERALD

I'm... OK.

(beat)

That cocksucker Crowder is bragging in the papers like he's Lee Fucking Harvey. I mean, Lee Fucking Oswald. I mean—

Flummoxed, Gerald finishes his drink. A WAITER comes by to take an order.

GERALD (CONT'D)

What would you like, Wren?

WREN

How about a saketini?

GERALD

(To the Waiter)

A saketini and another Aviation.

The Waiter departs.

GERALD (CONT'D)

Morcilla and I had our differences, but she didn't deserve to be mowed down like that. Anyway, I was already working out a settlement with her that would leave me and my company financially viable.

WREN

I didn't know that.

The Waiter brings the drinks. Wren takes a sip.

GERALD

Let me put it this way: I would never wish Morcilla dead, but now that she is, I have to move on. I want to be with you. What can I say – it's the truth. I love you, Wren.

Wren twirls her cocktail, an absent-minded look on her face.

GERALD (CONT'D)

From the moment I met you.

WREN

I-- Me too, Ger. I just wish--

She shakes her head.

GERALD

--Wish what?

WREN

I wish that bastard Sinisa would go away forever and leave me alone.

Gerald takes her hand.

GERALD

I think he will. I have a good feeling.

EXT. - HOTEL/ROOFTOP POOL - NIGHT

Alone by the pool, on a peaceful moonlit evening, Gerald and Wren make love.

INT. - HOTEL - DAY

Gerald and Wren eat room-service breakfast in Wren's room. They both wear plush terrycloth robes and goofy-looking slippers supplied by the hotel.

GERALD

Wren, do you remember that jerk who worked for me? The one I told you about who downloaded kiddie porn onto his computer?

WREN

Did you finally fire him, Ger?

Gerald sucks air through his clenched teeth.

GERALD

No. He-- he committed suicide. In the office. He hung himself. I guess he was desperate. Maybe I was too harsh on him.

Wren is taken aback. Gerald solemnly sips his tea and stares out the window, expecting inquisition from Wren.

WREN

That's, I don't know... crazy. I'm speechless.

GERALD

Now that Morcilla's funeral is over, I might come in for some scrutiny from the investigators just because of the sheer oddity of two people I know dying on the same day. The detective in charge of Oscar's suicide might try to make a federal case. I'm sure I'll be okay, but in the meantime, I don't want to arouse suspicion by having you too close. We can't be together for a while, Wren. Do you understand?

WREN

I'm not sure. I guess so.

GERALD

You know that every husband becomes a prime suspect when his rich wife dies unexpectedly - especially if he immediately takes up with a younger, more beautiful woman. It screams motive.

WREN

But your wife was killed by a sniper. A random thing.

GERALD

Yes, but you know how overzealous the cops can get.

WREN

Not really.

GERALD

Look, it'll just be for a little while until the dust settles. Then we can be together.

WREN

What am I supposed to do, Ger? Where am I supposed to live? I can't stay in the hotel any longer. It's driving me crazy.

GERALD

I have a plan.

INT. GERALD'S OFFICE – DAY

Gerald speaks on the phone at his desk.

GERALD

That's right. Three-month lease on the yellow guest house overlooking the river. My lawyer will transfer the whole rent tomorrow.

(beat)

Dominique Francon. F-R-A-N-C-O-N.

Gerald hangs up. Paul KNOCKS and enters.

PAUL

You wanted to see me, Gerald?

GERALD

I think we should acquire some heavy equipment of our own to use on the museum project. We'd save money over the long run.

PAUL

Good idea, Gerald.

Gerald hands a flyer to Paul.

GERALD

I see that a construction company called TS Erection is having a fire sale. I'd like you to go to the auction next month and bid on the grader. I can go up to $15K.

PAUL

Sure thing, Gerald.

(beat)

Janet told me to tell you that a Detective Dunn is here. He wants to talk to you.

GERALD

Again? Jesus. Alright, have her send him in.

INT. GERALD'S OFFICE - DAY (LATER)

Detective Dunn sits across from Gerald at his desk. Gerald pays half-attention to what Dunn says.

DUNN

Our IT guys finished removing all the pornography from your database.

Gerald fiddles with a pen.

DUNN (CONT'D)

I probably shouldn't tell you this Mr. Pfalzgraf, but your buddy Oscar was found guilty of feeling up girls in the subway when he was a minor.

GERALD

He's not – he wasn't – my "buddy," Detective, but thanks.

DUNN

Sure thing.

(beat)

Are you seeing anyone now, Mr. Pfalzgraf? Socially, or otherwise?

GERALD

My wife is recently dead. I'm grieving. Have you ever heard of something called the "grief process?"

DUNN

Yes, I have.

Dunn fixes his gaze at Gerald who eventually relents.

GERALD

No, I am not seeing anyone now, if that's any concern of yours.

DUNN

I must say, Mr. Pfalzgraf, I was rather hoping we'd find a more compelling reason behind the death of Mr. Dupree than just some basic boring troubles at work. But that's just me.

GERALD

Well, I--

DUNN

--The secret of life is to appreciate the pleasure of being terribly, terribly deceived. Do you know what I mean?

GERALD

Umm... not really. Is that another one of your quotes?

DUNN

Oscar Wilde. A Woman of No Importance. Gee, I really had you pegged as someone who'd be familiar with his work.

INT. CORONER'S OFFICE - DAY

C.U. of the Coroner's report for Oscar Dupree on a computer screen; "Suicide" is typed into the space marked "Cause of Death."

EXT. HUDSON RIVER PARK - DAY

Wren stands by the railing in the Hudson River Park looking out across New York Harbor on a breezy day. Wearing the same uniquely purplish suit as when he met Sinisa at the Borgata Hotel, Gerald approaches unnoticed from behind and wraps his arms around her. He kisses her on the ear.

GERALD

Hello, luscious.

WREN

Mmm... hello, lover. Hug me tighter.

GERALD

Did you know the nautical term "fathom" originally meant a hug?

WREN

No, I didn't, Mr. Pfalzgraf. Were you a sailor? What else do you know?

Gerald points to a ship sailing on the Hudson River.

GERALD

See those people on that ship, Wren? They're standing on the fo'c's'le.

Wren turns and faces Gerald.

WREN

Fo'c's'le? How do you spell that?

GERALD

I'm not sure. I can never remember if there are three apostrophes or only two.

The couple stroll hand-in-hand along the river front.

GERALD (CONT'D)

I'll miss you, Wren. I'll be going crazy without you.

WREN

Me too, Ger. Are you sure this is the best thing to do?

GERALD

Right now, at this moment, no. But we both know we have to separate for a while. Until things get back to normal.

(beat)

You're going to love that little village up there on the Hudson, Wren. The place I found for you is really quite charming.

WREN

I hope I don't forget how to make a Gibson while I'm in the sticks.

A brisk wind kicks up, driving Wren into Gerald's arms.

WREN (CONT'D)

Ooo, warm me up.

Gerald embraces Wren tightly. She puts her hands in his pockets to warm them, and after a moment takes out a $500 chip from the Borgata Hotel casino.

WREN (CONT'D)

Where'd you get this, Ger?

Gerald takes the chip and examines it like it's a foreign object.

GERALD

Wow, 500 dollars. Geez, uh, that must be from, uh, that time I went to an architect's conference in Atlantic City. I guess I haven't worn this suit in, like, five years. I wonder if the chip is still good.

Wren takes notice of Gerald's purplish patterned suit.

INT. DIVE BAR - NIGHT

FLASHBACK.

SINISA

Yeah, I met some pompous asshole at the Borgata named Garcia-- wait, that's not it.

Sinisa pulls out the business card and looks it over.

SINISA (CONT'D)

Geraci. Some slick motherfucker in a purple suit.

EXT. HUDSON RIVER PARK - DAY

BACK TO SCENE.

WREN

(Tentative)

Um, Gerald, I know this sounds weird, but would you happen to know anyone named Geraci by chance?

Gerald fakes thinking for a second, then shakes his head.

GERALD

No, never met anyone with a name like that. Why do you ask?

WREN

Just wondering. I thought you might know him, but if you don't, you don't.

GERALD

Who is he?

WREN

I'm not sure. I'm kinda afraid to find out.

GERALD

That doesn't make any sense, Wren.

WREN

I suppose you're right.

The ship on the river BLARES its foghorn. Gerald takes Wren back into his arms and kisses her passionately.

INT. HOTEL - DAY

Wren packs clothes when her cell phone RINGS.

WREN

Hello?

INTERCUT WITH POLICE STATION

INSPECTOR REINKING

Is this Wren Colfax?

WREN

Yes. Who is this?

INSPECTOR REINKING

I'm Inspector Reinking of the NYPD. Your name and phone number were in the possession of Mr. Sinisa Ražnatovi. Would you be able to come to the station and answer a few questions for us?

WREN

I don't know. I really have nothing to do with him. Is he in trouble again?

INSPECTOR REINKING

You could say that. How about it, Ms. Colfax. Can you stop in for a few minutes?

WREN

I'd rather not. I'm getting ready to go on a vacation, uh, trip.

INSPECTOR REINKING

Well, I don't want to force you to do anything. It's just that now Mr. Rażnatovi is dead--

WREN

--Dead? Oh my god!

INT. POLICE STATION - DAY

Inspector Reinking and Wren meet in the Police Station.

INSPECTOR REINKING

We found him at the bottom of the stairwell. He hit his head on a radiator and almost certainly died instantly. Toxicology reported a significant concentration of alcohol and drugs in his system.

WREN

Well, it doesn't surprise me he'd go out that way. He was a consummate abuser of drugs... and other things.

INSPECTOR REINKING

Other things? You?

WREN

What did you want to talk to me about?

INSPECTOR REINKING

What did Mr. Ražnatovi do for a living?

WREN

As far as I know, he beat up people for money and sold drugs.

INSPECTOR REINKING

Did he make good money?

WREN

My god, no. He was broke most of the time. Last I knew he owed some guy a lot of money.

INSPECTOR REINKING

Like how much?

WREN

He told me $100,000. And I believed him. Although the last time I saw him he said he had a job lined up that would help him clear his debt. I suppose that was just another one of his fantasies.

INSPECTOR REINKING

I'm not so sure. After he died, we found a substantial amount of cash in a brief case in his apartment. I can't tell you the exact amount but it was in the thousands.

WREN

Really?

INSPECTOR REINKING

Do you know of anyone who might've paid him the cash?

Wren shakes her head.

INSPECTOR REINKING (CONT'D)

Or who he might've owed money to?

WREN

Possibly some mobster he worked for. I'm really not sure.

INSPECTOR REINKING

I see. The money was hundred-dollar bills wrapped in ribbons with the Borgata logo.

WREN

Borgata?

INSPECTOR REINKING

Does that mean something to you, Ms. Colfax?

WREN

I, uh, recall Sinisa saying he was going to meet someone at the Borgata who wanted him to do a job.

INSPECTOR REINKING

Do you remember the contact's name?

WREN

(Hesitating)

No. I'm... I don't remember. I'm sorry.

INSPECTOR REINKING

C'mon. Think.

WREN

I... Can't remember.

(beat)

Can I go now, Inspector?

INSPECTOR REINKING

I suppose so.

He hands her his card.

INSPECTOR REINKING (CONT'D)

Here's my card. If you remember any details, especially the name of the guy Mr. Ražnatovi was supposed to meet at the Borgata, you give me a call.

WREN

I will, Inspector.

INSPECTOR REINKING

Thank you for coming down today. Where are you going for vacation?

WREN

I'm not sure I can go now.

Wren departs. Inspector Reinking addresses his companion Inspector.

INSPECTOR REINKING

I'd say she pretty much confirmed the money is a payoff to some mob criminal. Plant the RFID with the cash and let's see who comes looking for it.

INT. GERALD'S OFFICE - DAY

Gerald works at his desk. Janet calls to him over the intercom.

JANET

(Over intercom)

Gerald, there's a Ms. Francon here to see you. She doesn't have an appointment.

GERALD

(Into intercom)

Francon? Um, OK, tell her I'll be right out.

INT. PFALZGRAF OFFICES/LOBBY - DAY

Gerald enters the Lobby where Wren waits for him.

GERALD

Wren, uh, Ms. Francon. What are you doing here?

Wren is about to answer when Gerald, noticing Janet's interest in their conversation, cuts her off.

GERALD (CONT'D)

Let me take you to that property we discussed.

EXT. MADISON SQUARE PARK - DAY

Gerald and Wren sit together on a bench.

GERALD

I thought you'd be on your way to the apartment upstate, Wren. What's going on?

WREN

I got a call from the police this morning. Sinisa's dead.

GERALD

Dead? How'd that happen?

WREN

He fell down the stairs. He was stoned and must have slipped.

GERALD

Why did the police call you?

WREN

Gerald, do you know someone named Geraci?

GERALD

Why are you asking me that again?

WREN

Sinisa told me he met a man named Geraci at the Borgata Hotel. Someone who was paying him to do, well, something illegal I assume. The police found a lot of money in Sinisa's apartment. The money came from the Borgata.

GERALD

So?

WREN

Sinisa said Geraci wore a fancy suit. Kind of like the one you wore the other day. And then I found that chip in your pocket. Do you really not know who Geraci is?

GERALD

Listen to me. Sinisa's dead, Wren. I love you and want to marry you. I know a lot of people - some good, some bad. Would it really matter to you whether or not I knew this guy Geraci?

Wren contemplates the question, then strokes Gerald's face.

WREN

Not really.

GERALD

Then, I don't know him.

Wren embraces Gerald and kisses him.

WREN

I love you too, Gerald.

INT. TRAIN STATION - DAY

Gerald accompanies Wren and her luggage to the track where the train to the Hudson Valley awaits departure.

GERALD

I'm going to miss you more than I can imagine, Wren. But it's only for three months.

WREN

It'll feel like three years, I know it. What are you going to do without me, Ger?

GERALD

Cry a lot.

WREN

Oh, my.

GERALD

I also have to attend the trial of that cretin Crowder. It starts in a month and I'll have to give victim's testimony at some point. Shit. Do you believe that bastard now claims he wasn't there the first day of the shootings?

WREN

It's all so awful, Ger. I don't envy you at all. I'll think about you day and night.

GERALD

In three months, you'll be back in my arms. I'll introduce you to all my friends. We'll travel. It'll be great. I'm so happy.

An ANNOUNCER calls 'all-aboard'; Wren departs for the train.

INT. GERALD'S HOME - DAY

INSERT TITLE CARD: "SIX MONTHS LATER"

Gerald carries Wren across the threshold, followed by the Butler who schlepps a bunch of luggage.

GERALD

Welcome to your new abode, Mrs. Pfalzgraf. How about fixing us some drinks?

WREN

With pleasure, Mr. Pfalzgraf.

Gerald puts Wren down and she heads to the kitchen. Gerald paws through a pile of mail. He stops to open an important looking letter from the D.A. He reads it.

D.A. (V.O.)

Dear Mr. Pfalzgraf - As you are a victim of Silas Crowder's capital crimes, I want to be the first to inform you that Mr. Crowder's new lawyer has filed an appeal. The appeal is based on new evidence uncovered since the guilty verdict was rendered three months ago. Although I cannot go into specifics, the new evidence consists of rifle rounds found from the second day of the shootings that do not match those from the first day.

Wren exits the Kitchen and places a Gibson on the coffee table. Gerald watches her walk out onto the balcony. Her beautiful silhouette contrasts with that of Morcilla's we saw in the beginning. He goes back to reading the letter.

D.A. (V.O.) (CONT'D)

Mr. Crowder's lawyer intends to assert that his client is not guilty of the shooting that killed your wife and another victim. Rest assured that the New Jersey State Police and Warren County detectives will pursue with vigor the identity of a second shooter, should one exist, who was responsible for your wife's murder. If you have any questions or concerns, please contact my office.

Gerald returns the letter to the envelope. He admires Wren on the balcony for a moment. She turns and blows him a kiss.

GERALD (V.O.)

What a Prince would do now?

Gerald sips his Gibson, his face a mix of triumph and impending doom.

FADE OUT.

THE END

DOUBLE BLIND TEST

After a professional mediator is conned by identical twin businessmen who sought her help to resolve a dispute, she meets another woman in a suspiciously similar circumstance, and the two team up to take down the con artists.

Double Blind Test – A Treatment

Act I

THE time is the present; the place is New York City – JFK airport to be exact. Tracy Shepard, a stylish woman in her 40s paces anxiously among other would-be airline passengers waiting on standby to board an early morning flight to LA. As a professional mediator on contract to two companies doing business in the fast-growing nanotechnology industry, she is due this morning to lead a meeting to resolve a dispute between the feuding high-tech firms: NanoNano and PicoTech. Consistently organized and reliably punctual, Tracy has arrived late to the airport, and her tardiness has put her seat in jeopardy. After cajoling the gate agent unsuccessfully to pull a dead-heading flight attendant off the plane, Tracy is ready to throw a fit when a rumpled, slightly overweight middle-aged man intercedes and makes a chivalrous offer. He is Fischer Cuttbate, a passenger on the flight to LA. "I don't mean to butt in, but I couldn't help overhearing your predicament, ma'am. I'd be happy to trade my seat with you for one on the next flight. I'm in no hurry." Impressed by Fischer's uncommon generosity, and a bit smug that she triumphed over the gate agent in the end, Tracy swaps tickets with Fischer and boards the plane. Tracy waves to Fischer as she enters the jetway in time to make her important meeting as her good-Samaritan saunters off to an airport bar.

In LA, Tracy enters a conference room and is met by Ron from NanoNano, a large man suffering from acromegaly – a growth disorder that distorts his hands and face. Tracy mentions she almost missed the flight, and Ron offhandedly replies that he's aware of it. She's about to inquire as to how he knows, but she's interrupted. Tracy starts the meeting by introducing herself to the heads of the two companies: Matt Blankenshein of NanoNano, and Sumner Fogle of PicoTech. Matt is a confident, young entrepreneur accustomed to wealth and privilege, a man who sees no boundaries. Fogle is the opposite: a portly businessman in his sixties who cautiously, patiently worked his way to the top from the rank and file in staid companies of the past. Each man is accompanied by several executives, all men. The tensions in the conference room are high. Responding to a testosterone-fueled outburst contesting her credibility, Tracy makes it clear to all that this morning she's the one in charge. She declares, "I could ask all of you to lay your cocks on the table and I'll choose the winner with a ruler... or you can shut up for a nanosecond and let me outline a plan that no one will like but no one will completely despise either." Unaccustomed to being berated – by a woman no less – the men shut up and take their seats like chastened schoolboys.

Tracy presents a compelling case to NanoNano and PicoTech on the financial and strategic virtues of accepting her proposals. Both companies compete in the fast-growing nanotechnology industry, and while the two battle each other they are vulnerable to competitive encroachment by upstarts. Not yet ready to capitulate, the executives argue and sling insults across the table, as well as at Tracy, but her methodical, even-keeled temperament prevails. In the end, Matt and Fogle agree on Tracy's resolution; deep down both CEOs recognize NanoNano came out ahead. After Fogle and his team somberly leave the conference room, Matt congratulates Tracy on her tenacity. "Impressive, Ms. Shepard. You've got quite a pair for a lady." Tracy is unfazed by the cocky remark, for she's encountered Matt's type many times before in her mediation dealings: the brash young, full-a-cum, hot-shot son of privilege. Not that she finds Matt unattractive – quite the contrary. She remains cool. "I'm glad you're glad, Mr. Blankenshein." When Matt inquires about Tracy's next mediation gig, she replies playfully, "As I recall, it's a dispute over oil leases in Texas. Someone probably laid pipe where they shouldn't have." Tracy's double-entendre delights Matt. Later that evening as Tracy sips a fruity cocktail by the hotel pool, she takes a call from Matt who invites her to meet him the next day. She informs him that she's taking an early flight back to New York the next morning. Flattered and not wishing to burn any bridges, Tracy tells Matt, "Next time."

The following morning in LAX, Tracy walks onto a jet en route to New York City when to her surprise she encounters Fischer sitting in her row in first class. With more time now, she thanks him effusively for giving up his seat for her. She also emphasizes that tardiness is not one of her traits, blaming the late arrival on her usually-reliable limo driver. Fischer replies that giving up his seat really wasn't a big deal. "My meeting with the venture capitalists wasn't until the next day." The mention of "venture capitalists" intrigues Tracy who inquires to the nature of Fischer's business. He explains that he and his identical-twin brother Fletcher own a small bio-tech laboratory called RodCone that is developing a therapy for a rare eye disease: retinitis pigmentosa. Tracy is taken aback. This exact disease afflicts her widower father Charles, a former physics professor at Columbia University who is now completely blind and essentially house-bound in a modest New York apartment. She presses Fischer for information and learns that progress on the promising retinitis therapy is at a standstill because Fletcher opposes the infusion of cash from outside investors. Fischer expresses his irritation toward his brother's intransigence – especially because Fletcher is a hands-off partner who contributes little to the business operations, despite being a fifty-percent co-owner.

Concerned that a therapy capable of helping her father may never come to market, stymied by a dispute between the two brothers, Tracy offers her mediation services at no charge. Fischer insists on paying something for the effort, and he and Tracy settle on $1,000. After shaking on the deal, Fischer invites Tracy to come by the lab's office sometime to hear a presentation on the retinitis therapy.

Back in New York, Tracy visits her father Charles in his modest brownstone apartment in Upper Manhattan. Sitting together in the living room, Tracy recounts her conversation with Fischer regarding the retinitis therapy, including the news that the progress has stalled due to the fraternal dispute. Charles implores Tracy to help mediate the dispute to which she replies, "That's what I hope to do. I'm planning to go to Jersey in a few days to meet with the brother." Later, while tidying up the kitchen Tracy discovers an old pistol in a cabinet drawer. Fearful that her father might one day descend deeper into depression and commit an act of suicidal desperation, Tracy stows the pistol in her purse.

Some days later, having decided to accept Fischer's offer to hear a presentation Tracy makes a trip to the lab offices where she meets RodCone's business director and their chief scientist. Fischer greets Tracy and escorts her into a conference room. The chief scientist proceeds to explain the nature of the disease and the technology behind the therapy. After the presentation Fischer reiterates his concerns about financing, and predicts his recalcitrant brother will refuse to meet with Tracy. Tracy informs Fischer, "Would it surprise you if Fletcher already agreed to meet with me?" Fischer is impressed. As Tracy prepares to leave, the business director says he will email the presentation file to her.

Back in her stylish Sutton Place apartment, Tracy finally works up the nerve to deal with the pistol she confiscated from her father's kitchen drawer. Following the instructions she located on the internet, Tracy safely pops out the clip. Sadly, she places the pistol and the clip in her closet. Returning to her computer, Tracy sees that RodCone's business director has emailed the presentation file as promised. She prints it out.

The next day Tracy shows up at Fletcher's rustic bungalow in New Jersey. After making Tracy wait on the porch while he finishes a phone call Fletcher calls her in, only to treat her shabbily. Believing Tracy to be one of Fischer's tools of persuasion, Fletcher challenges her motivations and credentials. Even after Tracy portrays herself as merely a disinterested party seeking nothing more than a satisfactory compromise to the brothers' dispute, Fletcher behaves rudely, going so far to question her fascination with retinitis pigmentosa. "Why do you care so much about this? Does someone you know have retinitis or something?" Tracy snaps back at the dismissive provocation, putting Fletcher down hard with the facts of her own father's struggles with the disease. Tracy is about to storm out when Fletcher begs for forgiveness. He admits his demeanor was uncalled-for; his arrogance shamefully mounted as a shield against what he believed to be a crass ploy engineered by his brother. Haltingly, Fletcher implores Tracy to stay. Sensing contrition, or perhaps an opening to influence a weakened opponent, Tracy agrees.

Fletcher reveals some interesting news to Tracy: while Fischer and the lab scientists have been developing a therapy to address retinitis pigmentosa, Fletcher and an outside collaborator have been working on an actual cure for the insidious eye disease. Fletcher explains that a cure is better for the patient, but that a therapy which must be administered daily makes more money for the company. Fletcher contrasts his vision of producing a one-time cure with Fischer's greedy approach of milking suffering patients forever. And there in a nutshell is the real source of their dispute. He despises the venture capitalists that his brother wants to tap. "It's only money to them." Furthermore, Fletcher reveals his admittedly paranoid suspicion that Fischer is manipulating the lab's books to secure an advantageous position should the therapy prove a financial success. Tracy isn't sure what to make of things now. Perhaps her preconceived notions about Fletcher as a contrarian Luddite were misguided.

Noticing a vintage electric guitar in a stand, Tracy asks Fletcher whether he plays. He explains that he purchased the guitar many years ago. "It's the same kind that Keith Richards plays, a 1955 Telecaster." Fletcher proceeds to play the opening bars of a Rolling Stones tunes. Tracy is impressed by Fletcher's remarkable fidelity to the original.

On the train ride back to New York, Tracy thumbs through the presentation emailed to her previously. After reaching what should have been the end of the presentation, Tracy discovers a number of additional pages containing financial data marked "confidential." It appears they have been appended accidentally. Back home in front of her computer, Tracy concludes that Fletcher's concerns about corrupt finances were legitimate; someone at the lab has in fact been cooking the books to Fletcher's disadvantage. Determined to warn Fletcher of the deceit, Tracy arranges to meet him again.

Fletcher shows up the next day for lunch at a tony Manhattan restaurant. He's decidedly underdressed for the venue, sporting worn jeans and a flannel shirt. In contrast, Tracy arrives impeccably turned out. Tracy shows Fletcher her analysis of the confidential financial charts, but he seems distracted. He'd prefer to learn more about Tracy. Discussing art, Tracy tells Fletcher she owns an original Kandinsky painting. Tracy already knows that Fletcher is a fan of Frida Kahlo as evidenced by his derivative painting she observed on an easel in his bungalow. Fletcher reveals that his own mother went blind with glaucoma, and Tracy summarizes her academic background, but as time fritters away, she feels compelled to circle back to the subject of their lunch meeting: potential fraud at the lab. Finally, Fletcher concedes he should consult a forensic accountant.

A week later, Tracy is in hot West Texas mediating the dispute over oil leases she had previously mentioned to Matt. During a much-needed break from the childish behavior of the so-called professional company executives, she checks in with her assistant who informs her she received a call from someone at RodCone. Tracy returns the call and learns from the receptionist that Fischer is unable to pay the $1,000 invoice for her mediation services. "The FBI raided our company and froze our accounts." Tracy asks to speak to Fischer only to learn he's on the lam – no one knows where he and his business director are. Tracy is floored.

Back in New York, sorting through a pile of mail, Tracy opens a letter from Fletcher that contains a note and a check. In the note he explains that he took Tracy's advice, hired a forensic accountant and discovering the depth of fraud, sadly called in the FBI to investigate. When he learned the FBI froze the lab's accounts he felt obligated to make good on Fischer's agreement to pay Tracy $1,000 for her services.

Later, Tracy visits her father, but she's subdued. The stress of the Texas mediation shows through; furthermore, in light of the demise of the lab, she now regrets that she built up the promise of the retinitis therapy. Charles senses Tracy's downbeat mood and suggests she take a break from the rat-race. "Find a nice man. Fall in love." Charles's advice only deepens Tracy's sadness. Always working, constantly on the go, 40-something Tracy doesn't need to be reminded that she's long neglected her love life. She changes the subject, informing her father that the next mediation involves professional football – a dispute that includes a college player, his agent, and the New York Jets. Charles is more interested in the status of the retinitis therapy. She dances around the troubles facing the lab, noting that Fletcher has some better ideas about a real cure. "He just needs money to get it rolling," notes Tracy. Her father replies, "Money? That's all? Why don't you help him out, Tracy?" Tracy demurs. She's not an investment banker. But to keep her father hopeful, she quickly adds, "Believe me Dad, when Fletcher gets further along, I'd be happy to invest. Helping to run a real business with real products would be a breath of fresh air."

Riding home in her limo from her father's place Tracy receives a call from Fletcher. He rambles on a bit about being foolish for not confiding completely in Tracy. Finally, Fletcher gets to the point: he invites Tracy to dinner where he will explain everything to her. Although booked wall-to-wall with meetings and engagements, Tracy accepts his invitation.

Fletcher meets Tracy at an upscale Manhattan restaurant for dinner. In a complete turnabout from the sartorial debacle he suffered at lunch some weeks earlier with Tracy, Fletcher makes amends by showing up in a stylish suit and tie. Dinner is served, along with copious amounts of fine wine recommended by the sommelier. Fletcher and Tracy talk about the demise of the lab, the fate of Fischer, the future of the therapy. Despite the dismal state of affairs Fletcher is upbeat. With some prodding from Tracy, Fletcher finally reveals the reason he summoned her to meet with him. "I know I led you to believe I was just messing around, because I didn't want anyone to know about it, but I'm on the verge of a real cure." Up to this point, Tracy assumed Fletcher was light-years away from developing his visionary cure, but with success looking on the horizon, Tracy is ecstatic. Tracy learns that while Fischer was a profligate soul, Fletcher invested his inheritance and is now prepared to plow $1 million into the cure. Tracy assumes a mil is sufficient to proceed but Fletcher corrects her, explaining that with new hiring, equipment and insurance costs he will need another million. And he surprises Tracy with his intention to meet with a venture capitalist firm the following day, despite his stated revulsion for their practices. "It seems that's the only way research turns into a product," comments Fletcher, "unless you're a multi-billion-dollar pharmaceutical company." Before Tracy, now modestly inebriated, can react to what appears to be a risky plan, Fletcher compliments her well-defined legs and sexy feet. The remark catches her off-guard, and for the first time in decades, she feels like a bashful, little girl.

After dinner, Tracy and Fletcher stroll the periphery of Central Park. Tracy kisses him and invites him home to check out her . . . Kandinsky. In the throes of making love, Tracy spots a truly remarkable sight: a snake tattooed on Fletcher's penis.

The next morning, hungover and feeling quite washed out, Tracy struggles to get out of bed. Fletcher has already showered and gotten dressed. After fetching aspirins and water for Tracy, and helping her to the window for a breath of fresh air, he reminds her of his meeting with the venture capitalist firm. Tracy fears Fletcher is ill-equipped to go toe-to-toe with the VCs who will undoubtedly strike a deal that disadvantages him. She offers – insists, really – to accompany him to the meeting. Fletcher is relieved to know Tracy the mediation expert will be there to support him.

Later in the afternoon, Fletcher and Tracy meet the VCs in a mid-town hotel conference room where they receive a decidedly one-sided offer. As Tracy suspected, the VCs peg Fletcher for a business novice and try to play him for a patsy. They challenge him on the wisdom of developing a cure when a lifelong therapy seems more lucrative. Fletcher reacts angrily to this same line of reasoning that drove a wedge between him and Fischer. Sensing no worthy proposal is forthcoming, Tracy abruptly cuts the meeting off and sends the VCs packing. After the VCs leave, Tracy turns to Fletcher: "They'll rip you off." Fletcher is both angry and downbeat, at a loss now as to where he can secure funding. Tracy responds quickly, "From me, Fletch. Let me be your angel investor." The unexpected proposal from Tracy brightens Fletcher's demeanor ten-fold. "You'd loan me the money?" Fletcher asks. "No, Fletch, not loan. Invest. I would take an equity position." They resolve to get their lawyers together to hammer out a deal.

A week or so later, the big meeting commences. Fletcher's people propose a deal to Tracy that is essentially structured as a loan. Tracy reminds them that she's interested solely in taking an equity position. She gets an offer of stock, but Tracy counters with an unexpected proposal whereby the new company would instead grant her stock options that if exercised after an IPO could conceivably make her the majority shareholder. Fletcher's people recoil at the proposal, but she's not yet finished. She also demands a seat on the board. They counsel Fletcher on the risks, but when he signals his satisfaction with the arrangement, they back off. The deal is sealed.

The next day Tracy lunches with her lawyer to go over the finer points of the deal. Her lawyer notes that Fletcher's counsel wants to set up the first board meeting in a week, but Tracy reminds her that she'll be out of town in the coming weeks on the big football negotiation.

Tracy hits the road to conduct shuttle diplomacy among the

star college football player, his aggrieved agent, and the New York Jets front office. Things go poorly at first when the agent and the football player's father get into it, but Tracy senses from the interactions that the agent is the most vulnerable of the parties. Later she meets him one-on-one and makes a monetary offer for him to go away. In an indignant response the agent threatens to go to the press with a smear against the football player's father. Unimpressed, Tracy comes back with a claim that a techie she knows has already hacked into the agent's computer and found nothing that would support the agent's threat. She adds that the hacker, however, did discover some child pornography on his laptop. The agent vehemently denies it, but he soon understands that Tracy has the tools to make life pretty miserable for the agent if he doesn't capitulate. The mediation quickly wraps up when the agent grudgingly accepts some go-away money.

Act II

Back home at last, Tracy prepares for the board meeting. She's excited about getting the operation underway – and about seeing Fletcher again. After Tracy's driver drops her off at the lab building, Tracy notes the piss-poor condition of the lobby. She trudges up the stairs to the second floor and finds the door to the lab offices removed. She peers inside and finds the lab office a mess; it looks like a gut renovation is in progress. A spooky cleaning lady informs Tracy that the previous tenants left abruptly and the owner is prepping the space for a new tenant. Shocked, Tracy runs down the stairs, nearly tripping in her sexy heels, and heads for a nearby bistro where she orders a stiff drink and phones her lawyer. Within minutes her lawyer calls back with disturbing news: the phone numbers for Fletcher's people have been disconnected, the lab office had been rented month-to-month for the past four months, and Fletcher's bungalow in Jersey is available to lease. Realizing the worst, Tracy instructs her lawyer to collect as much information she can gather. She hangs up, gulps her drink and simmers at the notion that she's just been scammed out of $1 million.

Tracy visits the FBI where she lays out for an agent the history of events leading up the scam. In the course of recalling the details it suddenly occurs to her that the financial information she thought she had received "in error" from RodCone's business director had in fact been planted purposefully to drive her to sympathize with Fletcher's situation. Angry, she recounts the story for the agent, including the fact that the FBI had raided the lab. The agent runs a quick computer check then informs Tracy that no such raid took place. The whole thing was a set up. The agent has Tracy work with a composite artist to develop a likeness of the twin brothers. In the course of developing a composite drawing, the artist questions whether Fletcher and Fischer were the same person. Tracy is taken aback, but she grudgingly acknowledges she has never seen them together. When the artist asks if the con man has any distinguishing marks such as a tattoo, Tracy, too ashamed to reveal the snake on his penis, quietly replies, "None that I know of."

Tracy's less-than-encouraging experience at the offices of the FBI drives her to hire a private investigator. In her apartment with the PI, Tracy recounts the details of the sordid con game and makes it clear that she expects results from the PI. She offers a bonus for quick resolution. Like the composite artist, the PI surmises that the "identical twins" are actually one man. He goes on to postulate that Fletcher/Fischer employed a sizable gang to pull off the scam, including hiring people to take seats on the plane to LA the day she met Fischer to ensure first class was sold out when she arrived. Adding to the grim situation, he suggests possible involvement of her limo driver which would explain her uncharacteristically tardy arrival at the airport that fateful day. Most disturbing for Tracy though is the PI's belief that someone connected to one or both of the nanotechnology companies in LA was part of the scheme. The monumental extent of the scam saddens and inflames Tracy. As Tracy escorts the PI to the door, she feels compelled to provide an added detail she'd kept from the FBI. "One more thing I forgot to mention. Fletcher has a snake tattooed on his… um, penis". Trying not to react inappropriately, the diligent PI makes a note and departs. Tracy crumples in tears.

Time has passed without progress on the case. Tracy has lost her burning desire to mediate all sorts of disputes, preferring to walk the park, do crossword puzzles, spend time reading in quaint bistros in her tony neighborhood. With income flat-lining and her bank account depleted to the tune of $1 million, Tracy puts her beloved Kandinsky on the auction block. A visit to her father's place is somber. She hints that things are a bit down for the moment due to a bad investment decision. Always concerned for his daughter, Charles advises a stiff-upper lip.

Tracy would rather make things right, suggesting a vague desire to seek and exact revenge. Back home after the visit with her father Tracy speaks to the PI who has no new news to offer. Discouraged, Tracy peruses news on the internet. She perks up upon spotting a small business item: NanoNano, Matt's technology company, has successfully gone IPO.

The next morning, Matt takes a call from none other than Tracy – the woman who helped him resolve the ugly dispute with his competitor; the woman to whom he granted some early stock shares as compensation for her efforts. A sum now worth tens of thousands of dollars. After a bit of small talk, Matt invites Tracy to come to the new headquarters relocated to San Diego for an IPO party where she can meet the executive team. Recalling her PI's assertion that one or more people employed by the warring companies might be part of the scam, Tracy gladly accepts the invitation. It's an opportunity to ferret out some intel first-hand. She also looks forward to seeing Matt again; she felt some chemistry with the younger man during the LA mediation. And she caught him ogling her legs – a sure sign that romance is in the cards.

Seated with Matt and a handful of company executives at the party, Tracy makes mental notes of the topics her table-mates discuss, but nothing pointing to a lead is forthcoming. As it turns out, every person at the table is a frat-boy chum of Matt's or an arm-candy girlfriend – with the exception of Marilyn, Matt's VP of Human Resources. As the discussion moves to the vagaries of the stock market, Marilyn jumps at the opportunity to insert herself into the conversation. She commiserates with the others about her under-water stock options from a previous employer, but she remains optimistic for she is about to invest in a small biotech firm working on a therapy for acromegaly which could be a goldmine if successful. She mentions that Ron – the large man suffering from the disease whom Tracy first met the day of the mediation – brought the idea to her. Marilyn continues, referring to the scientist seeking her investment. "Calvin is close to a cure for acromegaly, but his twin brother won't help him get the money to move it along. His brother wants to develop a pill you have to take every day. Calvin's ready to go to clinical trial but he's stuck. He doesn't really want to deal with VC's."

Astonished to hear a tale eerily similar to the one that nearly ruined her life, Tracy can't help blurting out, "Marilyn, did this Calvin guy have a snake tattooed on his co...?" She stops just short of making a complete fool of herself at the table, belatedly substituting the word "collar" for "cock." Gobsmacked, Marilyn says nothing. Matt teases, "I thought you were going to say 'cock.' A tattoo on the dude's cock." The guests snicker while Tracy ardently denies the assertion. Despite the teasing, Matt is attracted to the stylish, older Tracy and he makes a point to get some private face-time with her after dinner. He mentions that he read an article about her in *Forbes* magazine which portrayed Tracy as a cunning, effective negotiator – even a bit Machiavellian. It's a trait Matt finds sexy. "I bet you could persuade a man to do anything you want," posits Matt, suggesting she's angling for a seat on the board. She responds that, in fact, the company could use someone like her on the board.

Impressed with Tracy's confidence and assertiveness, Matt invites her for a ride in his yacht the next day, but she must decline (again) as she plans to fly out early the next morning.

Tracy visits the women's room on her way out of the restaurant and runs into Marilyn who sheepishly confides that, yes, Calvin has a snake tattooed on his, um, cock. The women decide to retreat to a quiet bar to talk through this bizarre coincidence. Tracy explains her situation but Marilyn is reluctant to accept the idea that she too is the target of an elaborate scam. To express the full gravity to Marilyn, Tracy provides details, including the painful revelation of her own loss of $1 million. Tracy describes some of Fletcher's quirky characteristics that bear a remarkable similarity to Calvin's behavior – including his guitar-playing prowess – which convinces Marilyn that the two men are one and the same. But whereas Marilyn is happy simply to have avoided a catastrophe, Tracy calls upon her to assist in the takedown of the con man. Marilyn demurs but Tracy is insistent. After Tracy learns that Marilyn was set to meet Calvin in the near future for dinner in Jersey to make a six-figure investment, she insists Marilyn go through with the plan. In this way Tracy can re-establish contact with her nemesis. Marilyn resists at first, but finally agrees to help when Tracy articulately elucidates the evils of letting a scumbag like Calvin continue his nefarious ways. Marilyn asks, "How are you going to get him to confess?" Tracy replies coldly, "I'm a professional negotiator, Marilyn. I'll negotiate for it."

Still in San Diego, Tracy calls Matt to let him know she decided to stay in town after all. Reinvigorated by the hope that she may finally take down Fletcher, and sensing potential romantic chemistry with Matt, Tracy proposes a rendezvous. Matt eagerly invites Tracy for a ride on his 130-foot Astondoa yacht. They visit Catalina and cruise by Coronado Island. Tracy remarks that the Hotel Del Coronado reminds her of Billy Wilder's movie "Some Like it Hot." The mere mention of the classic comedy encourages Matt to go off on the genius of Wilder. Tracy notes that her father is also a devout fan of the influential Hollywood director. A promising first bond is formed between Tracy and Matt. Knowing Matt has read the article in *Forbes* magazine about her, Tracy feels obligated to counter the cut-throat image portrayed in the magazine. She doesn't want Matt to draw the wrong conclusion about her personality. For the first time, Tracy allows her vulnerability to come to the surface. Matt gently places his finger on Tracy's lips, cutting her off. He leans forward and kisses her, then leads her to the master cabin.

Act III

Some weeks later, as planned, Marilyn has dinner with Calvin, and per Tracy's directions Marilyn has seen to it that her companion is thoroughly drunk. In his inebriated condition, Calvin will be easier for Tracy to deal with later.

Back at Calvin's home, he fumbles with his keys before finally stumbling in. Marilyn looks plaintively over her shoulder toward the driveway, then follows Calvin in, closing the door behind her. Calvin heads for the bedroom, stripping off his clothes as he weaves through the hallway. Marilyn goes into the bathroom, locks the door and calls Tracy. "Where are you?" whispers Marilyn. "Right where I'm supposed to be – parked next to your car." Marilyn enters Calvin's darkened bedroom where he's sprawled out naked, waiting for the services of his woman. But instead of hopping into bed, Marilyn informs the drunken Calvin that she has to go. She scoops up his clothing and makes for the door. Calvin slurs some words of protest, but he's too drunk to mount a case to convince Marilyn to stay. As Marilyn marches out the door Calvin calls out, "What about the money?" And after she leaves the house, he mumbles to himself, "What the fuck's wrong with that bitch?" to which Tracy, standing tall in the doorway, retorts, "The better question would be 'what the fuck is wrong with you'?"

Perhaps expecting his mark to show up one day to vent anger and seek recompense, Calvin (who is also Fletcher) casually informs Tracy that the money he scammed from her has long ago been split up and spent. Lying in bed in the dark, he asks her to lock the door on her way out. Tracy has other ideas. She flips on the light which temporarily blinds Fletcher. A moment later, when his eyes can tolerate the light, he sees Tracy pointing a pistol at him. It's the pistol she confiscated from her father's kitchen drawer months earlier. Suddenly, Fletcher is a bit more compliant. Given that the money is gone, he asks what she expects him to do. Tracy is ready with an answer. She tosses a paper bag onto the bed which bounces, suggesting heft. Fletcher takes up the bag and removes a pair of sheet metal cutters. As Fletcher confusedly handles the cutters, Tracy notes matter-of-factly, “I read somewhere that Keith Richards' middle finger is insured for one point six million.” Suddenly it dawns on Fletcher: Tracy expects him to lop off his finger as penance for his sins. He pleads with her but she’s adamant. “Put the fucking shears on your fucking finger. Now!” Fletcher complies, then pukes all over himself. As he stands there totally vulnerable, Tracy lays out the deal: cut off his finger or confess to his crimes on the video camera she has brought along. Fletcher begs, but when Tracy pushes him to cut off his finger, he becomes indignant. He’s thinking about calling her bluff. He taunts her, “You fell for a scam like a stupid schoolgirl.” Tracy takes the indictment personally and screams at Fletcher, “Cut off your fucking finger now or I will kill you! Or you can confess your--” She never gets to complete the demand, for Fletcher lunges at Tracy under the presumption that the gun ain’t loaded. In fact, Tracy also presumes it’s unloaded – that it’s just an intimidating prop she disarmed after taking it from her father’s house. But in an involuntary reaction to Fletcher’s sudden movement, Tracy squeezes the trigger and delivers a round through his throat. A round that she had no idea was present in the chamber when she popped out the clip. As Fletcher’s life wheezes out of the bullet hole, Tracy runs to the bathroom and throws up. When she regains her composure, Tracy slowly reenters Fletcher’s bedroom and observes the corpse splayed out, his tattooed penis exposed like a taunt. The vision enrages her. Tracy impetuously grinds the point of her stiletto heel into Fletcher’s shriveled scrotum. The act serves to inspire a plan for escape. Tracy rushes about Fletcher’s house wiping off doorknobs and furniture. When she’s convinced that evidence of her presence there has been thoroughly expunged, Tracy heads to her car where Marilyn has deposited Fletcher's clothes, including the pair of pants containing his cell phone. Tracy bolts the scene and drives down the dark country road. After a mile, she pulls off into a pine grove. Tracy performs some jumping jacks, then makes a furtive 911 call using Fletcher's cell phone. Breathing hard and adding a little-girl lilt to her voice, Tracy explains to the 911 operator that she's just escaped from a rapist's house after shooting him with his own gun. She adds that she's now lost in the woods and believes that the wounded rapist is in pursuit. The operator instructs her to keep the phone active: "We can track your location with it." Concerned that she might be hanging on too long, Tracy gives up a phony name then drops the still-active cell phone onto the pine needles. She gets back in her car and exits the scene. On her way back from Jersey to the Upper East Side of Manhattan, Tracy makes a detour where she tosses Fletcher's wallet onto the curb of a street in a dicey neighborhood, hoping to confuse law enforcement. Eventually, she crosses the George Washington Bridge where in mid-span she tosses her father's pistol out the window into the depths of the Hudson River.

Back in her apartment, Tracy examines her body as though looking for a wound. In the background, water fills the bathtub. Tracy climbs into the bathtub with a glass of vodka. Relaxed finally, she leaves a message on Matt's phone: "I miss you. Call me when you can. I want to see you again soon. I need a hug."

The next morning the news of the mysterious young girl who shot a would-be rapist is all over the TV. The coverage comports with the circumstances that Tracy strived to engineer.

Back in San Diego, Tracy the shareholder discusses company strategy with Matt the CEO. She raises the topic of a potential new market for Matt to consider – cosmetics made using nanotechnology – and takes the opportunity to raise a concern in Matt's mind over the general lack of female representation in his executive ranks. "You may want to promote one of your women execs in advance of entering the female-oriented cosmetics market," advises Tracy, knowing full well that Marilyn is the sole candidate in NanoNano. Matt agrees to look into it. Tracy leaves Matt to meet up with Marilyn. The last time Tracy and Marilyn were together was at Fletcher's house in Jersey the night Tracy plotted to extract a confession from him. That's what Marilyn thinks happened. Tracy is on her way to break the shocking news to Marilyn about the demise of poor Fletcher/ Calvin, the vile con-man.

Tracy arrives at the restaurant to find Marilyn at the bar enjoying a cocktail. Tracy orders a stiff one. Marilyn is anxious to hear all about the juicy details of Fletcher's drunken confession and the subsequent investigative actions of the FBI. She blathers on for a minute, imagining the look on Fletcher's face when Tracy dropped in on him with video camera in tow. Finally, Tracy interrupts. "Things didn't go exactly quite as planned. He's dead. I shot him. I had to shoot him." As Tracy expected, Marilyn freaks out. "You know I didn't want to get involved from the beginning. Now you've connected me to a homicide." Tracy explains how the police believe an anonymous girl killed Fletcher, and that so far things look as though the story will stick. Tracy adds that everything will be OK as long as Marilyn cooperates by staying cool and keeping her mouth shut, but Marilyn is not satisfied. She wants something from Tracy. "You need my cooperation? OK, you're a big-time negotiator, Tracy. Negotiate for it."

Tracy, expecting this type of pushback from Marilyn, supplies something of value in exchange for Marilyn's cooperation. Tracy had already planted the idea in Matt's head. "What do you know about nanotechnology and cosmetics, Marilyn?"

Back in New York, Tracy, Matt and Tracy's father Charles watch an old Billy Wilder movie – "Ace in the Hole." After it's over and Tracy retreats to the kitchen, Matt hands Charles a large engagement ring he intends to give to Tracy the next time she's in San Diego. Charles is overcome with joy, as he envisions his busy, type-A daughter finally settling down to experience happiness with someone who loves her.

One month later, Matt hosts another big dinner in San Diego for his employees and their guests to celebrate a superb year for the company. The band plays as the guests dine on fine cuisine. Tracy, Marilyn and several execs sit with Matt at the head table. One of the execs notes that Ron, who had departed NanoNano to take a job with PicoTech, had just been arrested for having child pornography on his company computer. Everyone at the table, with the exception of Tracy, is shocked at the man's ignoble downfall.

Matt taps a glass, capturing the attention of the room. The band stops playing. Matt informs the audience that NanoNano has just signed a huge contract with the government which will ensure healthy financial results for the foreseeable future. He adds that the cash flow will enable NanoNano to pursue research on rare eye diseases. The guests applaud; Tracy smiles with satisfaction. Matt then calls on Marilyn to stand. "I'm thrilled to announce that Marilyn Jenkins has been promoted to General Manager of our soon-to-be operational facility in Malaysia where we will commence our cosmetics operation." Marilyn accepts the applause from her peers. Matt goes on to encourage anyone who wants to speak to Marilyn to do so now. "Marilyn leaves for Kuala Lumpur tomorrow morning and we won't be seeing her much around here after that." Tracy smiles imperceptibly at the notion that Marilyn will soon be on the other side of the world, out of sight and out of mind.

After dinner Tracy retreats to the women's room and like before, she spots Marilyn in the mirror behind her. Marilyn, a bit tipsy and visibly agitated, declares, "I earned my promotion, Tracy. I suggested the idea of cosmetics with Matt a long time ago, just so you know." Tracy couldn't care less. But when Marilyn blurts out, "I don't want anyone thinking you had something to do with my promotion, like payback for saving your ass on that Calvin thing," Tracy loses it. She checks under the stalls for the tell-tale feet of others who may be in the restroom, finding no one. Irritated at Marilyn's loose lips, Tracy upbraids her. "You're a General Manager now, Marilyn. You got what you wanted. Don't blow it." Marilyn needs to know that Tracy believes she earned the promotion, but Tracy rebuffs the entreaty. Instead she strongly advises Marilyn to keep her trap shut, for which she will be rewarded. When Marilyn inquires as to the source of Tracy's ability to deliver rewards, Tracy announces that Matt has proposed marriage. Not only that, Tracy is taking a seat on the board. With that, she leaves Marilyn dumbfounded in the ladies' room.

A supremely satisfied Tracy dances with her dashing young fiancé as the company party winds down, secure in the knowledge that Marilyn will soon be half a world away.

Epilog

A year later, Matt and Tracy's father watch TV together. Wearing thick glasses as an aid to his partially recovered eyesight – thanks to innovations pioneered at NanoNano – Tracy's father enjoys seeing a movie for the first time in years. Just as Tracy brings in some sandwiches for her men, her phone rings. It's her former PI with some startling news: he's come upon a lead in the con game perpetrated upon Tracy. He's identified a murder victim with curious tattoo of a snake on his penis. Tracy tries to persuade the PI to leave the case alone as she no longer cares about it – at least that's what she wants to convey. Instead, Tracy's resistance to pursuing the lead strikes the PI as somewhat strange. She insists he drop the investigation, so he hangs up – but not before leaving her with the distinct impression he intends to continue pursuing leads regardless.

Tracy takes a seat with her father and new husband as they watch "Double Indemnity," Billy Wilder's superb tale of connivance and downfall. Her mind is elsewhere – will the PI connect the dots? What else can she do but fret and wait? She asks her father the name of the movie. "Double Indemnity," he replies, to which Matt adds casually, yet ominously, "A scam leads to murder."

DOUBLE BLIND TEST

FADE IN.

INT. JFK AIRPORT - DAY

A female GATE AGENT stands behind an airline counter scanning the floor for stragglers, one of whom is FISCHER, an ordinary looking white man in his 30s. A few PASSENGERS on standby shift around anxiously. The Gate Agent makes an announcement over the intercom.

GATE AGENT

(Into microphone)

This will serve as the final boarding call for Delta flight 701, nonstop to Los Angeles, departing at seven o'clock from Gate B20. All ticketed passengers should proceed at once to the gate.

The moment the Gate Agent takes her thumb off the mike, TRACY gets in her face. Tracy, a tall, professional-looking woman in her 30s wears a stylish black suit cut above the knee, and expensive heels that show off her toned legs.

TRACY

You've got to let me on that flight. I absolutely have to be in LA by noon. I'm mediating a dispute--

The Gate Agent turns away, disinterested in listening to the pleas of a latecomer.

GATE AGENT

--Impossible.

TRACY

I know you're deadheading at least one stewardess. Give me her seat and send her on the next flight.

The Gate Agent serves Tracy a look.

GATE AGENT

We don't call them stewardesses anymore.

Tracy glowers at the Gate Agent. Before tempers flare out of proportion, Fischer steps up to the counter. In heels, Tracy is inches taller.

FISCHER

I don't mean to butt in, but I couldn't help overhearing your predicament, ma'am. I'd be happy to trade my seat with you for one on the next flight. I'm in no hurry.

TRACY

Really? Oh, my. That's very generous of you sir, but I wouldn't want you to miss your flight.

FISCHER

It really is no trouble, ma'am, no troub--

Tracy extends her hand which Fischer shakes.

TRACY

--Tracy Shepard.

FISCHER

OK, Tracy. No trouble at all. I know all about deadlines and business commitments and that kind of stuff. Take my place, I insist.

TRACY

Why, I can't thank you enough, Mister--

FISCHER

--Cuttbate, Fischer Cuttbate. I go by Fish.

TRACY

Really? Fish? I mean, thank you so much... Fish.

Familiar with how rich people always get their way, the Gate Agent dangles the boarding pass for Tracy to grab. Tracy walks to the jetway and just before disappearing waves to Fischer. Fischer waves back and walks toward an airport bar.

INT. CONFERENCE ROOM/LA - DAY

Two groups of BUSINESSMEN mill around on opposite sides of a long conference table, talking, drinking coffee, eating bagels and donuts. Members of each group occasionally glance with contempt at their counterparts across the table. Tracy is at the head of the conference table, checking her watch. RON, a big man suffering from acromegaly approaches.

RON

Ms. Shepard? I'm Ron Slomsky, CFO for NanoNano. We're glad you could make it out here on time.

TRACY

So am I. I almost missed the flight.

RON

That's what I heard.

(beat)

I mean--

TRACY

--You did? Who told--

MATT, late-20s, handsome, stylish haircut, elegantly casual clothes, interrupts.

MATT

--Hi. Matt Blankenschein, CEO and founder of NanoNano. Can we get started?

TRACY

Let's go.

Matt addresses the crowd.

MATT

OK, everyone. Take a seat and try not to defile one another. You all know why we're here. This is Tracy Shepard. She's going to mediate the dispute between our companies. I'm Matt Blankenschein of NanoNano and this fine gentleman...

Matt gestures to FOGLE, a 60-year-old portly businessman sporting a comb-over.

MATT (CONT'D)

...is Sumner Fogle, Chief of PicoTech.

FOGLE nods to the rest of the Businessmen.

MATT (CONT'D)

You wanna say anything, Sumner?

FOGLE

Just this: Can we stop fucking around and get on with business?

TRACY

OK. Thanks for that input, Mr. Fogle.

Tracy addresses the audience.

TRACY (CONT'D)

Gentlemen, together you own 65 percent of the nano-technology market. Congratulations. Of course, you want more. Greed is good, right? That's what they say in the movies.

(beat)

Let me tell you something: lust is more powerful than greed. Greed clarifies, but lust compels. The greedy die with the gout, the lustful go out in the saddle. While you all sit here in this stuffy conference room, enjoying artisan bagels and fair-trade coffee, your competition - however meager at the moment - is chasing after your clients with a steely hard-on. Lusting after your business.

The Businessmen look around uncomfortably at each other. Did she just say "steely hard-on?"

TRACY (CONT'D)

The world of nanotechnology is moving fast. You're losing share while you lock heads over patent violations, employee poaching, slimy marketing campaigns--

FOGLE

(Points at Matt)

--Just so you know, it was NanoNano that escalated this when they hacked into our database and stole the design specs--

BUSINESSMAN #1

--That's bullshit and you know it, Fogie! One of the assholes you fired posted those specs on Slashdot--

TRACY

--Come now, gentlemen, that's not how you're going to resolve--

BUSINESSMAN #1

--Yeah!? And what do you propose, Mrs. Mediator?

TRACY

Well, you could all lay your cocks on the table and I'll choose the winner with a ruler... or you can shut up for a nanosecond and let me outline a plan that no one will like but no one will completely despise either.

Tracy scans the Businessmen sternly, leaning forward supported by both hands on the table. The Businessmen sit back ready to hear the proposal.

TRACY (CONT'D)

Good. Now let's look at the net present value of the damage each of you will inflict on each other absent a resolution.

Tracy presses a button, projecting a graph on a screen.

TRACY (CONT'D)

The y-axis is in millions of dollars.

DISSOLVE TO:

INT. CONFERENCE ROOM/LA - DAY (LATER)

Without sound Tracy lectures the Businessmen who then engage in a vigorous argument. Tracy balls them out but two of them begin jostling. Tracy shakes her head and smirks at the childish behavior. Ron separates them and fellow Businessmen lead the two jostling fools back to their seats. Tracy resumes her presentation. Fogle walks to a corner of the Conference Room and lights a cigarette. Matt follows him. The two begin a conversation.

INT. CONFERENCE ROOM/LA - DAY (LATER)

Tracy sits near Matt who surreptitiously ogles her feet. Fogle fiddles with a pen.

TRACY

OK, so it all comes down to NanoNano licensing a couple patents as penance for...

(Quotes with fingers)

... "borrowing" the design specs from PicoTech. No more talk about stealing.

MATT

Listen. It's been a very long day. What's a couple patents between enemies. I'm not going to speak for Sumner, but he and I--

FOGLE

--You're gonna speak for me anyway, aren't you Blankenshein?

MATT

Me and Sumner are copacetic - right Summy?

Fogle grimaces, then relents.

FOGLE

Shit. Yeah. Copa-fucking-cetic.

TRACY

Fantastic. Shake on it.

After the two exchange a perfunctory handshake, Fogle and his team of Businessmen beat a hasty exit. Matt lingers by Tracy.

MATT

Impressive, Ms. Shepard. Tracy. You've got quite a pair for a lady.

TRACY

Well, I guess I'll take that as a compliment.

MATT

If someone told me yesterday that I'd be shaking hands today with that mick leprechaun, I'd' have shit in his hat. But it's a good deal. Hell, I'm glad the whole fucking episode is finally over.

TRACY

I'm glad you're glad, Mr. Blankenshein.

MATT

Matt.

(beat)

Yeah, I'm glad it's over. Now we can proceed to Defcon One - nuclear winter for PicoTech. What's next for you, Tracy?

TRACY

Me? Go back to the hotel. Shower off the coating of testosterone. Have a cocktail by the pool.

MATT

No, I meant--

TRACY

--My next mediation? As I recall, it's a dispute over oil leases in Texas. Someone probably laid pipe where they shouldn't have.

Matt grins.

EXT. FANCY LA HOTEL - NIGHT

Casually dressed, Tracy lounges with a cocktail by a lighted pool as swells swim and carouse. At a cabana nearby, FAMOUS MOVIE PEOPLE argue over the terms of a movie contract. Tracy shakes her head at what seems to be a looming disagreement seeking a resolution. Her cell phone RINGS.

TRACY

Tracy Shepard.

(beat)

Oh, hello, Matt.

(beat)

Tomorrow? I'd love to, but I'm flying back to New York early.

(beat)

OK. I promise. Next time I'm out this way. Yes. I will. Thanks.

INT. JET - DAY

Tracy walks onto the Jet bound for JFK looking sharp and confident. A slouching, rumpled-looking Fischer sits in the aisle seat of first class reading a newspaper. Tracy is surprised to see him.

TRACY

Fisch...er? Is that you?

Delighted to see Tracy again, Fischer folds his newspaper and straightens up from his slouch.

FISCHER

Well, good morning, Tracy. How are you? Did you make it on time to your meeting the other day?

Fischer stands to let Tracy pass in front of him.

TRACY

Excellent. And yes, thanks to you I made my meeting.

FISCHER

(Sniffing)

Mmmm... Van Cleef and Arpels?

TRACY

That's right. Very good.

Tracy takes her seat by the window.

TRACY (CONT'D)

I can't tell you enough how grateful I am to you for giving up your seat. You're my white knight, Fischer. I wish I could make it up to you.

FISCHER

Think nothing of it. My meeting with the venture capitalists wasn't until the next day. And please, call me Fish.

Tracy kicks off her designer shoes. Fischer notes the fine definition of her feet.

TRACY

You know, Fish, I travel all over the country for my business, and that was the first time I almost got bumped. My driver overslept and I got to the airport just before the flight took off.

(beat)

I wouldn't want you to think I'm some kind of a scatterbrain.

FISCHER

Hey, it can happen to anyone, Tracy. Bottom line: you got on the plane and made your meeting. Someone else might've caved in and waited on standby - or worse, gone home and cried about it. Your perseverance paid off.

Tracy smiles in appreciation for the compliment.

INT. JET - DAY (LATER)

Tracy listens to music. Fischer reads "A Life Decoded." Tracy studies the book cover, then pulls out the earbuds.

TRACY

You had a meeting with venture capitalists? What sort of business are you in, Fischer?

Fischer puts down the book.

FISCHER

I co-own a biotech firm with my twin brother Fletcher. RodCone Laboratories. I'm sure you've never heard of it.

Tracy shakes her head.

FISCHER (CONT'D)

We're developing a therapy for a rare ophthalmologic affliction, and so far, all the preliminary test results are encouraging.

Fischer retrieves a business card and hands it to Tracy.

FISCHER (CONT'D)

We're about ready to start clinical trials. That's when the serious financing is critical, hence my meeting with the VCs.

TRACY

What's the rare eye affliction?

FISCHER

Retinitis pigmentosa.

TRACY

My God!

FISCHER

It's a progressive retinal dystrophy.

TRACY

I know!

FISCHER

It starts with tunnel vision and usually leads to total blindness.

TRACY

I know! My father has it. He's essentially blind now, poor man. He used to teach Physics at Columbia. But now...

Feeling weepy, Tracy turns aside a moment before continuing.

TRACY (CONT'D)

I'm so excited you're working on a cure. What kind of results have you seen so far?

FISCHER

Well, first off, it's not a cure. It's a therapy. Patients would have to take a pill every day. But back to your question: the results are remarkable. Up to 75 percent regeneration of retinal cells.

TRACY

That sounds impressive. So, what did the VCs say, Fish? When will you start the clinical trials?

FISCHER

That's the problem. My brother Fletch doesn't want to bring new investors into the business. He's worried they'll take over and interfere with the research.

TRACY

Oh, no.

FISCHER

He means well I suppose, but he has no concept of what it takes to launch a new drug into the market. The VCs are hot for the project, but Fletch won't budge. And without the funding, we're stuck.

TRACY

Why don't you bring in the VCs anyway? Go around your brother.

FISCHER

Fletch and I inherited the business from our father. He set it up so we each own exactly 50 percent of the shares. I can't make a major decision like bringing new investors in without Fletch's vote.

TRACY

I see.

FISCHER

What really pisses me off - excuse me - what irritates me most is that Fletch is completely hands-off. He never gets involved in day-to-day operations. I haven't even seen him in three months.

Silence as Fischer sulks and Tracy mulls the possibilities.

TRACY

Y'know, Fish, I'm a pretty good professional mediator. I help resolve differences for a living. Perhaps I could be of assistance in getting your brother to change his mind. I really would hate for progress on your new drug to grind to a halt.

(beat)

Besides, I owe you one for giving up your seat the other day.

FISCHER

Really, Tracy, you don't owe--

TRACY

--I want to help Fischer. I really do. My father... Let me help you on this.

FISCHER

Well, OK. That would be great.

TRACY

Perfect.

FISCHER

I bet top mediators like you charge more than the value of a first-class seat. Let me at least pay you something.

TRACY

That's not--

FISCHER

--I insist.

TRACY

Well, if it'll make you feel better, let's say... $1,000?

FISCHER

Deal!

TRACY

My favorite word.

EXT. JFK AIRPORT - DAY

Fischer is on the sidewalk talking on a cell phone. Tracy struts out of the airport pulling a stylish suitcase and heads directly for her waiting limo where a DRIVER stands by the open back door. Fischer spots Tracy and runs to her just as she steps into the limo.

FISCHER

Tracy!

TRACY

(Startled)

Fish?

FISCHER

I was wondering, Tracy, if you'd like to see a presentation on the eye drug. I'd love to tell you all about it. Interested?

TRACY

Sure. That'd be great.

FISCHER

Alright. I'll set it up.

The Limo drives off into a sea of yellow cabs.

INT. LIMO (TRAVELING) - DAY

Relaxed in the back seat, Tracy speaks on the phone.

TRACY

(Into phone)

I can't go to Texas next week. I have that other thing.

(beat)

Alright. Pull the base research on the shale oil contracts. What else, Carla?

Chuckling, she cups the phone and calls to her Driver.

TRACY (CONT'D)

Yusef, take the Whitestone.

(Into phone)

The owner of the New York Jets? Player contract issue, right? OK. Did you tell my father I'm coming over?

(beat)

Thanks, Carla.

EXT. WHITESTONE BRIDGE - DAY

Tracy's Limo crosses the bridge.

EXT. PARKING GARAGE - DAY

Fischer shuffles to a crappy car covered in pigeon droppings and throws a piece of luggage into the truck. He hops into the driver's seat, turns the key and hears a series CLICKS Fischer bangs the steering wheel with both hands.

EXT. DAD'S BROWNSTONE - DAY

Tracy's limo pulls to the curb in front of DAD's Brownstone. The Driver opens the door and Tracy proceeds up the steps to the door. She pulls keys from her purse, unlocks the door and enters.

INT. DAD'S BROWNSTONE/KITCHEN - DAY

Tracy walks in and places her purse on the kitchen counter.

TRACY

Dad? It's me. Where are you?

O.S. a toilet FLUSHES followed by the SOUND of water running then a THUMP of an object falling on the floor.

DAD (O.S.)

Damn it!

TRACY

Dad? Are you alright?

INT. DAD'S BROWNSTONE/BATHROOM - DAY

Dad stands at an old-fashioned pedestal sink gripping it with both hands for support. He is frail-looking and wears a belt and suspenders. His blind eyes wander.

DAD

Tracy Rae? I'm in here. I dropped the soap. Can you help me find it?

Tracy enters the Bathroom, locates the soap, rinses it off and places it in Dad's palm.

TRACY

I'll be in the living room. Do you want anything from the kitchen?

DAD

How about some juice? I'll be out in a jiff.

Tracy rubs Dad's shoulder and pecks him on the cheek.

INT. DAD'S BROWNSTONE/KITCHEN - DAY

Tracy roots around in the refrigerator and pulls out a quart of milk. She sniffs it and recoils. Tracy dumps the lumpy contents down the sink and reaches into a drawer for a towel. Hidden under the towel is a semi-automatic pistol. She's disturbed at the presence of a weapon.

Dad feels his way into the kitchen, running his hand along the wall.

DAD

So nice of you to visit me. What's new, Tracy Rae?

Tracy quickly stows the pistol in her purse.

TRACY

Nothing special, Dad.

She pours a glass of juice, takes Dad by the arm and leads him out.

INT. DAD'S BROWNSTONE/LIVING ROOM - DAY

Dad grabs at the air around him until he latches onto the arms of his chair. He sits down with an audible SIGH. Tracy hands Dad the glass of juice and takes a seat nearby.

TRACY

Well, maybe one thing. I met the owner of a bio-tech lab here in the City. He's working on a cure, or a therapy, something - for retinitis.

Dad jerks his head from side to side like a lizard, attempting to pinpoint his daughter's exact whereabouts.

DAD

Really!? That's fantastic! When will it be available?

TRACY

They're almost ready to go to clinical trial, but they need a cash infusion. The owner wants to bring some venture capitalists in, but his brother doesn't want to. Right now, they're stuck.

DAD

Hell, Tracy. You're a mediator. Can't you get them to agree?

TRACY

That's what I hope to do, Dad. I'm going to Jersey in a few days to meet with the brother.

DAD

Tell them I'll be a volunteer.

TRACY

Okay, Dad. But it's still experim--

DAD

--It's been four years since I've read a book, or seen your face. Please, I'll happily be their guinea pig. Tell them.

INT. OFFICE BUILDING/LOBBY - DAY

The Lobby of the Office Building is a dusty, cramped, poorly lit space. A doorman's desk sits by the wall unattended. Tracy scans the environs then steps up to a glass case displaying the names of various businesses that occupy the building. She spots the entry "RodC ne Labs - Suite 212."

EXT. SUITE 212 - DAY

Tracy stands outside a plain door with the number 212 stenciled on it. She presses a button and is buzzed in.

INT. SUITE 212 - DAY

Tracy walks into Suite 212 which is occupied by a few WORKERS who sit at steel desks arranged in a row. A RECEPTIONIST stands and greets Tracy.

RECEPTIONIST

Ms. Shepard? Mr. Cuttbate is expecting you. Can I get you something to drink?

TRACY

Nothing, thanks.

The Receptionist leads Tracy toward the Conference Room. She glances down at Tracy's shoes.

RECEPTIONIST

I love your shoes, Ms. Shepard. Blahniks?

TRACY

Christian Louboutin.

INT. SUITE 212/CONFERENCE ROOM - DAY

The Receptionist escorts Tracy into the Conference Room and leaves. Three men who are seated at the long conference table stand up to greet Tracy. They are Fischer, his BUSINESS DIRECTOR and his CHIEF SCIENTIST. The Business Director is mid-30s, dressed in a dark business suit. Sixty-something Chief Scientist wears a cliché white lab coat.

FISCHER

Tracy. I'm glad you could make it. Can I get you something?

TRACY

No thanks, Fischer. I'm good.

FISCHER

OK, Tracy, I know you're busy, so we won't waste any time. Our chief scientist will give you a high-level overview of our research. I think you'll be impressed.

TRACY

I hope so.

FISCHER

Yes... And then when you meet with Fletcher, you'll be fully prepared.

The Chief Scientist presses a button on the lectern causing the lights to dim. A gruesome picture of a needle piercing an eyeball appears on the screen. Tracy recoils in disgust.

CHIEF SCIENTIST

This is how some researchers have foolishly tried to cure retinitis pigmentosa, Ms. Shepard.

TRACY

(Grimacing)

Good lord.

CHIEF SCIENTIST

We're working on a better way. A therapy. A pill that patients will take every day to gradually improve and maintain the quality of their vision. Here's what we're doing.

The Chief Scientist clicks a button and a ball-and-stick model of a molecule appears on the screen.

CHIEF SCIENTIST (CONT'D)

This is a protein called rhodopsin.

DISSOLVE TO:

INT. SUITE 212/CONFERENCE ROOM - DAY (LATER)

A large "?" appears on screen. Fischer raises the lights.

CHIEF SCIENTIST

Any questions, Ms. Shepard?

TRACY

I don't know. I guess not. That was pretty technical, but I think I got the basics. Really remarkable.

FISCHER

It's expensive work, Tracy. We really need to get Fletch on board with the VCs. I hope you can use your mediation magic on him - although I wouldn't be surprised if he refuses to see you.

TRACY

Would it surprise you if Fletcher already agreed to meet with me?

FISCHER

You mean he--

TRACY

--I'm taking the train to Hamilton Square tomorrow morning.

FISCHER

Wow. You're good.

Tracy smiles, pleased to receive Fischer's praise. She shakes hands with the principles and heads for the door. Just before exiting the Business Director intercepts her.

BUSINESS DIRECTOR

Thank you for coming by today, Ms. Shepard. I'll email you a copy of the presentation.

FISCHER

Let me know how you make out with Fletcher, Tracy.

TRACY

I certainly will. Bye bye.

INT. TRACY'S APARTMENT - DAY

Tracy enters her spacious apartment on Sutton Place with its handsome view of the Queensborough Bridge. An original Kandinsky painting hangs on the wall. Tracy checks mail.

INT. TRACY'S APARTMENT/BEDROOM - DAY

Tracy sheds her clothing. She places her expensive shoes into a slot in her closet which holds 100 pairs.

INT. TRACY'S APARTMENT/BATHROOM - DAY

Tracy lounges in a luxurious bath.

INT. TRACY'S APARTMENT/BEDROOM - DAY

Wearing a terrycloth robe, her hair wrapped with a towel, Tracy reaches into a dresser drawer, gingerly removes her father's pistol by the grip and carefully looks it over.

INT. TRACY'S APARTMENT - DAY

With the pistol atop her desk Tracy sits in front of her laptop typing.

TRACY'S P.O.V. - GOOGLE SEARCH BAR

Into which she types "how to disarm a pistol"

BACK TO SCENE.

Tracy studies the laptop screen, clicks on a website and reads the instructions. Holding the pistol at arm's length while pointing it at the floor she turns her head to the side and hesitantly presses a button causing the magazine to pop out and fall to the floor. Shaking her head sadly she retrieves the magazine and stashes it and the pistol into her drawer.
Tracy then turns her attention to the laptop.

TRACY'S P.O.V. - EMAIL PROGRAM

Where a long list of emails awaits her attention, among them one from Fischer's Business Director titled "RodCone Presentation."

BACK TO SCENE.

Tracy prints out the document.

EXT. FLETCHER'S BUNGALOW/PORCH - DAY

Toting a rich-looking alligator briefcase, Tracy rings the door-bell. After a moment during which Tracy paces the porch, FLETCHER opens the door. He holds a telephone to his ear. Fletcher's dirty blonde hair is combed straight back, and he sports huge, boxy eyeglasses. Tracy extends her hand.

TRACY

Good afternoon, Mr.--

FLETCHER

--You're early. Can you wait here until I'm done with my call?

Fletcher shuts the door in her face.

EXT. FLETCHER'S BUNGALOW/PORCH - DAY (LATER)

Tracy paces the porch, checks her watch, and just as she's about to give up, Fletcher opens the door. Tracy turns around and steps up.

FLETCHER

I'm ready now Mrs. Shepard.

TRACY

Ms. Shepard. Tracy Shepard. How do you do, Mr. Cuttbate.

Tracy extends her hand again. Fletcher hesitates, then belated shakes it. Fletcher turns and Tracy follows him in.

INT. FLETCHER'S BUNGALOW - DAY

Fletcher's Bungalow is cluttered with books and magazines, an electric guitar, and an easel propping up a painting of a surgical-like image vaguely reminiscent of Frida Kahlo's painfilled self-portraits. Tracy examines the surroundings.

TRACY

What a pleasant house you have here, Mr. Cuttbate.

FLETCHER

No, it's not.

(beat)

Have a seat.

Tracy looks around for the least-grungy chair and sits down, placing her briefcase on the floor. Fletcher plops into an over-stuffed divan.

TRACY

I saw a very interesting presentation about your company's drug the other day. It seems like it could be revolutionary. But I'm just a layperson. What's your assessment?

FLETCHER

It has its pluses and minuses.

TRACY

Do you think it's ready for clinical trials?

FLETCHER

Maybe.

SOUND - TELEPHONE RINGING O.S.

Fletcher rises and exits. Irritated, Tracy wanders around the room, picking up some magazines on the coffee table. She runs her fingers across the strings of Fletcher's electric guitar. Fletcher returns, startling Tracy.

FLETCHER (CONT'D)

Sorry about that. Where were we?

The two retake their seats.

TRACY

We were talking about... the drug. Is it ready to be tested, in your opinion?

Fletcher waits a long time to respond.

FLETCHER

Possibly.

TRACY

Look, Mr. Cuttbate. I only came--

FLETCHER

--Why did you come out here? Why do you care so much about this, Mrs. Shepard? I don't suppose you know someone with retinitis?

TRACY

(Angrily)

Yes, as a matter of fact I do. Someone I love very much. My father. And it disturbs me greatly that a promising cure might not see the light of day because you can't come to terms on something as mundane as financing. It's a goddamned shame.

Tracy stands abruptly and reaches for her briefcase. Fletcher's imperious demeanor melts into that of a chastened school-boy.

FLETCHER

Wait. Please don't go, Ms. Shep... Tracy. I... I'm really sorry for acting like a jerk. I mean it... sincerely. Please, sit down. Fischer didn't tell me your father has retinitis.

(beat)

Can he... see at all?

Tracy shakes her head.

FLETCHER (CONT'D)

I'm so sorry to hear that. Please, Tracy. Don't go.

Tracy sits back down slowly.

FLETCHER (CONT'D)

Can I get you something to drink? Please?

INT. FLETCHER'S BUNGALOW - DAY (LATER)

Tracy sits next to Fletcher on the divan sipping lemonade from a glass. A notebook full of mathematical equations and scribbles sits open on the coffee table.

FLETCHER

I suppose Fischer's illustrious scientist told you all about the wonderful therapy he's working on. The daily regimen?

TRACY

Mmm-hmm. I got a copy of his presentation yesterday.

FLETCHER

A therapy... not a cure. You understand the difference, right? Kind of like blood pressure medicine, or Somavert - you have to take it every day for the rest of your life. And if you stop taking it, you regress. Understand?

TRACY

I understand.

(beat)

What's Somavert?

Fletcher squirms a moment.

FLETCHER

Uh, it's, uh, a treatment for acromegaly. Anyway, what would you say if I told you I'm working on an actual cure for retinitis?

Fletcher taps the notebook proudly.

TRACY

Really? That's fantastic.

FLETCHER

Not according to Fischer. You see, a life-long therapy stands to make a hell of lot more money than a short-term cure. He and his men don't want to sell a cure. Not good business.

TRACY

But--

FLETCHER

--I'm against Fischer's plan to bring in the venture capitalists because they don't care about cures and quality of life and all that shit... excuse me. It's all about the money to them.

TRACY

Hmmm. I can see your point. How far along are you with your cure?

Fletcher looks down at his hands sheepishly.

FLETCHER

Well, uh, it's in the early study phase. Not too far along, actually.

(beat)

If I could only get the money to take it all to the next level... I wish I was good with business like my brother.

(beat)

Fischer never lets me see any of the company's finances. For all I know, he's gonna cut me out of the action if his drug gets FDA approval and RodCone goes public.

TRACY

Do you really think that's a possibility?

FLETCHER

I wouldn't put it past him.

TRACY

That's a pretty seri--

FLETCHER

--Listen, Tracy. I behaved like a boor earlier because I thought you were just another one of Fischer's mind-games. But I know you're here because you're genuinely interested in a cure for this terrible disease. More lemonade?

TRACY

Sure.

Fletcher pours some lemonade into Tracy's glass.

FLETCHER

It was nice of you to come all the way out here. I thought it would be a waste of time, but I'm glad I got the opportunity to explain my side.

TRACY

Me too.

FLETCHER

Uh, Tracy, don't tell Fischer about what I said about him cutting me out of the action. I shouldn't have mentioned that. And don't tell him about my work on a cure either. It's way too soon for that, OK?

TRACY

If you say so. It's important that my clients trust me.

FLETCHER

I trust you, Tracy.

TRACY

Well, thank you.

Tracy scans the room and sets her eyes on the guitar.

TRACY (CONT'D)

Do you play the guitar, Fletch?

FLETCHER

Yeah, a little. Well actually, I've been playing since I was about nine. I bought that Fender 20 years ago at an auction - it's the same kind that Keith Richards plays. 1955 Telecaster.

Fletcher walks to the guitar. He turns on the amp and plugs in the cord which emits a SCREECH. Tracy looks on with concern that he might actually start playing. A horn HONKS O.S.

TRACY

I really should get--

Fletcher faithfully plays the first bars of "Honky Tonk Women." Tracy nods, impressed.

FLETCHER

--Who's your favorite rock star, Tracy?

TRACY

Geez, that's tough. I was a Bowie fan as a kid. Ziggy Stardust period, y'know, glitter--

Fletcher plays the opening chords of "Moonage Daydream."

FLETCHER

(Singing)

--I'm an alligator. I'm a mama-papa coming for you.

Fletcher nods to Tracy who hesitates at first then blurts out the next lyric.

TRACY

(Singing)

I'm a space invader, I'll be a rockn-rollin' bitch for you.

Fletcher nods encouragingly.

FLETCHER

(Singing)

Keep your mouth shut, you're squawking like a pink monkey bird. And I'm busting up my brains for the words. Keep your 'lectric eye on me babe.

TRACY AND FLETCHER

(singing)

Put your ray gun to my head. Press your space face close to mine, love. Freak out in a moonage daydream!

Tracy laughs happily and applauds.

TRACY

Wow, Fletch. You're really good. Do you play in a band?

FLETCHER

Not anymore. No time.

Tracy reaches for the glass of lemonade, just as a car horn HONKS O.S. She glances at her watch and bolts upright.

TRACY

Shit! The train back to the City leaves in 20 minutes. I'm sorry, Fletch, I've got to go. I enjoyed spending the afternoon with you.

Fletcher places the guitar back on its stand.

FLETCHER

Me too. But I'm glad it turned out better than it began.

Fletcher escorts Tracy to the door.

EXT. FLETCHER'S BUNGALOW/PORCH - DAY

Fletcher shakes Tracy's hand.

FLETCHER

Have a good trip back to the city, Tracy.

TRACY

Thanks, Fletch. I will.

Fletcher watches Tracy walk to a cab waiting at the curb. He continues to watch as the cab drives down the lane and out of sight, then he walks back inside, singing to himself.

FLETCHER

(Singing)

Don't fake it baby. Lay the real thing on me.

INT. TRAIN (TRAVELING) - DAY

Tracy sits in a first-class seat reading Fortune as the train lumbers along. She puts down the magazine, retrieves the printout of the RodCone Labs presentation and thumbs through the material until she reaches a page with a big question mark like the one at the end of Torrent's pitch. Tracy discovers several additional pages marked "Confidential" that contain business spreadsheets.

INT. TRACY'S APARTMENT - NIGHT

Tracy sits at her desk, poring through the business spreadsheets and consulting her laptop. She sits back and shakes her head. She circles some numbers and writes the word "WTF" next to them.

Tracy's laptop makes a "ping" SOUND. She sees an email has arrived from Knecht.

TRACY'S P.O.V. - EMAIL

Which reads "Dear Ms. Shepard, I accidentally sent you the wrong file yesterday. Please discard it and replace it with the corrected version which I have attached. Let me know if you have any questions. Sincerely, Chad Knecht."

BACK TO SCENE

Tracy shakes her head contemptuously.

INT. UPSCALE BAR AND GRILL - DAY

Fletcher, dressed way too casually, and Tracy, looking sharp, arrive at the Bar and Grill. The MAITRE'D escorts the odd couple to a table in the back. He holds the chair for Tracy while casting a disapproving gaze toward the unkempt Fletcher. He presents menus and leaves.

FLETCHER

I'm sure you already guessed this, but I'm not used to going to nice restaurants, especially not with a well-dressed, beautiful woman. I hope I'm not embarrassing you too much, Tracy.

Tracy rolls her eyes as if it's the most ridiculous thing she's ever heard.

TRACY

I'm just glad you could meet me on such short notice. I really thought we should get together right away. It's about the financials of RodCone Labs.

A WAITER arrives. Fletcher picks up the menu.

WAITER

Pardon me, madame, sir. Would you care for sparkling, still, tap?

Tracy looks to Fletcher, but he's engrossed in the menu.

TRACY

Still, please.

FLETCHER

What's con-fit?

WAITER

Cone-fee, sir, is the French method of preparing salted duck legs in rendered fat.

Fletcher snaps the menu shut.

FLETCHER

Sounds good, that's what I'll have. Tracy, what about you?

Unprepared to order so quickly, Tracy fumbles with the menu.

TRACY

I'll have the... uh, the tuna, medium rare.

WAITER

Very good, madame, sir.

The Waiter leaves with the menus.

FLETCHER

What's the bad news you came to tell me, Tracy? I assume it's something bad, right?

Tracy pulls the RodCone presentation from her purse and lays it out on the table. Fletcher cranes his neck to view it.

TRACY

Chad Knecht emailed me these confidential spreadsheets by mistake.

FLETCHER

Jesus, what is all this stuff?

Tracy points to a chart with a butter knife.

TRACY

In this column are actual expenses, and the one next to it seems to contain fabricated expenses. And these figures here are used to calculate a phony I.R.R.

FLETCHER

What's that?

TRACY

I.R.R? Internal rate of return? It's kind of like N.P.V... uh, net present value—

FLETCHER

--How do you know all this gorp?

TRACY

I have an MBA. I worked at Solomon Brothers before I started my own mediation company.

FLETCHER

MBA, huh? I'm impressed. Where from?

TRACY

Columbia. My father was a physics professor there.

(beat)

Aren't you concerned about what might be going on at your company? What Fischer might be involved in? It might be serious fraud, Fletch. What are you going to do?

The Waiter arrives with the food.

FLETCHER

Have a nice lunch with you.

TRACY

Seriously, Fletch. I'm concerned for the cure. And for you too, of course. Maybe you should hire a forensic accountant before the whole enterprise folds up and you lose everything.

FLETCHER

You're probably right. I'll call my lawyer. I sure hope Fischer's not involved. That would disappoint me, but not really come as a big surprise.

Fletcher hacks at the duck leg. Tracy places a luscious piece of fatty tuna into her mouth.

FLETCHER (CONT'D)

When I was a little boy, my mother - rest her soul - told me I was the first to be born. She told me when I was born Fischer was holding my heel. I think that says it all.

Confused, Tracy tilts her head.

FLETCHER (CONT'D)

Jacob and Esau? Genesis, chapter 25?

(beat)

Never mind.

Tracy and Fletcher eat quietly for a moment

TRACY

I couldn't help noticing the painting in your den, Fletch. It kind of reminds me of Frida Kahlo. Did you paint it?

FLETCHER

Yeah. I know it looks like I copied her style, because I did. After Mama went blind--

TRACY

--Your mother was blind?

FLETCHER

Yeah. Glaucoma. Anyway, I came to appreciate how painful blindness can be. That's what I was trying to capture.

(beat)

I bet you know a lot about art, Tracy. Do you have a favorite artist? Van Gogh? Rembrandt?

TRACY

I guess I would say... Wassily Kandinsky.

FLETCHER

Who?

TRACY

Kandinsky. He was a Russian artist. I have one of his paintings.

Tracy sips her water, trying not to come off as an art snob.

FLETCHER

Kandinsky? I'm going to look him up. Is that with a "C"?

TRACY

"K".

FLETCHER

Maybe I can see it sometime.

TRACY

Uh, sure. Maybe. Sometime.

INT. OFFICE BUILDING - DAY

Tracy talks on a cell phone while pacing the lobby of a large Office Building in Midland, Texas.

TRACY

I'm still waiting for those gas-well leases. I need 1997 through 1999.

(beat)

Hot? Shit, it's already 103 and it's only 11 o'clock. What else?

(beat)

RodCone Labs? What do they want?

(beat)

Well, if it's urgent, alright. Send me those leases ASAP.

Tracy hangs up, takes a seat in a mid-century modern chair facing a fountain and makes another call.

RECEPTIONIST (O.S.)

RodCone Laboratories. How may I help you?

TRACY

This is Tracy Shepard. Someone there asked me to call? Something urgent?

RECEPTIONIST (O.S.)

Oh, yes. Thank you, Mrs. Shepard. It's been a hectic day. Let me check my notes.

(long pause)

I'm afraid we can't remit the money for your bill. The one for $1,000 for... let me see... for alternative dispute resolution? You sent us an invoice last week - well, I'm afraid we can't pay it.

TRACY

Why not?

RECEPTIONIST (O.S.)

We can't pay for anything right now. The FBI raided our company on Monday and froze our accounts.

Tracy leans forward in the low-slung chair, dumbfounded.

TRACY

What happened? What's going on? Let me talk to Fischer... Mr. Cuttbate. I'm a friend of his.

RECEPTIONIST (O.S.)

No one knows where he is. Mr. Cuttbate disappeared before the FBI came in. So did Mr. Knecht.

TRACY

I don't... I mean... Well, if he comes in have him call me.

RECEPTIONIST (O.S.)

I'm sorry, Mrs. Shepard, I have to go.

TRACY

Holy shit.

JFK AIRPORT - DAY

Jet lands on the runway.

EXT. TRACY'S APARTMENT BUILDING - DAY

The limo pulls to the entrance of Tracy's apartment building. She strides past the DOORMAN into the building.

INT. TRACY'S APARTMENT - DAY

Tracy sits at her desk inspecting the mail. She tosses one piece after another into the trash can, stopping at a particular envelope. She slits open the envelope and pulls out a check and a letter.

FLETCHER (V.O.)

Dear Tracy, I took your advice and hired a forensic accountant to analyze the charts you gave me. Unfortunately, you were right: someone at the lab was keeping two sets of books. I decided to call the FBI. I know now that many people were involved, including my brother. I also learned the lab can't pay its bills, so please accept the enclosed personal check from me for $1,000 to cover the fee you and Fischer agreed to. Sincerely, Fletcher Cuttbate.

Tracy sits back in her chair and twists her hair.

INT. DAD'S BROWNSTONE/LIVING ROOM - DAY

Tracy and Dad sit together on the sofa.

TRACY

Honestly, Dad, you wouldn't believe the way these so-called business leaders behave. Sometimes I feel like I'm deciding who gets to play with the dump truck in the sandbox.

DAD

Why don't you cut back on the work? Take a rest. Travel.

TRACY

I already travel too much.

DAD

Find a nice man. Fall in love.

TRACY

I don't know... I'd like... It's just sometimes I... I don't know what's wrong.

Tracy looks down at the floor and rubs her hands together, then not wanting to be a buzzkill, perks up.

TRACY (CONT'D)

You know what they say: a hard man is, I mean a good man is hard to find.

(beat)

Hey Dad, have you ever heard of Woody Johnson?

DAD

Sure. He owns the Jets.

TRACY

Well, my next assignment - should I choose to accept it - is a contract dispute involving the Jets and some high-flying college fullback or hunchback or--

DAD

--Whatever happened to that lab that was working on a retinitis cure?

TRACY

Uh, they, um, they're still trying to figure it out.

DAD

Oh.

TRACY

But, one of the owners is working on something even better. He just needs money to get it rolling.

DAD

Money? That's all? Why don't you help him out, Tracy?

TRACY

Geez, Dad. I'm not a banker. Besides, he's still far from getting anything into the market. It'll take time.

DAD

I see. Well, actually, I can't.

Tracy checks her watch.

TRACY

I gotta go, Dad. Talk to you later.

Tracy kisses her father's cheek.

DAD

Let me know how the big football player affair turns out.

INT. LIMO (TRAVELING) - DAY

Tracy receives a phone call.

TRACY

Hello?

INTERCUT with Fletcher's Bungalow.

FLETCHER

Tracy, it's Fletch. How're you? Is this a good time to talk?

TRACY

Sure. I'm heading home. You really didn't have to send me--

FLETCHER

--I've got something important to tell you, Trace. I feel a little stupid for not confiding in you before, knowing now what a fine woman you are.

TRACY

What are you talking about, Fletch?

FLETCHER

Can you meet me Friday night for dinner? I have some things I'd like to show you. My treat.

TRACY

I, uh, I have to check with my secretary, y'know. She manages my calendar.

FLETCHER

Oh.

(beat)

OK.

TRACY

Screw it. Yes, Fletch, I would love to have dinner with you. I'm intrigued. Where shall we meet?

EXT. UPSCALE RESTAURANT - NIGHT

Tracy waits on the sidewalk, dressed to kill. From O.C. Fletcher walks toward Tracy.
He also looks uncharacteristically sharp in a double-breasted suit, white shirt and stylish tie. Tracy spots him but isn't sure it's him - he looks too good.

TRACY

Fletch?

FLETCHER

Wha'dya think, Trace? Do I look better than I did last time?

TRACY

Wow, you look great. I'm stunned. I mean, you look sharp.

FLETCHER

It's an Armadillo ZEG-na suit.

TRACY

(Chuckling)

Very nice.

FLETCHER

Needless to say - but I'll say it anyway - you look gorgeous Trace. I hope you like the restaurant.

TRACY

I know I will.

Tracy loops her arm underneath Fletcher's and they walk into the Restaurant.

INT. UPSCALE RESTAURANT - NIGHT

Fletcher and Tracy sit across from one another at an elegantly set table eating artistically presented food. Wait-staff come and go, filling water glasses, pouring wine.

TRACY

So, after yet another sexist remark about me in front of a client, I decided to quit the world of investment banking and try mediation instead.

FLETCHER

What're you working on next, Tracy?

A WAITER pours the last of a bottle of wine.

WAITER

Excuse me, sir. Would you care for another bottle?

FLETCHER

Sure.

The Waiter leaves with the empty bottle.

TRACY

Mediating a 3-way dispute with the New York Jets, a college football star and his aggrieved agent.

FLETCHER

Kinda like Jerry Maguire, huh?

TRACY

Probably not. This agent sounds like a whiny loser. But I can easily imagine college-boy shouting "show me the money!"

The Waiter returns with a bottle of wine and shows Fletcher the label.

FLETCHER

Is that the same stuff as before?

WAITER

Certainly, sir. Château d' Armailhac, 1996.

The Waiter pours the wine and departs.

TRACY

Fletch, where do you think Fischer went? What's going to happen to the lab - and all the retinitis research?

FLETCHER

I honestly don't know, Trace. Deep down Fischer's a good man. Maybe he got in over his head. No doubt that bastard Knecht was behind it.

(beat)

All this drama throws RodCone Labs into Limbo.

TRACY

It's so sad. I suppose the pressure warped his judgment.

FLETCHER

Doesn't make any difference now. Whether Fischer was a dupe or the mastermind, if they find him, he'll probably do time.

(beat)

Our assets are frozen and the creditors are starting legal action.

(beat)

This rabbit is really good. I never had it before.

TRACY

You're amazing, Fletch. You're so calm. How do you do it? If it was me, and my company was in deep trouble, and my brother was on the lam, I'd be going crazy.

FLETCHER

I'm optimistic.

TRACY

How come?

The Waiter arrives with food.

FLETCHER

Is that the venison? It looks like pudding.

INT. UPSCALE RESTAURANT - NIGHT (LATER)

Fletcher and Tracy have moved along into the meal.

FLETCHER

You remember those equations I showed you back at my house? Those weren't just theories. A colleague at Penn State is helping me test formulas on animals. The results are more than promising. We're close to a real cure for retinitis pigmentosa, Tracy.

TRACY

I don't understand. Are you saying--

The Waiter arrives.

WAITER

--Excuse me madame, sir. May I bring another bottle of wine.

TRACY

No thank--

FLETCHER

--Absolutely.

The waiter departs.

FLETCHER (CONT'D)

I know I led you to believe I was just messing around, because I didn't want anyone to know about it, but, yeah, I'm on the verge of a real cure.

TRACY

My God, Fletch! That's fantastic! An actual cure. Why didn't you show the formula to Fischer? Oh wait, right, not good for business.

(beat)

I think all this wine is going to my head.

The waiter returns, pops the cork and refills the glasses.

FLETCHER

That's one reason. But when I learned he was talking to venture capitalists, I got worried. Why share a good thing with a bunch of clowns who know the cost of everything and the value of nothing?

TRACY

So sayeth Oscar Wilde.

Tracy takes a swig of wine.

FLETCHER

Did he say that? Damn, I thought I came up with it.

INT. UPSCALE RESTAURANT - NIGHT (LATER)

Tracy picks at a dessert. A half-drunk snifter of Cognac sits nearby, and she's a bit tight. Fletcher drinks bourbon from a rocks glass.

TRACY

Y'know, my dad wants t' volunteer t' be a test subject.

FLETCHER

Well, just like with Fischer's therapy, I have to line up funding for clinical trials. That ain't cheap.

TRACY

What're you gonna do? How're you gonna get the money, Fletch?

FLETCHER

After my father died, he left Fish and me each a half million dollars in stocks and bonds. Fish spent a good chunk on toys and nice furniture. I denied myself the comforts of life and invested. You've seen my dumpy house. Would you believe I have more than a million dollars in savings?

TRACY

Really? That's fantastic. So, when will you start the clinical trials?

FLETCHER

After I line up another mil. It'll cost at least two to get going. I have to hire some people, buy insurance, post a bond, deal with a shitload of FDA bureaucracy.

(beat)

That's why - don't laugh - I'm meeting with a new vulture capital firm tomorrow.

TRACY

What? You're gonna take VC money? I don't und--

FLETCHER

--As much as I despise them, it seems that's the only way research turns into a product. Unless you're a multi-billion-dollar pharmaceutical company. I don't have a choice, really.

TRACY

Gee, Fletch. I don't know...

The Waiter drops off the check. Fletcher pulls out his wallet and counts out large bills. Tracy sips her Cognac.

FLETCHER

Can I ask you a question?

TRACY

You jus' did.

FLETCHER

Huh? Oh, I get it.

TRACY

(Giggling)

I'm sorry, Fletch. What is it?

FLETCHER

How do you keep your legs in such great shape? You must work out, or swim a lot. You have the most gorgeous legs I've ever seen. And your feet--

Taken aback, Tracy is uncharacteristically flummoxed.

TRACY

--Well, uh, thank you, Fletch. I try. I'm... I'm glad you noticed.

Tracy looks down like a shy schoolgirl and awkwardly examines a fingernail. After a moment, she pushes her hair away from her eyes and smiles.

TRACY (CONT'D)

Ready to go?

EXT. UPSCALE RESTAURANT - NIGHT

Fletcher and Tracy stroll the sidewalk outside the Restaurant. Tracy touches Fletcher's shoulder and he turns toward her. As Tracy is taller by a few inches, Fletcher looks up into her somewhat glassy eyes. After a moment, she kisses him on the lips.

TRACY

Would you like to see my apartment? I could show you my Kandinsky.

INT. TRACY'S APARTMENT/BEDROOM - NIGHT

Tracy and Fletcher roll around naked in her bed. Tracy moves her head down low. Suddenly, she sits up.

TRACY

Oh my God! Where did you ever...?

The outburst at first startles Fletcher, but he quickly chuckles knowingly.

FLETCHER

It was after a Lou Reed concert--

TRACY

--I didn't know you could get a tattoo on your, um—

FLETCHER

--Penis? Yeah. I guess anything's possible when you're wasted enough. One of my buddies picked out a design of a snake and the guy tattooed it around like it was climbing a tree. It hurt like hell the next day when I sobered up.

TRACY

(Laughing)

I can imagine. Lie back. I wanna try something.

FLETCHER

Uh oh.

TRACY

You said you admire my feet. I caught your brother staring at them, too. This foot-fetish thing must run in your family.

FLETCHER

Could be.

TRACY

I can peel a banana with my feet.

FLETCHER

Really?

TRACY

Lie back.

Fletcher lies back and a moment later lets out a moan.

INT. TRACY'S APARTMENT/BEDROOM - DAY

Tracy lies in bed motionless. Fletcher tiptoes quietly out of the bathroom fully dressed. Tracy rolls onto her right side and faces Fletcher, groaning in agony.

TRACY

Fletch? What are you doing?

FLETCHER

Good morning, Tracy. I didn't mean to wake you. How're you feeling?

TRACY

Ugh... terrible. I never should've had that second Cognac.

Tracy sits up, then abruptly lies back down.

TRACY (CONT'D)

Ooh... I feel awful.

Suddenly, Tracy bolts past Fletcher into the bathroom. Retching SOUNDS O.S.

INT. TRACY'S APARTMENT/BEDROOM - DAY

(LATER)

Tracy limps from the bathroom licking her lips. Fletcher waits for her with a glass of water and aspirins.

FLETCHER

I'm sorry you feel so bad. Let me help you back to bed.

Fletcher takes Tracy's arm and walks her toward the bed.

TRACY

I'll be OK. Just let me rest by the window. Would you open it?

Fletcher leads Tracy to a lounge chair and opens the window. He places the glass of water and aspirins on a nearby table.

FLETCHER

I had a wonderful evening, Trace. I'll call you later and let you know how things went with the VCs.

Tracy sits up quickly

.

TRACY

I forgot. When is your meeting?

FLETCHER

Three o'clock.

TRACY

Where?

FLETCHER

The Marriott Marquis.

TRACY

I'd like to go with you.

FLETCHER

Really? I mean, that's OK. You don't have to do that - I can manage. Besides, you don't feel well.

TRACY

VCs... They'll want to... I'll feel better by 3.

FLETCHER

Are you sure? I can handle it.

TRACY

I'm sure you can. Still though, I'd like to help. I'll try to get some sleep. I'll be better by 3.

FLETCHER

Really, I--

TRACY

--Don't do anything without me!

INT. HOTEL CONFERENCE ROOM - DAY

Two VCs, both men in their 50s dressed in dark suits and armed with reams of market data sit on one side of a conference table. Tracy and Fletcher sit on the other side. Tracy appears a bit haggard.

VC 1

Tell me, Mr. Cuttbate. Why do you want to develop a cure when a daily regimen seems the better way to go?

Fletcher angrily slams his palm on the table; he's ready to walk out of the conference room. Tracy gently reaches for Fletcher's forearm and coaxes him back into his seat.

TRACY

Development of a cure for retinitis pigmentosa is non-negotiable. Period. No life-long therapy. That's not the objective of Mr. Cuttbate's company.

VC 1

And why, may I ask, Mrs. Shepard, is that not the objective?

TRACY

Providing a cure is the right thing to do--

VC 2 grins derisively.

TRACY (CONT'D)

--and the clinical trials for a cure will cost significantly less than the trials for a therapy. The time to market will be reduced by a factor of two. The risk of competitive encroachment will be reduced dramatically. Get it?

VC 2 stops grinning. He glances nervously at VC 1 and rummages through his charts and tables.

VC 2

Well... I'm not so sure... I don't know... about that...

After uncomfortable rambling from VC 2, VC 1 intervenes.

VC 1

OK, look. You're the scientific expert Mr. Cuttbate. We're just simple financiers. Far be it from us to tell you how to conduct R&D. If you think a cure is a better play than a therapy, so be it.

Fletcher looks over at Tracy and smiles at the display of her business acumen. She remains stoned faced, refusing to look at Fletcher.

VC 1 (CONT'D)

So, Mr. Cuttbate, do we have a deal? Or at least the foundation for a deal?

Fletcher is about to respond when Tracy speaks up.

TRACY

Mr. Cuttbate will take it under consideration. That's all.

Tracy stands up abruptly and extends her hand, indicating to everyone's surprise that the meeting is over. The VCs file out of the conference room, grumbling and visibly annoyed. When they are gone, Tracy turns to Fletcher.

FLETCHER

What the hell, Tracy?

TRACY

Be cool, Fletch. Those people are just like the VCs your brother courted. Vultures. There's no upside for you and your company in any of their proposals.

FLETCHER

I don't know--

TRACY

--Trust me, they'll rip you off.

FLETCHER

So where am I going to get the funds to go on? I'm out of ideas.

TRACY

From me, Fletch. Let me be your angel investor. You have a million, you need another million. Well, I've got a million. What do you say?

FLETCHER

You? You'd loan me the money?

TRACY

No, Fletch, not loan. Invest. I would take an equity position. If you're interested, we'll assemble our lawyers to work out a mutually beneficial arrangement.

FLETCHER

I don't know what to say. I'm speechless.

TRACY

Remember, Fletch, I expect to make money on the cure, too.

FLETCHER

Of course, of course. I'll call my lawyer right away. How about tomorrow?

TRACY

Let's make it next week, Fletch. I have to check on my guy's availability.

FLETCHER

Whatever you say, Trace.

(beat)

This is so great. Let's celebrate. Have a drink with me?

TRACY

Now? It's only 4:30.

Fletcher shrugs "so-what".

TRACY (CONT'D)

Oh, what the hell. I'm mostly recovered from last night. Where do you want to go?

EXT. OFFICE BUILDING - DAY

Tracy and her lawyer HANNAH exit the limo and walk to the Office Building. Hannah is the same age as Tracy, much shorter and dressed in a dark, conservative suit. She carries an over-stuffed briefcase.

INT. OFFICE BUILDING/LOBBY - DAY

HANNAH

What a dump.

Hannah starts for the elevator, then sullenly heads for the stair-well when she notices Tracy already climbing the stairs.

INT. SUITE 212 - DAY

Fletcher stands by the open door. Tracy appears, followed closely by Hannah. Fletcher ogles Tracy's feet for a moment. Noticing, she grins imperceptibly.

FLETCHER

C'mon in Tracy. I'm playing receptionist today. I had to let our girl go.

TRACY

Nice to see you again Fletcher. This is my lawyer, Hannah Goldman. Hannah, meet Mr. Cuttbate.

Hannah puts down the briefcase and shakes Fletcher's hand.

HANNAH

How do you do, Mr. Cuttbate.

FLETCHER

Doing fine. Let's go to the conference room. I can't wait to do this. I'm so excited, Tracy.

INT. SUITE 212 CONFERENCE ROOM - DAY

Two middle-aged men, ANDREWS and ZWIEBEL, wait inside. Andrews is gaunt, Zwiebel is well-tailored and chubby. Both stand when Fletcher, Tracy and Hannah walk in.

FLETCHER

Gentlemen. This is Tracy Shepard, my angel investor. And Hannah Goldman, her lawyer.

Fletcher points to each man in succession.

FLETCHER (CONT'D)

That's Arthur Andrews, my accountant and Bernard Zwiebel, my attorney general.

After all parties shake hands and nod heads, they sit at the conference table. It's Tracy and Hannah on one side and Fletcher and his team on the other. Hannah opens her laptop. Andrews consults some papers.

ANDREWS

RodCone Labs has filed for bankruptcy under Chapter 7. Liquidation. Mr. Cuttbate has formed a new corporation, Cuttbate Associates which will purchase the key assets of the defunct RodCone Labs. Equipment, computer programs, and most importantly, six patents. Office furniture and the like is going on the auction block.

Tracy nods. Hannah takes notes on her laptop.

ZWIEBEL

Mr. Cuttbate here is the sole owner of the molecular models and mathematical formulations for the retinitis cure. RodCone Labs has nothing to do with this intellectual property, so no legal or financial claims can be attached to it by some pissed-off creditor.

TRACY

Very good.

ANDREWS

The incorporation bylaws state that Cuttbate Associates will have three board seats. Right now, Mr. Cuttbate is the Chairman and Zwiebel here is holding a seat temporarily, leaving one seat open. The company has issued a million shares to Mr. Cuttbate with a par value of $1, and is authorized to issue up to another ten million shares.

FLETCHER

About that open board seat--

ANDREWS

--Ms. Shepard, I understand you've expressed an interest in making a substantial investment in Cuttbate Associates. I've recommended to Mr. Cuttbate that his company issue $1 million in 20-year Class A debt paying 3.875 percent over Treasuries.

TRACY

I didn't come here to loan money, Mr. Andrews. I came to take an equity stake. Mr. Cuttbate already knows that's my position, and so do you, so let's just cut the crap.

FLETCHER

That's right, Art. I already told you that.

ANDREWS

I'm merely stating what I recommended to you, Mr. Cutt--

ZWIEBEL

--Mrs. Shepard, Cuttbate Associates is prepared to issue a second lot of 999 thousand shares to you in exchange for your $1 million investment. Under no circumstances will Mr. Cuttbate relinquish majority ownership of his company.

TRACY

I understand and appreciate your position, Mr. Zwiebel, as Fletch's legal advisor. But I have an alternative proposition to make. Grant me ten million options at 10 cents exercisable upon IPO--

ZWIEBEL

--Well, I... uh, um--

Zwiebel looks at Andrews for some guidance. Hannah peers up from her laptop and smirks at the floundering lawyer.

TRACY

--And appoint me to the open seat on the board. Cuttbate Associates needs someone like me on the executive team.

ZWIEBEL

Now, Mrs. Shepard--

TRACY

--Ms. Shepard.

ZWIEBEL

I'm sorry, Ms. Shepard. Now, Ms. Shepard--

TRACY

--Mr. Cuttbate, what do you think?

Fletcher looks at his advisors who glare back at him.

FLETCHER

Well, Tracy... uh, Ms. Shepard, there's no major difference, at least to me anyway. Either way the retinitis drug can go to clinical trial. That's all I want.

ANDREWS

You know, if your company goes public, Ms. Shepard here stands to become the majority shareholder.

FLETCHER

Yeah, I know Art. If - a big "if" - we go public. In the meantime, Tracy here is sticking her neck out a long way. It seems reasonable that she should be rewarded if it pays off.

Silence for several seconds. Tracy nods to Hannah.

HANNAH

If you are amenable to Ms. Shepard's offer, I'll deliver the detailed term sheet. Do you have a printer here somewhere, or did you lose it in the fire sale?

Both Andrews and Zwiebel look down and shake their heads at Hannah's impudent remark. Tracy isn't pleased.

TRACY

Just email it to them, Hannah.

INT. TRACY'S APARTMENT/BEDROOM - NIGHT

Tracy lies in bed, speaking on the phone while the SOUND of shower water splashes O.S.

TRACY

That's right, Dad. Yeah. The retinitis cure is going forward.

(beat)

I know. Yeah. The new company secured enough financing for... That's right. The trials will start... Well, I made a small investment myself. Yeah.

The splashing shower water SOUND O.S. ceases. The SOUND of a shower door opening O.S.

TRACY (CONT'D)

I have to go Dad. Listen, I'll be on the road a lot over the next couple of weeks. That football player thing I told you about. Yeah, me too. Bye.

Tracy hangs up the phone. Fletcher walks into the bedroom with a towel twisted high around his head and another wrapped around his waist. He wears a pair of Tracy's high heels.

FLETCHER

How do you walk in these things?

TRACY

Be careful. They cost $1200.

FLETCHER

Are you kidding?

TRACY

Each.

(beat)

Turn around.

Fletcher turns 360 degrees.

TRACY (CONT'D)

Hmmm. They make your legs look pretty good, Fletch.

FLETCHER

Is that your secret?

TRACY

One of many. Come over here.

Fletcher lies next to Tracy on the bed wearing the shoes.

TRACY (CONT'D)

I'm really excited about the cure.

FLETCHER

Me too. Andrews thinks we can get things rolling in a couple weeks.

TRACY

Great. That's good timing because I'm going to be on the road a lot this coming month. I have to drive out to Jersey tomorrow morning to meet with the Jets' front office people. Then I have to fly to Dayton, Ohio of all places.

FLETCHER

Oh yeah. Jerry Maguire and the magical football player.

TRACY

Something like that. Did you know the name of the Jets' owner is Woody Johnson?

FLETCHER

Uh uh.

TRACY

Would you believe when I was in college, I had a dildo I nicknamed Woody Johnson?

FLETCHER

Seriously?

Tracy pulls out a dildo from her bedside drawer. She shows it to Fletcher who crosses his arms, reluctant to touch it.

TRACY

See. It looks like it's made out of wood.

Fletcher inspects the dildo hesitantly.

TRACY (CONT'D)

It came with a strap.

Fletcher's eyes widen in trepidation.

INT. RESTAURANT - DAY

Tracy and Hannah sit by the window at a tony midtown Restaurant. Each picks at food on tiny plates.

TRACY

I can't believe I have to fly through Atlanta to get to Dayton. What a pain in the ass.

(beat)

So, what's up with Cuttbate Associates? Everything cool?

HANNAH

Yes. Your bank wired the money this morning.

TRACY

Good.

HANNAH

The term sheet I got from Bernard Zwiebel grants you the options and the board seat. They propose comping you ten k for being on the board. You OK with that?

TRACY

Sure. I don't care. What else?

Hannah pulls out a folder of papers from her briefcase.

HANNAH

Here are the incorporation papers. Zwiebel set up the first board meeting for a week from yesterday--

TRACY

--No good. Have him move it out another week after I'm done with the football player thing.

(beat)

I want this company to succeed. I want that cure to fly through the FDA. What do you think of Zwiebel?

HANNAH

Seems competent.

TRACY

Cuttbate Associates is going to need a high-quality lawyer to deal with all the government red tape. I'm thinking of moving him out. I'll need your help.

HANNAH

Really? Of course. I can start--

TRACY

--Do some research on lawyers with pharmaceutical background and give me a list of five or ten good ones.

Hannah deflates.

HANNAH

Uh, sure. I'll get right on it.

INT. JET - DAY

Tracy sits in first class reading Sports Illustrated.

INT. DAYTON BAR - DAY

Tracy sits in a booth in the back accompanied by MILTON, a sports agent, BRADLEY, a college football player, and his father, HAL.

HAL

I spoke with the Jets' front office. They'll pay you off.

MILTON

That's not how business is done, my friend. Why am I talking to this douche-bag? Bradley signed with me.

TRACY

Hal, I told you not to talk to--

HAL

--That paper Bradley signed, that wasn't a contract.

MILTON

Like hell it wasn't.

TRACY

Gentlemen--

BRADLEY

--This whole thing is messing... I don't want to miss the first day of training camp.

MILTON

You shoulda thought of that before, sonny. I'm your agent!

HAL

Go to hell!

Hal stands like he's going to physically confront Milton. Tracy steps between them.

TRACY

Let's start over... again.

INT. JET - NIGHT

Tracy sleeps in first class with shades over her eyes.

INT. TRACY'S APARTMENT - NIGHT

Tracy shuffles into her apartment. She tosses the key on the table and places her briefcase on the chair. The clock on the wall reads 12:30.

EXT. JETS FRONT OFFICE - DAY

With her briefcase in hand, Tracy walks toward the entrance of the Jets Front Office. Her cell phone rings and she stops to answer it.

FLETCHER (O.S.)

Tracy? Fletch. How're you doing?

TRACY

So-so. I'm about to go to a meeting.

FLETCHER (O.S.)

The football thing?

TRACY

Yeah. Can I call you later?

FLETCHER (O.S.)

Of course. I just wanted to make sure you can make the first board meeting later this week.

TRACY

Didn't my lawyer tell you? I'm not available until next week. After this I gotta go back out to Dayton.

FLETCHER (O.S.)

Next week, huh? OK. No problem. Glad I called. Have a nice time in Dayton?

TRACY

Nice time? Have you ever been there?

Tracy walks to the entrance of the Jets Front Office.

FADE OUT.

EXT. DAYTON BAR - NIGHT

Establishing shot of a typical sports bar.

INT. DAYTON BAR - NIGHT

Tracy and Milton sit together in the bar.

TRACY

You know the Jets are going to get what they want in the end.

MILTON

Probably. But it won't come free. I'll fuck over that little prick. And his asshole father too.

TRACY

How did you get to be so charming, Milt?

MILTON

Milton.

TRACY

Give me a dollar figure.

MILTON

You trying to bribe me?

TRACY

It's called indemnification.

MILTON

I have shit on his fucking father that will devastate Bradley.

TRACY

Ah, yes. You mentioned that to me. But I know you're bluffing.

MILTON

How so?

TRACY

Someone I know logged into your computer. The only devastating stuff he could find was a bunch of child pornography.

MILTON

That's a goddamn lie!

TRACY

That's what he told me. And he's very good at what he does, if you follow my meaning. He can make a computer appear to do anything.

MILTON

You fucking whore!

TRACY

Give me a number right now, or I'll drop a dime on your internet browsing habits.

MILTON

I have devastating information about Bradley's old man.

TRACY

You can't be Bradley's agent. Move on. Find another superstar to rep. You can do it.

MILTON

I'm ready to go to the New York fucking Post. It's devas--

Tracy folds her arms and glares at Milton.

MILTON (CONT'D)

--Alright. 200. Thousand.

Tracy sips her cocktail.

TRACY

35 it is. Thousand. Can I buy you another drink, Milt?

INT. TRACY'S APARTMENT - NIGHT

Tracy walks in, places her briefcase on the table beneath the Kandinsky and tosses a Jets jersey across a chair. She checks her answering machine.

ZWIEBEL

(Over answering machine)

Ms. Shepard. This is Bernard Zwiebel. Just a reminder that the board meeting is Thursday at one in the former RodCone Labs office. See you there.

INT. TRACY'S APARTMENT/BEDROOM - NIGHT

Tracy takes a stylish dress from her closet and lays it out on the bed. She retrieves a few pairs of shoes and matches them up to the dress, deciding on the appropriate pair. She makes a phone call.

TRACY

Carla? Sorry for the late call. Did you confirm my Botox appointment with Dr. Hammond?

Nine? Super. What about the spa?

(beat)

OK. What?

(Laughing)

None of your business little girl. Talk to you later.

Tracy hangs up the phone, looks at the dress-shoes combination and chooses a different pair.

EXT. OFFICE BUILDING - DAY

Tracy, looking sharp, steps out of the limo. Her Driver mans the door.

TRACY

Take the rest of the day off.

The Driver smiles and tips his hat. Tracy heads for the entrance.

INT. OFFICE BUILDING/LOBBY - DAY

Tracy sizes up the awful conditions of the Office Building Lobby.

She notices that the glass case with the names of various businesses still has the entry "RodC ne Labs - Suite 212." Tracy shakes her head in disgust at the piss-poor condition of the lobby, then heads for the stairs.

EXT. SUITE 212 - DAY

Tracy notices the door is missing. Her pace slows. She peers inside, then tentatively walks in.

INT. SUITE 212 - DAY

Suite 212 is a mess, looking as though gutted for renovation. Wearing expensive shoes, Tracy gingerly steps around detritus on the floor. SOUND of scraping O.S.

TRACY

Hello? Is anyone here?

The scraping stops. A CLEANING LADY steps out of a restroom.

TRACY (CONT'D)

Where is everybody? Isn't this Cuttbate Associates?

CLEANING LADY

(In Spanish)

They left. Now I have to scrape shit off their floor. Do you want to help me?

TRACY

Do you speak English?

CLEANING LADY

Si. Un poco.

TRACY

Where is everybody?

CLEANING LADY

Gone. Two weeks ago.

The old Cleaning Lady flashes Tracy a creepy toothless smile. Tracy bolts for the door.

INT. OFFICE BUILDING/STAIRWELL - DAY

Tracy runs down the stairwell, nearly tripping when her heel catches a loose tread.

EXT. OFFICE BUILDING - DAY

Tracy runs onto the sidewalk and scans the block. No limo. She walks briskly down the sidewalk.

EXT. BISTRO - DAY

Agitated, Tracy takes a sidewalk table at a BISTRO. A WAITRESS steps up to take an order.

WAITRESS

May I offer--

TRACY

--Bring me a double vodka.

The Waitress pirouettes and heads back toward the bar. Tracy takes out her cell phone and dials.

TRACY (CONT'D)

Hannah? What the fuck is going on with Cuttbate Associates!

At the next table a YUPPIE COUPLE with a TODDLER shush Tracy for the use of profanity.

TRACY (CONT'D)

Listen. Something is really wrong. The office is empty. No one is there except a cleaning lady.

(beat)

Meet me at the phony French bistro on Seventh.

The Waitress returns with the vodka. Tracy hangs up, takes a long drink, and lights a cigarette.

EXT. BISTRO - DAY (LATER)

Tracy and Hannah sit at the table; an ashtray holds several butts. Tracy nurses a drink; her hair is mussed. The Toddler plays in Tracy's purse.

HANNAH

Here's what I have so far. The Cuttbate website is down. I did a database search. The incorporation filing for Cuttbate Associates was rejected earlier in the week.

TRACY

Jesus.

HANNAH

I tried to contact Bernard Zwiebel and Arthur Andrews but their phones have been disconnected.

(beat)

Are you OK?

TRACY

Yeah. Go on.

Tracy takes a drink.

HANNAH

The lease on Suite 212 expired seven months ago. The rent was paid in cash on a month-by-month basis since then. The bungalow in Hamilton Square is currently available for rent.

TRACY

Good god. Listen, check through the records of all the people I met with regarding RodCone Labs and Cuttbate Associates. Find someone who can shed some light on this fuh--

Tracy glances at the Yuppie Couple who are staring at her.

TRACY (CONT'D)

--ugly mess.

Tracy rubs her temples. She lights another cigarette and sits back, resigned.

INT. FBI OFFICE/TAFT'S OFFICE - DAY

Tracy sits in the antiseptic FBI office of a SPECIAL AGENT who sports a conservative suit and military haircut. Tracy is dressed in a dark suit.

TRACY

I met this man, Fischer Cuttbate on a flight to LA. He told me his company was working on a cure - I mean a therapy - for an eye disease. It's the same disease my father suffers from.

The Special Agent nods sympathetically.

TRACY (CONT'D)

Anyway, Fischer told me his brother Fletcher was interfering in the business, so I agreed to try to sort it out for him, but what I discovered was that Fischer was trying to screw over Fletcher. Or so it seemed.

SPECIAL AGENT

How did you come to that conclusion?

TRACY

I mistakenly received...

Tracy hesitates.

SPECIAL AGENT

Yes?

TRACY

Uh, I received a spreadsheet that showed Fischer was cooking the books.

(beat)

Anyway, I passed on the information to Fletcher who then called the FBI and they shut down the company. Fischer disappeared. Then I found out from Fletcher that he had a real cure for the eye disease that he had kept secret from his brother.

(beat)

You have to understand Agent Taft... a cure for retinitis would be a godsend for my father. It would change his whole life. I had to see that it got developed.

SPECIAL AGENT

Completely understandable.

TRACY

So, I invested money - a million - into Fletcher Cuttbate's new company. Believe me, I did due diligence. My lawyer checked on patents, incorporation documents, tax data. Anyway, two weeks later I discovered it was a scam.

He offers a box of Kleenex. Tracy scowls

TRACY (CONT'D)

I don't cry.

(beat)

I'll see that the Cuttbates get the chair, or the needle, or whatever they use these days.

SPECIAL AGENT

OK, OK. We don't execute people for running scams, but I appreciate your outrage, Mrs. Shepard. Let's go back to the part about the FBI raid on, uh...

(Checks his notes)

...RodCone Labs. Tell me more about that.

TRACY

I got a call from the Labs' receptionist when I was in Texas.

The Special Agent works on his computer as Tracy speaks.

TRACY (CONT'D)

She told me that the FBI raided the place and that Fischer and his business director, Chad Knecht had gone missing. They couldn't pay for my--

SPECIAL AGENT

--There's nothing in our records about any raid on RodCone Labs, or any warrants on Cuttbate or Knecht. Nothing.

TRACY

N-nothing?

SPECIAL AGENT

It appears that not only was RodCone Labs a front, but that the raid was fabricated as part of the scheme to get you to ally yourself with the brother. I'm sorry, Mrs. Shepard. We'll initiate an investigation. I must tell you though that a con involving so many people in so many places over such a long period of time would have to have been perpetrated by a clever cast of characters.

TRACY

I... I... uh--

SPECIAL AGENT

--Do you have any pictures of the culprits?

TRACY

Uh, no. I don't.

SPECIAL AGENT

OK. Let's see if we can develop a composite picture of this guy Cuttbate.

INT. FBI OFFICE/FORENSICS UNIT - DAY

Tracy sits on an uncomfortable wooden chair across from a COMPOSITE ARTIST, a young woman in an FBI uniform. The Composite Artist sits in front of a computer screen.

COMPOSITE ARTIST

Before we get started putting together a composite sketch, give me some basics, Ms. Shepard. Hair color and style?

TRACY

Dirty blonde, medium length, combed straight back.

COMPOSITE ARTIST

Facial shape?

TRACY

Uh, oval-ish?

COMPOSITE ARTIST

Ears? Close to the head? Sticking out?

TRACY

Ears? I would say... normal. Not pasted to his head but not jug-eared either.

COMPOSITE ARTIST

Lobes?

TRACY

Geez. Lobes? Regular. I don't know.

COMPOSITE ARTIST

I know it's difficult, Ms. Shepard. If you had been robbed, we could show you a book full of mug shots--

TRACY

--I was robbed.

COMPOSITE ARTIST

I mean, robbed at gunpoint or something like that. There aren't too many mug shots of successful confidence men.

(beat)

I understand the person who conned you had an identical twin.

TRACY

That's right. Clearly, he was a party to the crime.

COMPOSITE ARTIST

Do you think it's possible these twin brothers were actually one man?

TRACY

What?

COMPOSITE ARTIST

Did you ever see them together?

TRACY

Well, no, I never did actually, y'know, see the two of them together. They didn't get along.

COMPOSITE ARTIST

I see. Before I forget, can you tell me: did either one of these men have any distinguishing physical characteristics that might help identify them? A scar, maybe, or a tattoo? Anything like that?

TRACY

Uh, um... Tattoos? No. No tattoos. None that I know of.

COMPOSITE ARTIST

Alright. Let's move onto the eyes. Color and shape?

INT. TRACY'S APARTMENT - DAY

Tracy and a PI sit at a table. Tracy hands the PI a thick folder.

TRACY

Here's everything I know. As I explained to you on the phone, I want this bastard Fletcher Cuttbate found and prosecuted. The FBI doesn't impress me.

PI

I understand, Ms. Shepard. My firm has a solid track record.

TRACY

On top of your fee, you can keep 25 percent of any money you recover as an added incentive. I expect results.

PI

From what you've already told me, Ms. Shepard, I am convinced that Fischer and Fletcher Cuttbate - no doubt aliases - are one and the same person.

Tracy shrugs.

PI (CONT'D)

Have you ever seen "Vertigo", Ms. Shepard? Great movie. Jimmy Stewart, Kim Novak, San Francisco?

TRACY

No.

PI

It involves a man who murders his wife with the cooperation of a woman who poses as her double. You should check it out sometime.

Tracy glances at her watch. The PI opens the folder.

TRACY

What else?

PI

How do you think this Cuttbate fellow knew to meet you at JFK airport and to be ready to forfeit his seat for you? That couldn't have been a coincidence.

TRACY

I don't have any idea.

PI

Well, I do. You said you were flying that day to meet with some clients in LA.

TRACY

That's right.

PI

My guess, Ms. Shepard, is that Cuttbate had a co-conspirator inside one or both of those companies. Someone who knew you were planning to fly that day at that exact time and on what carrier. You said you met Cuttbate again on the return flight. Coincidence? Not in my business. Nothing is a coincidence. Everything is planned.

Tracy nods sadly.

PI (CONT'D)

I'd even go so far as to postulate that members of Cuttbate's gang were on that plane to ensure first class was overbooked by the time you showed up at the airport. You told me your limo driver was late picking you up that morning. Do you trust him?

TRACY

(Flustered)

Well, I, never, uh--

PI

--I'll need a list of everyone who attended the meeting you had with these two companies. That's where I'll start. OK?

TRACY

Whatever you say. You're the expert.

Tracy escorts the PI to the door. They shake hands. As the PI steps out, Tracy pipes up.

TRACY (CONT'D)

One more thing I forgot to mention. Fletcher Cuttbate has a, um... he has a snake tattooed on his penis.

The PI raises an eyebrow slightly, takes out a pad of paper and writes a note on it.

PI

I'll check with some of the tattoo parlors and see if I come up with anything. Good day.

Tracy closes the door, cradles her head in her hands and bursts into tears.

FADE TO WHITE.

EXT. PARK - DAY

Tracy sullenly strolls the park in the drizzle.

INT. COFFEE SHOP - DAY

Tracy drinks coffee and works a newspaper puzzle.

INT. TRACY'S APARTMENT - NIGHT

Tracy is on the phone with her PI. From the intercut action it is clear she is not impressed with his status.

INT. AUCTION HOUSE - NIGHT

Tracy's Kandinsky is on the block. An AUCTIONEER drives up the price between two BIDDERS. The Gavel comes down.

EXT. TRACY'S APARTMENT (LOBBY) - DAY

Tracy stands by a saddened Hannah.

TRACY

Good luck, Hannah. If you need me to write a letter of reference, give me a call.

EXT. EMPLOYMENT OFFICE - DAY

Tracy's Driver, dressed in casual clothes instead of his uniform, walks up to the front door of the Employment Office holding a manila folder.

INT. DAD'S BROWNSTONE/LIVING ROOM - DAY

Tracy and Dad sit together on the sofa.

DAD

What's the matter, dear? You sound tired.

TRACY

Nothing. Well, maybe I am a bit tired.

DAD

You work too hard, Tracy. Too much traveling.

TRACY

Not really. I haven't been working too much lately. Not at all actually.

DAD

I don't get it.

TRACY

I made a bad investment decision, Dad. Lost some money. Kind of took the wind out of my sails.

DAD

Gee, I'm sorry to hear that.

(beat)

You don't need help, do you? I mean, you aren't in trouble, are you, dear?

Tracy hesitates

DAD (CONT'D)

Are you?

TRACY

No, no. Of course not, Dad. I'm just using the experience to reflect on what matters.

DAD

That's the way to go.

TRACY

Find a way to make it right.

DAD

Are you seeing anyone, Tracy?

Tracy stands and walks O.C.

INT. TRACY'S APARTMENT - DAY

INSERT: TITLE CARD "THREE MONTHS LATER"

Tracy sits at her desk in front of her laptop, scrolling through webpages while somber jazz music PLAYS in the background. She is dressed casually. The wall has a slightly faded outline where the Kandinsky once hung. The phone RINGS and she answers.

TRACY

Hello? Ah, Special Agent. Has it been another month already? Don't tell me, let me guess... Fletcher Cuttbate remains at large.

(beat)

Right, yeah, I know. I understand. Thanks.

Exasperated, Tracy hangs up the phone. She trains her attention back to her laptop. She stops scrolling and takes special notice of a business news headline on the screen.

TRACY'S P.O.V. – "NANONANO ANNOUNCES I.P.O."

INT. MATT'S OFFICE - DAY

Matt's Office is a sleek place, furnished in blonde, adorned with mid-century art. A flat-screen TV on the wall broadcasts silently. Matt sits at his desk casually browsing a brochure for Citation jets. A BUZZER sounds and Matt addresses his speakerphone.

SECRETARY (O.S.)

Mr. Blankenschein. A Ms. Tracy Shepard is asking to speak with you. She says she's done business with you in the past.

MATT

Sure. I know her. Great legs. Put her through.

(beat)

Tracy Shepard... the Medea of Mediation. How're you? What can I do you out of?

INTERCUT with Tracy on the phone in Tracy's Apartment.

TRACY

Calling to congratulate you on the IPO, Matt. Mazel Tov.

MATT

Why that's sweet of you Tracy. We're very happy how it turned out. What're your series B shares worth now? 50K?

TRACY

That's about right. Fifty.

MATT

You were a smart cookie to take your fee in stock instead of cash for that mediation session with PicoTech.

(beat)

If you don't mind my asking, how many shares did they give you?

TRACY

None. I took cash from them. I didn't think their future was as rosy as yours, Matt. I've read a lot about nanotechnology and I like what I see. I want to increase my stake in the company.

MATT

That's a nice vote of confidence. Listen, we're having a little dinner party next week to celebrate the IPO. Why don't you come out here as my guest? It'll be fun and you can meet the exec team.

TRACY

Meet the exec team. Oh, I can't think of anything I'd like to do more.

MATT

Did you know we moved our headquarters to San Diego? No core talent in LA. I'll have my admin send you the particulars.

TRACY

Sounds wonderful. Ciao, Matt.

INT. TRACY'S APARTMENT - DAY

Tracy hangs up the phone and smiles deviously.

EXT. SAN DIEGO INTERNATIONAL AIRPORT - DAY

A jet lands on the runway.

INT. SAN DIEGO RESTAURANT/DINING ROOM - NIGHT

Numerous ATTENDEES of the NanoNano IPO party enjoy meals at large tables in the San Diego Restaurant. Tracy sits on Matt's right at one of the tables situated in a prime spot, accompanied by six others: NanoNano EXECUTIVES and their WIVES and GIRLFRIENDS. Food has already been served and everyone eats. MARILYN, a bubbly, 40-year-old with salt-and-pepper hair sits across from Tracy.

MATT

Did anyone else order the burricotti with braised artichokes? These currants and the mint pesto really go well together.

EXECUTIVE #1

A far cry from crackers and Easy Cheese, huh Blankenshein?

MATT

Jesus. Don't remind me. That was the staple back at Stanford. There's something not quite right about aerosol cheese, but it makes sense when you think about it.

TRACY

I didn't know you were a Stanford grad, Matt.

MATT

Hell yeah, Tracy. All the good technology shit we enjoy today came out of Stanford. Google, GPS, spy satellites, the internet--

EXECUTIVE WIFE #1

--Easy Cheese?

MATT

(Chuckles)

Shit. Maybe. Wouldn't be surprised. The guys at this table, Tracy - my dream team, my brain trust - all Stanford boys.

MARILYN

I went to Vassar.

MATT

Oh, right. I forgot. Marilyn here is our VP of Personnel--

MARILYN

--Human Resources.

MATT

I brought Marilyn on board to hedge against a y-chromosome bubble. She came over last year from Oracle.

TRACY

Oracle. Must be a big change coming to a start-up.

MARILYN

Oh yeah. All good though. It's easy to get lost in big company bureaucracy. I needed something more personal. Besides, my options were under water.

EXECUTIVE #2

Join the club.

MARILYN

When I hired in, I got options at 45. Unfortunately, the next time the stock hit 45 was never.

MATT

I remember when Oracle dropped below eight bucks. I was gonna short the pig, but my old man advised me to load up on it instead. Hell, eight bucks? I picked up just about a million shares. Dumped it two years later when it hit 22.

Oohs and aahs from the Executive team.

MATT (CONT'D)

I bought the Astondoa with the proceeds. You should have seen the look on the dealer's face when I told him I'd pay cash for it.

The table laughs. Tracy rolls her eyes.

MATT (CONT'D)

I threw my dad a C-note for his sage advice.

Clapping now. Attendees at other lesser tables gawk enviously. After the table settles down, Marilyn presses on.

MARILYN

I'm hoping my financial luck will turn around. I've been talking to a biologist who's looking for an investor for his cure for acromegaly. Ron Slomsky introduced me to him.

MATT

(To Tracy)

Slomsky was our corporate strategist, but he quit and joined the enemy - PicoTech.

Boos and hisses.

MATT (CONT'D)

He has acromegaly. Huge hands, fingers like sausages. I think you met him in the mediation meeting last year. Looks a lot like that huckster on TV, uh... Tony Roma.

MARILYN

Tony Robbins. Anyway, this biologist - Calvin - is close to a cure for acromegaly, but his twin brother won't help him get the money to move it along. His brother wants to develop a pill you have to take every day. I guess that makes more money than a cure. Calvin's ready to go to clinical trial but he's stuck. He doesn't really want to deal with VC's - he calls them vulture capitalists.

EXECUTIVE #2

I resemble that remark, Ms. Jenkins.

MATT

Clinical trials are super expen--

TRACY

(animated)

--Marilyn, does this Calvin guy have a snake tattooed on his co--

The entire table stops what they're doing and looks at Tracy, waiting for her to complete the question. Finally, Marilyn replies hesitantly

MARILYN

--On his... what?

TRACY

On his, uh, collar... uh, collarbone?

MATT

Y'know, Tracy, I thought you were gonna say "a tattoo on his cock".

EXECUTIVE #2

Oh, for God's sake, Matt.

Some at the table smirk, but Tracy and Marilyn appear aghast. Marilyn avoids looking at Tracy.

MATT

I wonder if that would fuck up your sperm, you know, make you squirt ink like a squid.

Laughter at the table.

EXECUTIVE #2

Jesus, Matt.

Matt grins and reaches for a glass, annoyed to find it empty. He snaps his fingers at an ELDERLY WAITER

MATT

Garçon!

The Elderly Waiter cringes then turns and approaches Matt.

INT. SAN DIEGO RESTAURANT/DINING ROOM - NIGHT (LATER)

Dinner's over, the band plays non-intrusive music. Attendees of the IPO party mill around. Matt and Tracy stand off to the side alone.

MATT

A tattoo on some guy's cock?

TRACY

I never said that.

MATT

Yeah, but it sounded like--

TRACY

--I never said that.

MATT

OK. OK.

(beat)

Y'know, I read your book on mediation tactics. Very Machiavellian. I bet you could persuade a man to do anything you want.

TRACY

What do you think I want you to do?

MATT

Bring you into the action. Put you on the NanoNano board, perhaps?

TRACY

You could use someone like me on the board. Too many Stanford frat-boys on the team.

MATT

Yeah, you may be right. Where are you staying?

TRACY

I'm not. Taking the red-eye back to the city.

MATT

That's a shame. I was going to offer you a ride on the Astondoa. I'm taking her out tomorrow afternoon.

(beat)

It's a yacht.

TRACY

I know what an Astondoa is, Matt.

(beat)

Y'know, you're cute. The rich son of a rich father... squashing your competition, conquering the world. Young and fulla cum. I like that.

MATT

You'd better come back out here soon, Tracy. I want to talk to you some more.

Tracy walks toward the Lobby.

MATT (CONT'D)

Hey.

Tracy stops and turns around.

MATT (CONT'D)

Love the shoes.

INT. SAN DIEGO RESTAURANT/WOMEN'S ROOM - NIGHT

Tracy stands over a sink and washes her hands. She examines her face in the mirror. Suddenly she sees the image of Marilyn in the mirror fidgeting behind her. Tracy turns around and faces her.

MARILYN

Um, he does have a tattoo of a snake. On his ... y'know.

INT. SAN DIEGO BAR - NIGHT

Tracy and Marilyn sit in a booth drinking flowery cocktails.

MARILYN

Tell me, Tracy - you don't mind if I call you Tracy, do you? How did you know about the tattoo? Do you know Calvin?

TRACY

I don't know anyone named Calvin. And neither do you, Marilyn. This guy is using an alias. When I knew him, he called himself Fletcher Cuttbate. He had a twin brother, supposedly.

(beat)

What does he look like?

MARILYN

He's a bit taller than me. Shorter than you. Blondish hair. A little overweight.

TRACY

Uh-huh. Did you ever see Calvin and his twin together, in the same place at the same time?

MARILYN

Hmm. Now that you mention it, I don't think so.

TRACY

How odd. Listen, Marilyn, you're in the middle of being conned.

MARILYN

What?

TRACY

You're being conned. In the middle of an elaborate scam.

MARILYN

I've seen Calvin's work - his computer printouts, and stuff. I've spoken to his chief scientist. I've done my own research, Tracy. Ron Slomsky, who I worked with for almost a year, vouched for Calvin.

Tracy counts out the arguments on her fingers.

TRACY

Computer printouts? Easily fabricated. Chief Scientist? One of Calvin's stooges. Ron Slomsky? I met him during the mediation session between NanoNano and PicoTech. Most likely a co-conspirator. A common thread.

MARILYN

That's quite a theory, Tracy. Very "grassy knoll."

Tracy narrows her eyes with thinly-veiled contempt.

MARILYN (CONT'D)

Matt showed me a magazine article where they called you the "Medea of Mediation". Well, Medea was a jealous bitch.

TRACY

For God's sake, Marilyn, I'm not jealous. Forget that stupid magazine article. Listen to me. Calvin's story about cures and therapies is a scam. He's preying on your good nature, inventing a phony twin brother as a foil.

MARILYN

C'mon, Tr--

TRACY

--How much does he want from you?

Marilyn looks askance, checking whether anyone is listening. She scrunches down and whispers.

MARILYN

Two hundred and fifty thousand.

TRACY

Is that all? He wanted a million from me. And guess what - I gave it to the bastard. Two weeks later he and his entire charade of a business were gone. Disappeared. No trace. Do you get what I'm saying?

MARILYN

(Swallowing hard)

A million dollars?

TRACY

You're a smart woman, Marilyn. That's obvious. Think - deep down - do you really believe there are two different guys in the world with a snake tattooed on their junk? Two different tattooed-cocked breakthrough-drug-developers who have identical, greedy twin brothers?

MARILYN

Sounds impossible, I must admit.
(beat)
So, what do you want from me?

TRACY

I was supposed to fly back tonight but this is too important. Tell me more about Calvin. Ron Slomsky put you on to him. Then what?

MARILYN

I felt bad for Ron. I wanted to help.

TRACY

Help how?

MARILYN

I thought I could connect him to some investors, but Calvin was wary of them. He called them vulture cap--

TRACY

--Yeah, I know.

MARILYN

Then I thought, why not make an investment of my own.

TRACY

Persuasive little man, isn't he?

(beat)

I know you wanted to do good, Marilyn. I admire that.

Tracy sips her drink.

TRACY (CONT'D)

Um, you saw the tattoo so you obviously, y'know... Where did this take place?

MARILYN

I'm not going--

TRACY

--I'm saving your ass, Marilyn. You owe me details.

MARILYN

What for?

TRACY

I have to know. I have to know everything so I can get satisfaction. I got taken for a million, Marilyn. I have to try to get some of it back.

Marilyn slouches and sips her drink.

TRACY (CONT'D)

Please.

MARILYN

Alright. Jesus. I fucked him if that's what you're so intrigued about.

TRACY

Where was this?

MARILYN

His house... in a little town in Jersey. Calvin's attractive in a vulnerable sort of way.

TRACY

Well, I'll go along with that, I suppose. Tell me about his house.

MARILYN

Small place. Worn out furniture. Nothing special.

TRACY

What else?

MARILYN

He has a weird painting of a man with veins coming out of his eyes. Kinda creepy. Let's see... what else? Oh, he has a rare vintage electric guitar.

Tracy chuckles and shakes her head in disgust.

TRACY

I suppose he played rock tunes for you. Am I right?

MARILYN

Well, I mentioned I liked Boston. He played "More Than a Feeling." He's really pretty good.

Tracy Shepard, the "Medea of Mediation", feels pretty jealous now.

TRACY

Jesus Christ. That fucking bastard. What an operator. OK. I've heard enough. Calvin is Fletcher Cuttbate. No doubts.

MARILYN

Well, I have to admit it sounds convincing.

TRACY

Tell me you believe me, Marilyn.

Marilyn plays with her cocktail glass for a second.

MARILYN

Yeah, OK. I believe you.

TRACY

Finally. When are you meeting Calvin Shithead again?

MARILYN

Never. Not after all this.

TRACY

I mean, when would you have met him again if you hadn't found out what a scumbag he is?

MARILYN

I was supposed to meet him in a couple of weeks for dinner in Philadelphia, y'know, to, uh...

TRACY

To what?

MARILYN

Make my investment.

Tracy writes on a piece of paper and passes it to Marilyn.

TRACY

Take this. Now, listen carefully. I want you to accept Calvin's swell dinner invitation. Insist he take you back to his place in Jersey afterwards. And see to it he gets nice and drunk. I know he can pound the booze. I've seen him in action.

MARILYN

I don't und--

TRACY

--I need you to reconnect me with Fletcher, Calvin, whatever. I need to see him again. To get some restitution. To get him to confess to his crimes. To put an end this unfunny comedy of errors.

Marilyn scratches the back of her neck and nibbles on a cuticle. She sips her drink to delay responding.

TRACY (CONT'D)

I need your help. Please.

MARILYN

(Sternly)

I don't want to get involved.

TRACY

Hell, Marilyn, you are involved! You're vulnerable! We need to bring this bastard to justice before he fucks up any more women!

A few nearby PATRONS stop conversing among themselves and look over to size up Tracy's outburst.

MARILYN

Why don't you just call the police or the FBI? Why do you have to meet him in person?

TRACY

Do you know what Lex Talionis is?

(beat)

Never mind. Look, Calvin is a con artist, Marilyn. A very good con artist. He and his cronies left no tracks. I've been to the FBI already... they're stumped. So is my expensive PI.

(beat)

And even if I turned him over, they'd probably let him go for insufficient evidence. I've got to get him to confess on tape.

MARILYN

How are you going to get him to do that?

TRACY

(Smiling smugly)

I'm a professional negotiator, Marilyn.

INT. MATT'S OFFICE - DAY

Matt presses a button on his office phone.

MATT

(Into speakerphone)

Tracy Shepard. How was your flight back to Gotham City?

TRACY (O.S.)

(Over speakerphone)

I decided to stay. Your invitation for a ride on your yacht was too tempting. Of course, that's if you still want me to come.

MATT

(Into speakerphone)

I want you to come. I'll send a driver for you, Tracy.

TRACY

(Over speakerphone)

Should I buy some Dramamine?

MATT

(Into speakerphone)

The Astondoa is 115 feet long. You won't feel a swell... unless you want to.

INT. SAN DIEGO MARINA - DAY

Tracy struts into the Marina where Matt, drinking a Bloody Mary, awaits. She's decked out. He's a bit foppish in a maritime-inspired outfit. Matt stands and greets her.

MATT

Ms. Shepard. You look marvelous.

TRACY

Why thank you, Admiral Blankenschein.

MATT

Cute. If you're a good girl, I'll let you pilot her out of the harbor - of course, the real pilot has to stand next to you.

TRACY

That's OK, I'd rather hang out on the fo'c's'le.

(beat)

You do have a fo'c's'le, don't you?

Cocky Matt hesitates, flatfooted.

MATT

Um...

INT. YACHT (TRAVELING) - DAY

Tracy and Matt stand mid-ship by the rail looking out at the coast in the distance. Each holds a glass of red wine.

MATT

Why didn't you go back on the redeye, Tracy?

TRACY

What else? I succumbed to your irresistible charms. I also got into a long conversation with Marilyn last night and missed my flight.

(beat)

Your boat is amazing.

MATT

The Astondoa is a work of art. I christened her "Brobdingnagian".

TRACY

Ironic coming from the maker of Lilliputian devices.

MATT

Thank you! That was my intention. You're the only one who noticed.

(beat)

You're quite perceptive, Tracy. Maybe I do need someone like you on the board. What advice would you give a bright young CEO like me?

TRACY

Seriously? Let me think.

(beat)

Okay. I just want to say one word to you - just one word.

MATT

Yes?

TRACY

Are you listening?

MATT

Shit yeah, Tracy. What is it?

TRACY

(Gravely)

Plastics.

Matt stares dumbly for a split-second, then laughs.

MATT

That's good. You're good.

A moment of silence. Tracy smiles and sips her wine.

TRACY

Where are we, Matt?

Matt points to the horizon at the Hotel Del Coronado, its red shingles gleaming in the sunset.

MATT

That's Coronado Island. And that's the Hotel Del Coronado.

TRACY

Ah, the Del.

MATT

That's right. I'll bet you're a movie buff, aren't you Tracy? Plastics. You had me going.

TRACY

I know "Some Like it Hot" was filmed at the Del. My father is a huge Billy Wilder fan. I've seen all his movies probably a dozen times.

(beat)

Even though he can't see now, he still listens to the dialog and follows along.

MATT

Your father is blind? That's too bad. I'd like to meet him sometime. Chat about the classic American films.

TRACY

I know he'd enjoy that.

(beat)

This wine is excellent. What is it?

MATT

1997 Screaming Eagle. I have a case of 1992, but I like to save that for very special occasions.

The breeze kicks up. Matt drapes his sport coat across Tracy's bare shoulders.

TRACY

You have nice hands.

Matt looks down at Tracy's sexy feet.

MATT

And you have nice--

TRACY

--Matt, I know you read that silly article about me. Where they called me the "Medea of Mediation". I'm not like that. Really. In my business I have to project an image--

MATT

--I underst--

TRACY

--An image of impartiality. Y'know, I can never let my true feelings show through. That can make me appear cold-hearted--

MATT

--That's not--

TRACY

--I just want you to know that I'm really a very passionate person. It's just that my work has kept me so busy--

MATT

--Tracy--

TRACY

--And I have so much on my mind right now--

Matt gently places his finger on Tracy's lips, cutting her off. He leans forward and kisses her.

MATT

Would you like to go below deck? Relax a bit? Taste that '92?

Tracy turns her back on Coronado Island and embraces Matt.

EXT. PACIFIC OCEAN - DAY

The Astondoa cuts through the waters.

INT. PHILADELPHIA RESTAURANT - NIGHT

Marilyn and CALVIN (Fletcher) sit at a table near the wall and next to a potted plant. WAITERS remove the plates of food. A few PATRONS remain in the mostly empty Restaurant. STAFF mill around, checking watches, anxious to close up.

CALVIN

I gotta take a leak, Marilyn. Man, I'm pretty smashed. I hope you can drive. I'll be back in a minute. Get th' check, will ya?

Calvin weaves his way around the corner from the slick bar. When he's gone Marilyn dumps her vodka-tonic into the potted plant and refills it with bottled water. She hails the Waiter who arrives table-side.

MARILYN

Another Manhattan for him.

INT. PHILADELPHIA RESTAURANT - NIGHT (LATER)

Calvin returns to the table where a tall Manhattan straight up awaits him.

CALVIN

Wha' the fuck's this, Marilyn? I can't drink another one.

MARILYN

Are you sure, baby?

Fletcher slumps into his chair.

CALVIN

Well... maybe one more. But this's the las' one.

MARILYN

OK, baby. I just want to savor the moment. This is such a nice place and it's been such a nice evening... so far.

Marilyn flashes Calvin the sexy-eyes.

CALVIN

You're a - errrp - vixen, y'know that?

Calvin takes a sip and purses his lips.

CALVIN (CONT'D)

I jus' hope I don't fuckin' blow chunk.

EXT. CALVIN'S BUNGALOW - NIGHT

Calvin's Bungalow is similarly broken down as Fletcher's Bungalow was. Calvin fumbles with his keys as he attempts enter his Bungalow. After a moment he finally stumbles in. Marilyn looks plaintively over her shoulder toward the Driveway, then follows Calvin, closing the door behind her.

INT. CALVIN'S BUNGALOW - NIGHT

Calvin pivots clumsily, embraces Marilyn and plants a slobbery kiss on her lips. Marilyn stifles repulsion and finds the courage to press on with the plan. She puts her hand against Calvin's crotch.

MARILYN

Ooo, I feel something waking up. Why don't you get ready for bed, Cal, and I'll freshen up a bit? I missed you.

She squeezes Calvin's crotch again.

CALVIN

Ouch! Not so hard, Mare.

INT. CALVIN'S BUNGALOW/BATHROOM - NIGHT

Marilyn locks the bathroom door. She slowly washes her face and hands, then makes a cell phone call.

MARILYN

Where are you?

INTERCUT with Tracy in the Driveway of Calvin's Bungalow.

TRACY

Right where I'm supposed to be - parked next to your car. I saw you and Mr. Shitface go inside. Where are you now?

MARILYN

In the bathroom. He's in the bedroom. You better be on your toes. He's really drunk, but somehow, he's still able to get around.

TRACY

Yeah, amazing isn't it? I'll be ready, though. I've been ready. Is the door unlocked?

MARILYN

Yes. I made sure.

Marilyn hangs up the phone, takes one last look at herself in the mirror, breathes deeply and shuts off the light.

INT. CALVIN'S BUNGALOW/BEDROOM - NIGHT

Calvin's bedroom is dark. His clothes lie on the floor next to the bed. Marilyn sits on the mattress next to a naked Calvin.

CALVIN

What - errrp - took ya s'long, Mare?

Calvin reaches for Marilyn's leg.

CALVIN (CONT'D)

How come you're not undressed?

Marilyn collects Calvin's clothes.

MARILYN

I have to go, Calvin. I'm sorry.

Marilyn strides briskly out the bedroom with the clothes.

INT. CALVIN'S BUNGALOW - NIGHT

Marilyn approaches the door.

CALVIN (O.S.)

Wha' th'hell, Mare? Wha'd I do? D'I do sump'n wrong? Wha'bout the money?

Marilyn opens the front door.

INT. CALVIN'S BUNGALOW/BEDROOM - NIGHT

Calvin rolls out of bed and bangs his shin on a space heater.

CALVIN

Fuck! Fuckin' fuck that hurts!

SOUND - Door slamming O.S.

CALVIN (CONT'D)

Come back, Marilyn!

Calvin slumps onto the bed and rubs his shin, mumbling.

CALVIN (CONT'D)

(Mumbling)

Wha' the fuck's wrong wi'tha' bitch?

TRACY (O.S.)

The more appropriate question would be "what the fuck's wrong with you"?

(beat)

Hello, Fletch. How's the head?

Calvin (Fletcher) looks at a silhouette in the doorway of a tall, imposing female figure.

TRACY (CONT'D)

Aren't you going to say "hello" Fletch? Or would you prefer I call you Calvin?

FLETCHER

You found me. Congratulations. Wha' d'ya want, Tracy? Why're you here?

TRACY

I think you know why. Stand up and turn on the light.

FLETCHER

I'm goin' t' bed. I'm tired and a li'l drunk. Lock the door on your way out, please.

Fletcher flops back onto the bed and exhales long and loudly. Tracy flicks on the switch blasting the room in bright light; Fletcher shields his eyes.

FLETCHER (CONT'D)

Shut it off!

TRACY

I said stand up you misogynist piece of shit.

Fletcher stands up slowly after spotting Tracy pointing a pistol at him. It's her father's old semi-automatic.

FLETCHER

Easy, Tracy. Shit. What d'ya want? Your million dollars? I ain't got it. It got split up an' spent. I'm sorry, but tha's the way it works.

TRACY

Is that right?

Tracy notes the easel propping up the painting with veins coming out of eyes.

TRACY (CONT'D)

I see you're still ripping off Frida Kahlo.

FLETCHER

Why're you pointin' a gun at me?

TRACY

I came to negotiate for something that might make us whole again. You took a lot of money from me and you didn't hold up your end of the bargain. You let my father down, too. That wasn't nice, Fletch.

FLETCHER

Sorry.

TRACY

Tell me, how did you come to know my business? And my father's affliction? How did you put it all together?

FLETCHER

You're the Medea of Mediation, aren't you? I read all about you in that magazine. Interesting article.

Tracy smirks and shakes her head in disgust.

TRACY

You know, I've done some reading myself. I read that Keith Richards' middle finger is insured for one point six million. Did you know that? One point six mil. I'm sure you do, being such a big fan and all.

Tracy steps to the end of the bed and tosses a paper bag onto the mattress. It bounces, suggesting heft.

TRACY (CONT'D)

Open the bag, Fletch.

Fletcher hesitantly opens the bag and peers inside.

TRACY (CONT'D)

You're a very good guitar player, Fletch. I really enjoyed your performance that day I came out here to help you and your phony brother.

(beat)

You know, you may play like Keith Richards, but your middle finger isn't possibly worth as much as his. In fact, I bet your whole arm isn't worth as much as his middle finger. Still, I'm willing to accept a finger in exchange for the million you stole from me.

Fletcher removes a brand-new pair of sheet-metal snippers from the bag and looks at Tracy incredulously. She maintains her emotionless disposition. Fletcher's expression turns to horror.

TRACY (CONT'D)

Place the tool on your middle finger, Fletch.

Tracy extends her arms straight out, bringing the gun closer to Fletcher's face.

TRACY (CONT'D)

Do it now.

FLETCHER

Listen, Trace--

TRACY

--Put the fucking shears on your fucking finger. Now!

Tracy cocks the pistol. Fletcher cowers. He opens the snippers, then pukes all over his legs and feet. Tracy recoils.

TRACY (CONT'D)

I said "Now", you worthless piece of shit!

FLETCHER

C'mon—

TRACY

--Do it!

Fletcher slides the snippers onto his middle finger.

FLETCHER

(Whimpering)

Fuckin' bitch... fuckin' bitch.

Gripping the snippers, Fletcher stands before Tracy shaking, completely naked, hair tussled, chunks of barf spattered on his shins. Tracy grips the pistol steadily in both hands, her legs spread slightly for stability.

TRACY

Cut it off, Fletch. It's a good deal. Or I can lodge a bullet in your cranium.

FLETCHER

What kinda options are those?

TRACY

Fair enough. As a professional mediator I always like to offer my clients options. How about I let you confess your sins on tape? I have a video camera in my bag.

FLETCHER

You're a cunt, you know that? An evil cunt. You're mad at yourself - not me. You fell for a scam like a stupid schoolgirl. I don't owe you a fuckin'--

TRACY

--Shut up!

FLETCHER

Is that gun even loaded?

TRACY

Confess what you did to me--

Suddenly, Fletcher lunges at Tracy with the snippers. Tracy flinches. The pistol fires a bullet through Fletcher's throat and he falls to the floor, face up. He clutches his throat and writhes like a fish out of water.
A wheezy gurgling sound emanates from the hole in his throat, then a hiss, and then silence. Tracy drops the pistol and stares aghast at the body. She stoops down and reaches toward his neck to feel for a pulse, but stops short.

INT. CALVIN'S BUNGALOW/BATHROOM - NIGHT

Tracy throws up in the sink, runs some water, blots her face, and throws up again. She sits on the toilet, cradling her head.

INT. CALVIN'S BUNGALOW/BEDROOM - NIGHT

Tracy walks tentatively toward Fletcher's body. In death, he still grips the snippers. Tracy walks around to face him head on and spots his tattoo. She sneers, bends down and after a moment gouges Fletcher's face with her fingernails. Then she presses her spiked heel into his penis.

INT. CALVIN'S BUNGALOW - NIGHT

Tracy cursorily polishes door knobs and other surfaces to wipe away any fingerprints.

EXT. CALVIN'S BUNGALOW/DRIVEWAY - NIGHT

Tracy climbs into her car. Fletcher's clothes lie on the passenger seat where Marilyn stashed them. Tracy moves to pick up the pants but stops short. She takes a pair of gloves from the glove compartment and puts them on. Then she reaches into a pants pocket and retrieves Fletcher's cell phone. She starts the car and backs out of the Driveway.

EXT. HIGHWAY - NIGHT

Tracy drives down the dark, desolate highway, eventually pulling off into a Pine Forest.

EXT. PINE FOREST - NIGHT

Tracy turns off the lights and shuts off the car. She steps out, removes her heels and does a few seconds of jumping jacks. Puffing, she walks away from the car to place a call on Fletcher's cell phone.

911 OPERATOR (O.S.)

Nine one one. What's your emergency?

Tracy affects an agitated voice of a young girl.

TRACY

I need help! I just shot a guy who tried to rape me! I don't know where I am!

911 OPERATOR (O.S.)

Calm down dear. You say you shot someone? Is he dead?

TRACY

I don't know! I'm not sure! I'm afraid he might come after me!

911 OPERATOR (O.S.)

OK, dear. OK. Where are you? Where do you think you are?

TRACY

He attacked me! I ran out of his house into the woods. I'm lost! I think he's... oh my god!

911 OPERATOR (O.S.)

Stay where you are and leave your cell phone on. We can track your location with it. What's your name?

TRACY

Tiffany. He forced me to go with him. He was drunk. He attacked me with a big pair of scissors. I shot him with his gun.

911 OPERATOR (O.S.)

How old are you Tiffany?

TRACY

Sixteen.

Tracy drops the cell phone, still powered on, onto a bed of pine needles. Unintelligible squawking SOUNDS emanate from the cell phone. Tracy runs to the car.

EXT. HIGHWAY - NIGHT

Tracy peels out onto the highway.

EXT. TOWN - NIGHT

Driving through a dicey section of a Town, Tracy tosses Fletcher's wallet out the window into the gutter.

EXT. GEORGE WASHINGTON BRIDGE - NIGHT

Tracy throws the pistol out the window into the river below.

EXT. MANHATTAN RENTAL CAR GARAGE - NIGHT

Tracy hands the keys to an attendant.

INT. TRACY'S APARTMENT/KITCHEN - NIGHT

Frazzled, Tracy takes a bottle of vodka from the freezer and pours a stiff one which she downs in one gulp. She pours another.

INT. TRACY'S APARTMENT/BATHROOM - NIGHT

Tracy examines her body as though looking for a wound. In the background, water fills the bathtub. Tracy climbs into the bathtub with the glass of vodka. She stretches out.

INT. TRACY'S APARTMENT/BEDROOM - NIGHT

Tracy lies on top of the covers, dialing her phone. She receives a voice mail prompt from Matt.

MATT (O.S.)

Matt Blankenshein - leave a message.

BEEP sound over phone.

TRACY

Matt, Tracy. I'm missing you. Call me when you can. I want to see you again soon. I need a hug.

FADE TO BLACK.

INT. TRACY'S APARTMENT/BEDROOM - DAY

Tracy prepares for the day, applying makeup, getting dressed. The TV drones in the background. She steps around the bed and glances at the morning news report where a TV NEWSCASTER will soon hand off to a remote REPORTER.

NEWSCASTER

The Brooklyn DA's office is scheduled to make a formal statement at noon.

(beat)

Now let's go to Hamilton Square where our reporter is standing by.

Tracy stops and pays attention. The Reporter is about to lay out the findings so far, and will soon ask questions of a New Jersey State Police SERGEANT.

REPORTER

I'm standing on County Road 524 which runs past the pine forest you see behind me where State Police recovered a cellphone, they say might have belonged to a man who was killed last night in his home in Hamilton Square. According to 9-1-1 records a young girl called from this forest claiming a man had attacked her in his home with a knife. The man who police just found shot to death in his bedroom. I had a chance to talk to the New Jersey State Police earlier this morning and here's what she had to say.

TRACY

Shit.

SERGEANT

After receiving the 9-1-1 call, we dispatched troopers who followed the cell signal to the pine forest, where the phone was found lying on the ground. About an hour ago we discovered the body of a middle-aged man shot once through the throat.

TRACY

Shit.

REPORTER

Do the police have a positive ID on the victim?

SERGEANT

Not yet.

REPORTER

Did the cell phone belong to the victim?

SERGEANT

We think so. And other details cited in the 9-1-1 call match the scene we found at the house.

REPORTER

A source tells me the body of the deceased bore some marks. Scratches. Mutilation. Is that true?

TRACY

Shit.

SERGEANT

I'm not going to comment on speculation. Although I will say that it appears the victim turned the tables on the attacker.

REPORTER

What about the girl?

SERGEANT

Still looking for her. Undoubtedly, she was frightened beyond imagination.

REPORTER

I can't imagine. Thank you, Sergeant.

INT. JFK AIRPORT - DAY

Tracy hands a boarding pass to the same Gate Agent who gave her a hard time before.

GATE AGENT

Welcome, Ma'am.

Tracy walks a few steps toward the jetway.

GATE AGENT (CONT'D)

Glad to see you have your own ticket this time.

Tracy freezes momentarily at the cheeky remark, then proceeds down the jetway.

INT. MATT'S OFFICE - DAY

Tracy and Matt sit next to each other at a coffee table in Matt's big office nursing glasses of wine. Papers are strewn about the table.

MATT

I expect year-on-year revenue growth to exceed 150 percent, and if we get that contract with the Defense Department, we'll surpass our earnings per share target of nine cents.

TRACY

Have you looked at the cosmetics industry? I read that nanotechnology could be used to make some of the ingredients.

MATT

That's true, but we haven't focused there. Why do you ask?

TRACY

Just seems like a lucrative segment. Women are always open to trying new twists in makeup, cleansers and the like.

(beat)

Y'know, you may want to promote one of your female execs in advance of entering a female-oriented market. Your uber-male management team could be liability.

MATT

Well, we only have one female exec, but I'll definitely look into it.

Tracy looks at her wristwatch.

TRACY

Damn! I have to go Matt. Meeting someone for lunch.

Tracy stands, followed by Matt.

MATT

I'll pick you up at your hotel around seven? Do you have a place in mind for dinner?

TRACY

You pick, but I'd like to work up an appetite first. Got any ideas?

EXT. SAN DIEGO BISTRO - DAY

Tracy walks to the big plate-glass window of the Bistro and sees Marilyn inside seated at the bar with a drink in her hand. Tracy backs away and takes a couple of deep breaths.

INT. SAN DIEGO BISTRO - DAY

Tracy walks up to Marilyn and sits on a bar-stool next to her. Some BUSINESSMEN sit farther down the bar.

TRACY

Marilyn. So nice to see you again. Thanks for making the time.

The women exchange air-kisses.

MARILYN

No trouble at all.

TRACY

And thank you so much for helping me with Fletcher, Calvin, whatever.

A BARTENDER arrives.

BARTENDER

Good afternoon, ma'am. May I get you something?

TRACY

I'll have a Martinez.

MARILYN

I'll take another Dirty Shirley.

The Bartender acknowledges the orders and departs.

MARILYN (CONT'D)

How did your meeting go with Matt?

TRACY

Very well. We had a really nice conversation, and he didn't even bring up the tattooed collarbone incident.

Marilyn chuckles. A WAITER arrives and sets a plate of food on the bar between the women.

WAITER

Compliments of the chef, ladies. Mustard glazed pork belly, green lentils, eggplant caviar, and plums. Enjoy.

Marilyn spears one of the slimy-looking hors d'oeuvres and stuffs it in her mouth.

MARILYN

I didn't have time for breakfast this morning.

She spears another chunk and devours it like a hungry dog. The Bartender brings the drinks.

MARILYN (CONT'D)

I'm really anxious to hear how you worked things out with Calvin in the end. I'll bet he shit his pants when you walked into the bedroom.

(beat)

Oh wait, he wasn't wearing pants.

TRACY

Uh, Marilyn. I've got something--

MARILYN

--What did the FBI say? I'm ready to testify against that rat.

TRACY

Testify?

MARILYN

Yes. Of course. I want to face that bastard in court.

TRACY

Shit.

MARILYN

I hope he's not out on bail. God, maybe I should install a security system.

TRACY

Shit.

MARILYN

What's wrong?

Tracy takes a big gulp of her drink.

TRACY

I've got something to tell you about my encounter with Fletcher, uh, Calvin. Whatever.

(beat)

Things didn't go exactly quite as planned. Now be cool, Marilyn. Calvin, Fletcher. They're... I mean, he's... dead. I shot him. I had to shoot him.

Marilyn stops chewing and widens her eyes. After a second, she swallows the glob of food.

MARILYN

What!? You... you killed him?

The Businessmen look over. Tracy clutches Marilyn's forearm.

TRACY

Be cool, Marilyn. Jesus, do you want the whole place to hear you? I know this is unsettling.

Marilyn yanks her arm from Tracy's grip.

MARILYN

(Whispering)

Unsettling?

TRACY

Listen. I didn't plan on killing the fucker. I tried to reason with him, but instead of working with me he attacked me. He lunged at me with a knife... a sharp object. Do you understand? He tried to kill me. It was self-defense. I thought in his drunken condition he'd be easy to handle, but he caught me off-guard. I had no choice, Marilyn.

MARILYN

I... don't... know, Tracy. This is serious. You know I didn't want to get involved from the beginning. I told you that a million times. Now you've connected me to a homicide.

Tracy arches her eyebrows.

MARILYN (CONT'D)

OK - self-defense. But even if you did kill him in self-defense, everyone's going to think you killed him out of revenge for scamming you. And in two seconds, they'll connect me to the crime too - another ditzy broad who was sucked into one of his scams. It looks bad, Tracy.

(beat)

What were you doing there with a gun anyway?

TRACY

Doesn't matter.

(beat)

OK, it was for intimidation. I didn't know it was loaded. Honest. I popped out the magazine but... what difference does it make now? It's under control, Marilyn. The police think he was killed by a young girl. The weapon is gone. No one's going to connect us to it. I've been monitoring the local news, and that's the way the winds are prevailing. He was killed during the commission of debauchery. He attacked a young girl; she blew him away and stomped on his cock.

MARILYN

What!?

TRACY

We were never there, Marilyn. We're two successful female executives with better things to do than consort with a slug like Fletcher Cuttbate. Let's not descend into a folie à deux. I need your cooperation.

Marilyn samples her drink coyly, delaying a response.

TRACY (CONT'D)

Maril--

MARILYN

--You want my cooperation? OK, you're a big-time negotiator, Tracy. Negotiate for it.

TRACY

C'mon Marilyn. I saved you a quarter million dollars. Isn't that enough?

MARILYN

Funny, I don't feel any richer than I did yesterday. Besides, it's not about money.

TRACY

I see. Power, authority, position, status.

MARILYN

Something like that.

TRACY

Ultimately all negotiations come down to self-worth. How much of it you're willing to sacrifice... How much you can exact from someone else.

MARILYN

What are you going to do for me, Tracy?

Tracy plops an hors d'oeuvre in her mouth.

TRACY

Satisfy your sense of self-worth, of course. What do you know about nanotechnology and cosmetics, Marilyn?

EXT. PI's OFFICE - DAY

Tracy's limo pulls to the curb outside the PI's Office. A NEW DRIVER, a stocky, white man in a uniform opens the door. Tracy steps out.

TRACY

Stay here. This will only take a minute.

Tracy walks to the PI Office.

INT. DAD'S BROWNSTONE/LIVING ROOM - DAY

Tracy, Matt and Dad sit together on the sofa eating popcorn and watching "Ace in the Hole" on TV. Dad sits between Matt and Tracy.

CLOSE-UP - TV

Showing Kirk Douglas's character Chuck Tatum falling wounded to the floor, ending the movie.

BACK TO SCENE

DAD

How about that, Matt? Good movie, huh?

MATT

Very good. Great suggestion.

DAD

"I don't go to church. Kneeling bags my nylons". What a great line.

MATT

And the one about belts and suspenders. Genius.

Dad fingers his belt and suspenders sheepishly.

TRACY

While you two recap the entire movie, I'm going to make some coffee.

Tracy leaves.

DAD

Is she gone?

MATT

Yeah.

DAD

Tracy's a great woman, Matt. A real winner. I hope you respect that.

MATT

Sure. I most definitely do.

DAD

She works too hard. Never really had any lasting relationships. Maybe you can change that.

MATT

I think so.

Matt reaches into his pocket.

MATT (CONT'D)

I want to show you something. Hold out your hand.

Dad extends his palm into which Matt places a diamond engagement ring.

DAD

What's this?

MATT

What do you think it is?

DAD

Is this a diamond? It's too big to be a diamond.

MATT

That's what eight carats feels like.

DAD

Good God, Matt. Eight carats?

MATT

Shhh. I'm going to ask Tracy when she comes out to San Diego next week. Of course, I want your blessing.

Dad begins to tear up. His feeble eyes dart around.

DAD

Oh, Matt. Of course you have my blessing.

SOUND of cups clinking O.S. Matt quickly stuffs the ring back into his pocket. Dad blots his eyes. Tracy walks in carrying a tray with coffees and creamers.

TRACY

What's wrong, Dad?

DAD

Nothing dear. Something in my eyes.

INT. SAN DIEGO RESTAURANT - NIGHT

GUESTS of NanoNano sit at several tables at the same San Diego Restaurant where NanoNano celebrated its IPO party. Some Guests dance to Latin music. Matt and Tracy sit together at a center table with a few other EXECUTIVES including Marilyn.

INSERT: TITLE CARD "ONE MONTH LATER"

EXECUTIVE #1

Hey, did you hear about Ron Slomsky?

Most of the table pays attention. Tracy continues chatting with the person sitting next to her.

MARILYN

What?

EXECUTIVE #1

He got fired from PicoTech. Someone told me they found kiddie porn on his computer.

MATT

Jesus. What an asshole.

MARILYN

(Shocked)

I can't believe it.

Marilyn looks at Tracy who appears unsurprised at the sordid news.

MATT

Good thing he left us when he did. That kind of press we can do without.

Matt stands and taps his glass to attract the attention of the room. The band stops playing.

MATT (CONT'D)

May I have your attention everyone. We are gathered here today to celebrate the union of our fair maiden NanoNano and the deep-pocketed Department of Defense in the holy sacrament of government contracts. Hang on to your options, boys and girls.

The room erupts in applause.

MATT (CONT'D)

The contract will give us the cash flow us to pursue new avenues of R&D including cures for a variety of eye diseases - a market we believe is very lucrative.

More applause. Tracy nods sublimely.

MATT (CONT'D)

Now, I have another announcement to make. Marilyn, would you please stand up.

Marilyn stands and modestly clasps her hands in front of her.

MATT (CONT'D)

I'm thrilled to announce that Marilyn Jenkins has been promoted to General Manager of our soon-to-be opened facility in Malaysia where we'll start up our cosmetics operation. Marilyn brings enormous experience to the role, and we're happy to have such a talented woman on the senior executive team.

Marilyn acknowledges the applause.

MATT (CONT'D)

You all better get your face time in with Marilyn tonight. She leaves for Kuala Lumpur tomorrow morning and we won't be seeing her much around here after that.

Tracy smiles deviously. Guests step up to congratulate Marilynn.

INT. SAN DIEGO RESTAURANT/WOMEN'S ROOM - NIGHT

Tracy stands at the sink, examining an eyelash in the mirror. Like before, she sees the reflection of Marilyn watching her from behind. Tracy turns to face her.

TRACY

Hello Marilyn.

MARILYN

(Testily)

I earned my promotion, Tracy.

TRACY

Of course you did. Why would you even bring it up?

MARILYN

I suggested the idea of cosmetics with Matt a long time ago, just so you know.

TRACY

Insightful, Marilyn.

MARILYN

I don't want you telling people I asked you for help... I mean negotiated for... Shit!

Now that you're screwing my boss, I don't want anyone thinking you had something to do with my promotion. Like payback for saving your ass on that Calvin thing--

TRACY

--Jesus Christ, Marilyn! What's wrong with you? Did you drink too many Dirty Shirleys again?

Tracy bends down low to inspect the stalls for the telltale feet of accidental interlopers, finding none.

TRACY (CONT'D)

Look, you're a General Manager now, Marilyn. The biggest big-shot woman in nanotech. You got what you wanted. Don't blow it.

MARILYN

You don't think I deserve it, do you?

TRACY

C'mon, Marilyn. Deserve's got nothing to do with it. You should know that. You don't get what you deserve, you get what you negotiate.

MARILYN

Is that a fact?

TRACY

That's my experience.

MARILYN

I see.

TRACY

Just keep your big mouth shut, understand? Forever. You do that and I promise you'll do well in our company.

MARILYN

Huh? What? Our... what does that mean?

TRACY

Didn't you hear? Matt proposed last night and I said "yes".

MARILYN

Amazing.

TRACY

And I'm joining the board of NanoNano at the next meeting.

MARILYN

Unbelievable.

TRACY

Congratulations again on your promotion, Marilyn. Have a safe flight to Malaysia.

INT. SAN DIEGO RESTAURANT - NIGHT

Tracy and Matt dance among others to a Latin version of "Day and Night."

FADE OUT.

INT. DAD'S BROWNSTONE/LIVING ROOM - DAY

Matt and Dad watch TV together. Dad wears thick glasses.

INSERT: TITLE CARD "ONE YEAR LATER"

MATT

It's not too bright for you, is it?

DAD

No. I'm getting used to it. The picture is still a bit blurry but I ain't complaining. I forgot how sexy Barbara Stanwyck used to be.

Tracy walks in from O.C. with a plate of sandwiches. She sets the plate on a coffee table and rubs her father's neck.

TRACY

How's the movie, Dad?

DAD

One of my favorites.

Tracy smiles. Her cell phone RINGS and she answers.

TRACY

Tracy Shepard.

PI (O.S.)

Ms. Shepard, I'm the PI You hired to--

TRACY

--Yes, yes. What can I do for you?

PI (O.S.)

I have a solid lead. I came across a coroner's report. It mentioned that the deceased had the type of tattoo you described. He has to be your con man.

TRACY

I'm over that. I don't care anymore.

INTERCUT with the PI's office.

PI

I feel bad that I let you down. I want to complete the mission you hired me for.

TRACY

Well, I appreciate that, but I really just want to drop it.

PI

The guy was murdered. I've been looking through the police reports. No one was ever charged. If I can connect some dots back to the person who killed him, it may lead to your money.

TRACY

(agitated)

I just want to drop it, OK?

MATT

Something wrong, Trace?

Tracy walks into the Kitchen.

INT. DAD'S BROWNSTONE/KITCHEN - DAY

Tracy cups her hand around the cell phone.

TRACY

I stopped paying you a long time ago. Why are you still working on it?

PI

I don't get it, Ms. Shepard. Don't you want to find out if this guy is your con man? Gain some closure. Maybe get some of your money back.

TRACY

I'm happy now. I don't need closure. I don't need money. I just want to forget the whole thing. Understand?

PI

I suppose so.

TRACY

Thank you. I appreciate your diligence, but I think you should move on to another case.

PI

Interesting.

TRACY

What?

PI

Nothing. Sorry to have bothered you, Ms. Shepard. Have a nice day.

The PI hangs up.

TRACY

I didn't mean to sound-- Hello?

INT. DAD'S BROWNSTONE/LIVING ROOM - DAY

Tracy sits on the sofa; Matt puts his arm around her.

MATT

Who was that?

TRACY

No one. An old client. Whatcha watching, Dad?

DAD

"Double Indemnity."

MATT

A scam leads to murder.

C.U. of Tracy's fraught face.

FADE OUT.

THE END

OTHER BOOKS BY HERB SCHULTZ

Ronnieand Lennie

Ronnie and Lennie are identical twins fused in the womb and born into a world that is unprepared to separate them. The reason for their plight is vague and debatable, but one possibility wends its way throughout the narrative. Seemingly chained for life in a rural backwater of North Carolina, Ronnie and Lennie unexpectedly break free, but life apart is not all it's cracked up to be. Serious trouble descends upon our heroes, and they find themselves prisoners of another kind. A case of chronic adjustment disorder compels the twins to drastic action. Throughout the story we are introduced to a broad array of characters that influence the direction and speed Ronnie and Lennie take through life – a rudderless mother, a crazy groupie, an evil gambler, an unconventional doctor, to name just a few. *RonnieandLennie* is a funny, sad, vulgar story that spans decades and visits numerous venues as it chronicles the lives of two boys conjoined at the chest by a rogue band of flesh.

OTHER BOOKS BY HERB SCHULTZ

Architect's Rendition

All Gerald Pfalzgraf wanted was to be adored. That, and to possess all of his wife Morcilla's vast fortune. Was that too much to ask for? The founder of Pfalzgraf Associates, an exclusive Manhattan architecture firm catering to elite, wealthy clients, Gerald resents his wife's assertion that her financial support is fundamental to the firm's success – not because it's false, but because it's mostly true. Gerald has come to resent a lot of things over the course of twenty long years of marriage to Morcilla. He meets Wren, a beautiful, vivacious goddess half his age. Her jaw is perfect. He resolves to be with her. After obstacles to his happiness begin to pile up, Gerald tries his hand at architecting something different – a complex enterprise of mayhem. Guided by Machiavelli, his childhood hero, Gerald wields the tools of deception, manipulation and opportunism; he knows that men who seek to deceive will always find someone who will allow himself to be deceived. *Architect's Rendition* tells the story of an amoral man who tries to secure the life he always wanted to live by cutting a swath through a cast of misfit characters – the kind who allow themselves to be deceived.

OTHER BOOKS BY HERB SCHULTZ

Double Blind Test

Tracy Shepard is in the business of alternative dispute resolution – a fancy name for mediation. She is an expert in the art of negotiation, highly compensated by parties from all over the world – Fortune 500 companies, celebrities, wealthy families – locked in disagreement, burning cash on futile litigation, seeking another way out. Dubbed the "Medea of Mediation" for her drive and ambition, Tracy offers to help the owners of a small pharmaceutical lab resolve a difference between them that is holding up progress on a breakthrough drug. She is compelled to help the owners of the lab – identical twins named Fischer and Fletcher Cuttbate – because their drug is meant to cure an insidious eye disease that afflicts tens of thousands of people, including her father. Shortly after meeting them, Tracy becomes attracted to each Cuttbate brother for different reasons: Fischer for his gallantry and business acumen, Fletcher for his artistry and vulnerability. However, in the course of her mediation efforts she discovers disturbing evidence of fraud, and soon she finds that nothing is as it seems. *Double Blind Test* is a story of deceit, connivance, despair and lex talionis which posits this confounding question: What are the chances that two different men have the exact same tattoo . . . on their private parts?

OTHER BOOKS BY HERB SCHULTZ

Sometimes the Sun Does Shine There

Sometimes the Sun Does Shine There and Other Stories is a collection of five twisted tales of deceit, despair, decadence, derision and revenge. The anchor story presents Larry, a stooper who picks up discarded tickets at the Off-Track Betting parlor hoping to find a winner among the detritus. He is tormented by Vic, a vicious thug who puts him in the hospital where he meets a diligent worker and closet artist named Maddie. Larry soon discovers he is not the only victim of Vic's evil inclinations. A bizarre turn of events puts Larry in a position to rise up from the OTB floor and recover his dignity.

The other stories involve a grocery store robbery that exposes a fiend, a screenwriter on a mission who instead meets a minor character from a major motion picture, and a bratty bond trader who tries to mend a fractured relationship with his upstairs neighbor. The final story features two men who invent a device that scrambles their futures. Believing his business partner absconded with a valuable invention, the determined scientist embarks on a fruitless search which leads to his arrest for murder – thanks to the very device he invented.

Sometimes the Sun Does Shine There and Other Stories is the 2011 winner of the Indie Discovery Award for best short story collection.